The Book of
Hemyock

Heart of the Blackdowns

Compiled by Brian Clist & Chris Dracott

HALSGROVE

First published in Great Britain in 2001
Revised and reprinted 2012

DEDICATION
*To our wives, Mavis and Shirley,
for their support and forbearance.*

British Library Cataloguing-in-Publication Data
A CIP record for this title is available from the British Library

ISBN 978 0 85704 180 7

HALSGROVE
Halsgrove House,
Ryelands Business Park,
Bagley Road, Wellington, Somerset TA21 9PZ
Tel: 01823 653777   Fax: 01823 216796
email: sales@halsgrove.com

Part of the Halsgrove group of companies
Information on all Halsgrove titles is available at: www.halsgrove.com

Frontispiece photograph: *Mr Percy Sanders giving hot cross buns to the village children on Good Friday, 1962.
This was taken outside the Post Office which, in those days, also housed Mr Sanders' bakery.
The recipients of his buns are, left to right, back: Maureen Granger, Janice Fuller, Patricia Fuller, ? North, Malcolm Shire;
front: ?, Ivan Shire, Graham Howsam. The handcart had been used by successive bakers to deliver bread around the
village for many years but sadly was later stolen.*

Printed and bound in China by Everbest Printing Ltd

FOREWORD

In 2001 when I wrote the foreword to our new book *The Book of Hemyock* I said that the beginning of both a new century and a new millennium provided us with an excellent opportunity to produce a book about the history of our village and to discover how we can learn from the past to create a better future for our community, and that the village embodies a strange dichotomy: there is a continuum not only in the permanence of the townscape and the villagescape but also in the transience of the lives of the people who live there. Our book is an attempt to collect and collate some of the historical events that together have made Hemyock such a unique village.

Some 1000 copies of the book were printed, and it did not take long for them all to be sold. Over the years we have had numerous requests for the book to be reprinted. After eleven years our publishers, Halsgrove of Wellington have decided to reprint a new edition of *The Book of Hemyock* to celebrate the Diamond Jubilee of our Queen. The book is mainly the same as the original one, but it contains some four pages of new material to cover some of the events that have taken place over the eleven years since the first book was printed.

Two years ago another book containing fresh information about Hemyock was published privately, entitled *Make Hay Whilst the Sun Shines*. Copies are still available from myself, at 'Mountshayne', Hemyock EX15 3QS.

Brian Clist
2012

An early view of Hemyock from Castle Hill showing, from left to right, the Cattle Market, Parish Church, Catherine Wheel and the Wesleyan (Methodist) Church.

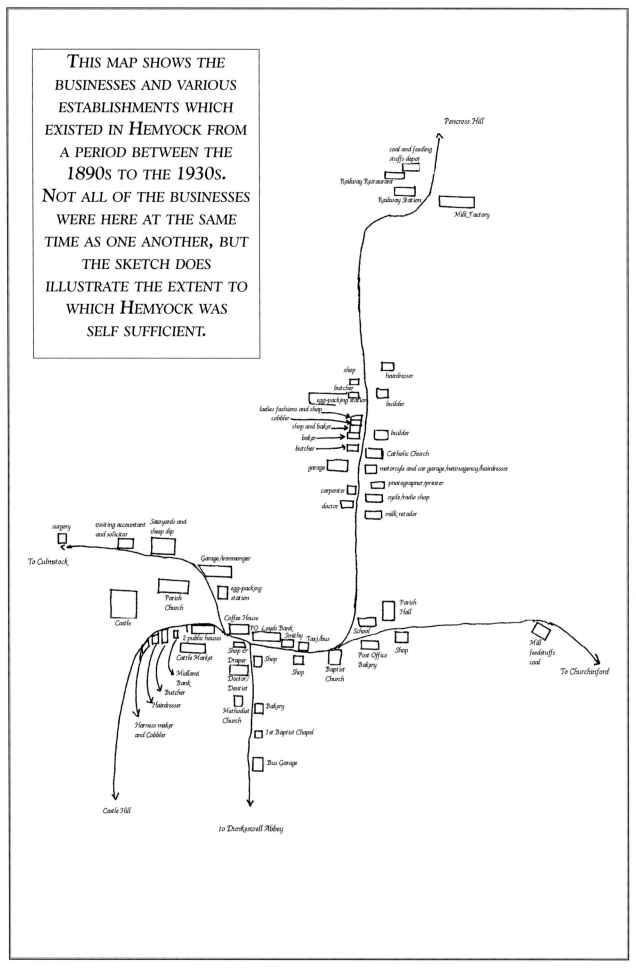

THIS MAP SHOWS THE BUSINESSES AND VARIOUS ESTABLISHMENTS WHICH EXISTED IN HEMYOCK FROM A PERIOD BETWEEN THE 1890S TO THE 1930S. NOT ALL OF THE BUSINESSES WERE HERE AT THE SAME TIME AS ONE ANOTHER, BUT THE SKETCH DOES ILLUSTRATE THE EXTENT TO WHICH HEMYOCK WAS SELF SUFFICIENT.

Pencross Hill

coal and feeding stuffs depot

Railway Restaurant

Railway Station

Milk Factory

shop

butcher

egg-packing station

ladies fashions and shop

cobbler

shop and baker

baker

butcher

garage

carpenter

doctor

hairdresser

builder

builder

Catholic Church

motorcycle and car garage/newsagency/hairdresser

photographer/printer

cycle/radio shop

milk retailer

surgery

visiting accountant and solicitor

Sawyards and sheep dip

To Culmstock

Garage/ironmonger

egg-packing station

Parish Church

Castle

Coffee House

PO Loyds Bank

2 public houses

Cattle Market

Smithy

Taxi/bus

Shop & Draper

Shop

Doctor/ Dentist

Shop

Midland Bank

Butcher

Hairdresser

Methodist Church

Baptist Church

Harness maker and Cobbler

Bakery

1st Baptist Chapel

Bus Garage

Castle Hill

to Dunkeswell Abbey

School

Parish Hall

Post Office Bakery

Shop

Mill feedstuffs coal

To Churchinford

4

CONTENTS

Foreword 3

Acknowledgements 6

Introduction 7

Chapter One: Geology & Natural History 9

Chapter Two: The Early Days 13

Chapter Three: The Village & Its People 17

Chapter Four: Village Churches & Chapels 41

Chapter Five: Hemyock Castle 53

Chapter Six: The Milk Factory 59

Chapter Seven: Village Inns 73

Chapter Eight: The Culm Valley Railway 79

Chapter Nine: Culm Davy 87

Chapter Ten: Hemyock School 93

Chapter Eleven: Young Farmers 111

Chapter Twelve: The Defence of Hemyock 115

Chapter Thirteen: Entertainment 131

Chapter Fourteen: Sporting Life 139

Chapter Fifteen: Medical Care in Hemyock 149

Chapter Sixteen: Farming 153

Chapter Seventeen: Scouts & Guides 163

Chapter Eighteen: The Simcoe Connection 169

Chapter Nineteen: Echoes From 1900 175

Chapter Twenty: 'Perlycombe' 178

Twinning and the St Ivel Hall 180

The Twenty-first Century 181

Acknowledgements

There were so many people who helped us with the first edition of this book with the loan of photographs, postcards etc and, of course, personal knowledge. They were: Roy Barton, Janice Bawler, Barbara and Les Bowden, Margaret and David Bromwich, Ted Collins, Eileen Doble, Pamela Dowson, Sylvia and Mike Eastick, John Eden, James Edwards, David Elkington, Peggy and Bill Granger, Dr.John Griffin, Cissie Gunn, Dennis Hart, Jim Hawkins, Hemyock BowlingClub, Betty Hill, Barbara Hole, Rita and John Hooper, Tom Humphreys, Phyll Kallaway, Joan and Fred Lawrence, Edna and Norman Lowman for providing so many photos from Edgar's ollection and Norman's own photos, Christine Mathews, Dr. Jonathan Meads, Margaret Mitchell, Eileen and Fred Perrott, Evelyn and Michael Pike, Caroline Pinder, Colin Popham, Brian and Paul Redwood, Jane and Keith Root, Patsy Ruffell-Hazell, Phyll and Les Salter, Margaret Sheppard, Brian Simpson, David Walker (photographer) from Wellington, Dulcie Webber, (for the loan of husband Harold's collection of photos from the early 1970s), Mabel Wheeler and Christine Young. Sadly some of these people are no longer with us. We are also extremely grateful to Eve Grosse for the drawings she prepared for the book. Our thanks also to Government of Ontario Art Collection in Toronto for permission to use the picture of John Graves Simcoe and to Michael Messenger's definitive book, *The Culm Valley Light Railway* for much of the information contained in Chapter 12. With this Diamond Jubilee edition our thanks to Shirley Dracott for a selection of photographs including the Jubilee events, Paul Steed and Hemyock.org, Neil Morralee, Mike Cooper and the Hemyock History and Archiving Association.

Introduction

In this book we have endeavoured to strike a balance between the old and the new, with text and illustrative material. As regards the latter we have been dependent on the number of post cards, photographs and ephemera kindly loaned to us by people who responded to our appeals. Our thanks to those concerned is conveyed in our 'Acknowledgements'. We have been very fortunate to be able to name nearly everybody in the photographs owing to the remarkable memories of a number of people. We have done our best to ensure that the names are correct and accurately spelt, if there any errors please accept our apologies.

We have drawn on a variety of historical records and documents in preparing this book, including the rare and exciting *Defence Returns* relating to Hemyock dated 1798 and 1803. Other records that have provided fascinating information include the old school log books, minute books for the Calf Club and certain sports clubs. Our story includes much about the ordinary everyday life of the village people, their social activities, sport, entertainment, their medical care etc. We have, as best we can, brought the Hemyock story up to date including The Diamond Jubilee Celebrations and in doing so have recorded something of Hemyock's more recent history for the benefit of future generations.

Chris Dracott
2012

Official unveiling of the 'WELCOME TO HEMYOCK' sign by Dr John Griffin (standing, right). Project co-ordinator John Hooper is on the left. Behind the sign from left to right are: Pamela Gubb, Barbara Bowden, Les Bowden, Dennis Gubb, Barbara Churchill, Ruth Brooks, Rita Hooper, John Churchill and Derek Brooks.

Early postcard of Hemyock looking north.
To the top left the range of hills terminates at Culmstock Beacon.

Early postcard of Hemyock looking south from Pencross. The Baptist Chapel can be seen almost in the
centre of the village. Many of the open fields are now occupied by houses.

CHAPTER ONE

Geology & Natural History

Hemyock is situated on the upper River Culm in the heart of the Blackdown Hills of the Devon/Somerset borderlands. For many years the distinct and beautiful scenery of this area remained largely unknown, not only to tourists visiting the West of England but also to many living in the West Country outside the Blackdown Hills. The sheer distinctiveness of the area, the geology, topography and natural history with unspoilt rural landscapes and stunning panoramas were to be recognised in the early 1990s when the Blackdown Hills were named an Area of Outstanding Natural Beauty (AONB).

The geology of the region, which has naturally played a major role in the development of Hemyock, is quite unique. A visitor seeing the Blackdowns for the first time would be struck by the flat-topped plateaux of the hills, three of which were utilised as airfields during the Second World War. One airfield, at Dunkeswell, just south of Hemyock, is still in use as an airfield although the aircraft using it have changed somewhat. These hills consist of upper greensand rocks of the cretaceous geological period, other examples of which in Britain include the Surrey Hills. Visitors to Hemyock and the Blackdowns in general, who are familiar with Surrey and the South East, are often heard to comment on the similarity of the scenery, with the exception of the flatness of the hilltops. The greensand of the Blackdowns is somewhat different in that it is a thick, massive, largely non-calcareous outcrop containing chert (a siliceous concretion similar to flint). To the north-west of Hemyock is a ridge of upper greensand which rises, at its highest point, Staple Hill, to 315 metres. To the south of this ridge the upper greensand outcrops have been eroded into the distinctive long, flat-topped ridges separated by deep combes.

Beneath the greensand are impermeable rocks, mainly Keuper marls. Where these rocks meet the greensand there is a series of spring lines which give rise to a number of rivers including the Culm which flows through Hemyock. The greensand is topped by a band of clay with flints and chert and in the valleys are deposits of gravel and alluvium. The chert and flints have been utilised by generations of farmers and builders for the construction of farmhouses, outbuildings and walls, etc.

Fossils are not abundant but some are to be found, very often within the flint concretions. Sea urchins and various types of seashell are not uncommon and provide evidence that many millions of years ago this whole region was part of a great sea. It will be many more millions of years before Hemyock disappears completely under the waters again, despite global warming and sundry other factors that continue to bring change to the planet.

The geology which has shaped the land in and around Hemyock has created a mixture of heath and moorland, permanent pasture wetland and woodland. Anyone approaching the village from the north would get an excellent feeling for the local geology by taking time to stop at the 'Welcome to Hemyock' sign and seat situated at the top of Pencross Hill. About 200 metres above sea level, the seat is located on a band of upper greensand with the higher ground behind capped by clay with flints. A few yards below the seat deposits of Keuper marl begin with a covering of valley gravel and topsoils. The band of marl deposits ends at the bottom of the hill where the alluvial deposits begin along the River Culm. Looking beyond the village, which is mainly built on the Keuper marl deposits the pattern continues upwards with upper greensand deposits, capped by clay with flints at Hackpen Hill (236 metres), Burrow Hill (219 metres), Lemons Hill (230 metres) and Ridgewood Hill (227 metres). Note the consistent height of the hills; there are no prominent peaks here.

Whilst contemplating the view from the millennium seat it is worth dwelling on the fact that this landscape took millions of years to evolve in geological terms. The field patterns and hedges, the woodlands and buildings took only 1000 years or more of activity by man to create, but man's efforts were to a large extent dictated by the geology.

Geology cannot, however, be blamed for the increase in the size of Hemyock. In common with many other villages throughout the country, new buildings have effected more change in the village over the past four or five decades than was to be seen over the previous four or five centuries. In the long term, Nature will inevitably have the last word; it always does, although dramatic natural changes to Hemyock are not visualised in the next million years or so… one hopes at least.

The geological make-up, geography and history of Hemyock have created a wide range of habitats for wildlife within the parish and with a bit of luck the individual who stopped at the millennium seat will have seen one of Hemyock's most exciting natural residents, a buzzard – or perhaps two – soaring above. An earlier traveller wrote a delightful description of the countryside in and around Hemyock which is quoted in the book *The Blackmore Country* by F.J. Snell and published in 1906:

The Culm is a little wandering river abounding with trout. Otters are hunted at Hemyock. Foxes are also found in the neighbourhood and on one occasion the noble wild red deer approached within five miles of us. Birds of all kinds are plentiful, and flowers abound. Bullfinches are a pest even among the apple trees. In my first walk I saw a kingfisher and a jay. The country exudes vegetation at every pore. The mildness of the climate by the fact that on Saturday last I saw in bloom the foxglove, poppy, primrose, wild anthernum and many other flowers. I saw a strawberry grown in the open; watched the bees on the mignonette beds and saw a wood-pigeon's nest with young…

It would be inaccurate to say that nothing has changed but Hemyock still retains much of the wildlife delighted in here. Within the parish are two commons which are nature reserves, Ashculm Turbary and Lickham Common. Both are leased by Hemyock Parish Council to the Devon Wildlife Trust. Ashculm Turbary is classified as a Site of Special Scientific Interest (SSSI) and enjoys an interesting history.

In the Hemyock Enclosure Award of 1836 five separate areas were retained as common land for the use of occupiers of tenements previously having no rights over the much more extensive commons and waste lands where 'the poor people residing with the sd(said). parish of Hemiock [could] dig and cut turf thereon for their own use.' These were called 'Turbaries'. Ashculm Turbary, at Simonsburrow (or Symonsburrow), north of Hemyock village, comprises 16 acres of heath, scrub and wet woodland; it is a predominately wet area and very difficult to walk over. The dominant grass is molinia, which forms large tussocks. There is an abundance of plant and other wildlife in what is an extremely important wet heathland community. Mammals to be seen include roe deer and foxes, and a wide variety of birds breed in or around the reserve. There is some public access to the reserve and a footpath nearby passing through very similar terrain. For lovers of the more adventurous walk this particular path is a must but beware; even wellington boots may not keep you dry at times.

The Lickham Common (or Lickham Bottom) Reserve located to the south-west of the village is somewhat smaller, being about ten acres in extent. It contains a variety of habitats on a north-west-facing slope. A stream flows along the greater part of the boundary and is joined by a small tributary in the north-east corner. There are many plants including bog myrtle, and the wooded area includes willow, birch, hazel and alder trees with the occasional oak. Mammals and birds abound. Buzzards have nested here, as also have kestrels and sparrowhawks which hunt in and around the reserve.

Beyond the boundaries of the nature reserves, Hemyock's wildlife remains diverse; badgers, foxes, rabbits, squirrels and roe deer are quite common. There are a number of badger sets but one mammal, the otter, has long gone from the River Culm, although they were once plentiful enough to command the attention of the Culm Valley Otter Hounds. Fortunately the otter is making a comeback in other parts of Devon and, one hopes, this species will make a welcome return to Hemyock's stretch of the Culm in due course. Now and then walkers exploring the locality on foot may be lucky enough (or unlucky depending on your point of view) to encounter that most beautiful of reptiles, the adder or viper. Grass snakes and slow worms are also to be seen, as well as frogs and toads, mice and voles.

Hemyock is particularly fortunate with its abundance of bird life. Birds of prey can often be seen soaring in groups of a dozen or more; as well as buzzards, sparrowhawks, kestrels, the occasional peregrine falcon and, more rarely, the hobby may be spotted. Every now and then ospreys have been known to spend a couple of days in Hemyock on their passage through the region. As with most places the occasional rarity turns up, including the European nutcracker, which is rather like a very large starling and has been seen both in the churchyard and near Mountshayne. There are quite a few enthusiastic bird-watchers in and around Hemyock and a good indication of just how much there is to be seen is provided by the following list assembled by a keen amateur ornithologist and his wife of the birds spotted in the small back garden of their Hemyock bungalow since 1983. The garden is situated at about 400 feet above sea level and has a bank with hedge to the west with a fairly mature oak tree in one corner. Bird boxes and feeders have been provided to encourage and sustain the avian visitors.

VISITORS SEEN REGULARLY EVERY YEAR

House Sparrow	Coal Tit	Swift
Dunnock	Long Tailed Tit	House Martin
Robin	Marsh Tit	Starling
Wren	Willow Tit	Magpie
Song Thrush,	Treecreeper	Jackdaw
Blackbird	Willow Warbler	Rook
Chaffinch	Garden Warbler	Carrion Crow
Greenfinch	Nuthatch	Great Spotted Woodpecker
Goldfinch	Siskin	Black Headed Gull
Bullfinch	Pied Wagtail	Wood Pigeon
Blue Titmouse	Grey Wagtail	Collared Dove
Great Tit	Swallow	Sparrow Hawk

OCCASIONAL / RARE VISITORS

Blackcap	Meadow Pipit	Mistle Thrush
Brambling	Fieldfare	Wheatear
Chiffchaff	Redwing	Hobby
Goldcrest	Pied Flycatcher	Kestrel
Yellowhammer	Spotted Flycatcher	Jay
Yellow Wagtail	Herring Gull	Tawny Owl
Linnet	Green Woodpecker	Cock Pheasant
Lesser Whitethroat	Lesser Spotted Woodpecker	and even a Male Mallard

OVERHEAD ONLY

Buzzard	Mute Swan	Lesser Back Backed Gull
Heron	Cormorant	and, of course, a cuckoo heard
Canada Goose	Lapwing	but never seen.

In addition two 'escapees' have appeared in this garden: a Ring-Necked Parakeet and a Grey Cockatiel!

This list of 66 species of birds observed in one small part of Hemyock gives some illustration of the wide range of bird life to be seen. Of the birds seen in the bungalow garden the following have actually bred in the garden over the years, blue and great tits, starlings (unwelcome visitors to the roof space for one year), wrens, robins and blackbirds.

The same property has been host to bats in the attic, sadly now moved on, plus other mammalian visitors such as mice, voles, foxes, badgers and hedgehogs.

The patterns of bird life has seen considerable changes over the past decade, not just in Hemyock but over the country in general. Our sample bungalow has seen increases in siskins and goldfinches for example but a great decline in song thrushes. Perhaps one day birds such as the red kite will be seen in the skies over our village. A species that was extinct in this country until recent years it has been re-introduced in parts of the Welsh Borders and the Chiltern Hills with considerable success so who knows what the future holds? One only has to think of a bird introduced into this country not so many years ago, the collared dove, to realise how rapidly and extensively a species can expand. There is certainly no shortage of collared doves in Hemyock.

The natural history of one species has not yet been referred to – man. Were there any of our species living in Hemyock prior to the days of Celt, Saxon and Norman? That question will be dealt with in the next chapter.

Hopefully this brief outline of the basic geology and natural history of Hemyock will give the reader some idea of what is to be seen and whet their appetites to explore the parish and see for themselves.

Sketches in this chapter (and throughout) by Eve Grosse.

An old picture of cottages at Cornhill, at the lower end of Castle Hill, looking towards Hemyock Castle.

The Sealed Knot group enjoy a weekend camp at Hemyock Castle, showing life as it might have been during the troubled days of the English Civil War.

The Sealed Knot group demonstrating the loading and firing of muskets.

CHAPTER TWO

The Early Days

In the Blackdown Hills there is some evidence of human habitation dating to the Mesolithic period some 7000 years ago. During the Neolithic (Stone-Age) period, 4500–2000BC, it is probable that there was human activity in the Blackdowns with the clearance of forest on the higher ground and the creation of trackways, together with some form of farming. However, there is no firm archaeological evidence of human activity during this period in Hemyock itself, with the possible exception of one site. On Hemyock Turbary are what may be the remains of a long barrow (burial chamber). At the site 13 huge stones are placed in an orderly fashion, suggestive of human effort rather than natural causes. The visitor looking at the size of the stones can only ponder on the effort taken to place them where they are. If they do not represent the remains of some prehistoric site, then what might they be? The very special atmosphere excites the imagination.

In the hills around Hemyock are a number of round barrows dating from the Bronze Age and a series of Iron-Age hill-forts, including those at Castle Neroche, Dumpdon and Hembury Fort which latter earthwork also shows signs of Neolithic activity and was used by the Romans for military purposes. With so much human activity in the Blackdown Hills during prehistoric times there can be little doubt that what became the parish of Hemyock was inhabited by ancient races and the blood of those early peoples flows in the veins of some Hemyock folk to this day.

It has recently been discovered that during the Iron Age (750BC–AD100), a great deal of iron smelting was carried on throughout the parish with a concentration of activity around Tedburrow. There is little doubt that the boundaries of the parish were much as they are at present from approximately this time. By Saxon times, c.900AD, there is written evidence identifying permanent features and describing the northern and western boundaries. These Saxon charters are not based on Hemyock but on the adjoining parishes of West Buckland, Wellington and Culmstock, but as the descriptions delineate their boundaries they must also define the boundaries of Hemyock. Around AD905 King Eadweard granted lands in West Buckland and Wellington to Asser (who wrote the biography of King Alfred), the Bishop of Sherborne. This starts at Leigh Hill, close to the Merry Harriers on the Clayhidon boundary. The charter, written in Anglo-Saxon, reads, 'Aerest uppan Dune aet Achangran' which translates as 'first up the hill at the hanging wood of oak trees'. What a superb description of that tree-covered steep greensand scarp slope with the oak trees hanging there as they still do! The land portion then leads along the ancient ridgeway road that runs from east to west where it meets the Hemyock boundary. This road was formerly an ancient trackway and not only the line of demarcation between two parishes but of two counties. It had been a track thousands of years before the arrival of the Saxons.

It had been the limit of King Ine's earlier Saxon conquest of the west, for it was here that the Britons (there must have been some Hemyock ones amongst them) prevented him from spreading both south and west from his base in Taunton. (A great barrow of stones was erected at Simonsburrow near Hemyock at about this time, which was, some say, built to honour a British leader 'Simon'. Others contend that it was the burial place of a Saxon warrior 'Sigemund'.) The charter describes the boundary here as 'of… adune on Sandford Landgemaere' (from the hanging wood of oak trees down to the bounds of Sandford) near what is now known as Sandford Point. The Saxon charter that describes the Culmstock boundary with that of Hemyock also dates from the early 900s. It starts at what the Saxons called the 'Hwyrfel' (a circular hill), now known as Broomfield Breach, where four parishes meet, those of Sampford Arundel, Wellington, Hemyock and Culmstock. Not only do these parishes meet here but so does the Devon/Somerset county boundary.

This junction was of extreme historical interest and must date from ancient times when 'parishes' and 'counties' were carved out from open country. Almost certainly connected with this, a few hundred yards to the north-west, is a circular banked enclosure, some 40 feet in diameter, with an internal ditch. The charter mentions a 'gewearc' (an 'old work') around here and so this structure must pre-date the time of the Saxons. The boundary of the portion of land then continues west along the top of Blackdown Common towards Culmstock Beacon, passing on its way a certain thorn bush that is named (thorns were often used as boundary markers because they could live to a great age) and on to 'peon mynet' (the end of the hill). The boundary then plunges south, down the hill, between Pitt Farm and Pithayne Farm, to a 'lacu' (a stream), which the boundary crossed. These are probably two branches of the River Culm. The next point to be mentioned contains a man's name 'Burgheard's Worpig' (Burgheard's worth or farm). One must assume this farm to be in the Straight Ash-Sidwells area of Hemyock. What is fascinating is that we know that at this time, in the late Saxon era, more than a century before the Normans came, Burgheard and his family were working their 'Worpig' just as their successors the Alfords and Dews do today.

Continuing south the boundary climbs up the side of Hackpen Hill, the top of which it meets at 'Rancomb', which could be Owlerscombe – close to the present Owleycombe. The boundary turns west, towards 'Hacapen' (the current Hackpen), where it becomes the boundary between Culmstock and Uffculme. Apart from Burgheard very few personal names survive from this period. One was an Anglo-Saxon lady called 'Sulca' who lived at some time between AD700–800. A wealthy landowner in the Culmstock and the Culm Davy area of Hemyock, she is thought to have been a person of religion, possibly a wealthy nun of some sort. She granted a lot of her land to Glastonbury Abbey.

Even if few personal names are known, evidence of the British and Anglo-Saxons are found in local names such as our river, the Culm, which is probably British, as is the 'Pen' (a head or top) of Pencross. Place-names containing 'hays' or 'hayne' or burrow' are Saxon. More will be said of place-names later.

The settlement pattern of our village and its hamlets, its long lanes leading to isolated farms, is almost entirely Saxon. One would like to think that the Britons and Saxons were able to live together in the same locality, for although their language, culture and methods of farming were completely different, the joint population was far too small for there to be any pressures of overcrowding. There would undoubtedly have been a degree of intermarriage and some of the descendants of these races live in Hemyock and the Blackdowns to this day.

Some time after the arrival of Sulca, Hemyock became a royal manor and another tier of local government was instituted, the 'hundred'. Hemyock Hundred consisted of seven parishes: Awliscombe, Buckerell, Clayhidon, Culmstock, Dunkeswell, Hemyock and Churchstanton. The Hundred Court, which continued for centuries, met every few weeks in the open air to settle local matters. More importantly information and orders from London could be disseminated quickly. The field in which the Hemyock Hundred Court was held can still be identified at the top of Madford Hill, and what is even more interesting is that many of the footpaths from the seven parishes still converge here.

More changes in both landownership and occupation are mentioned in the Domesday Book in 1086. The main manor was passed to Baldwin and details of those involved in the property can be found in the information on the smaller manors within the parish. We read that 'Otelin [held] Culm Pyne from Baldwin, Godwin held it before 1066' (in Anglo-Saxon times); similarly with Mackham, 'Hamo [held] Mackham from William. Aelmer held it before 1066'; and at Culm Davy, 'Oliver held Culm from Theobald, Colbnan held it before 1066'. Until 1066, when William the Conqueror invaded England, Godwin, Aelmer and Colbran were secure in their small manors in Hemyock. The Normans came and everything changed. Unfortunately history tells us no more; we have no idea what happened to them after they were removed, nor do we know what the ordinary inhabitants thought of their new Norman lords. We can be reasonably sure that Godwin, Aelmer and Colbran would have been occupying some land provided they were prepared to submit to their new Norman rulers.

Mention has already been made of Hemyock place-names and the information they provide. To give the reader some idea of the origins and meanings of place-names within the parish the following (which includes some farm names) is intended as a brief summary.

The name Hemyock is believed to originate from the British stream name 'Samiaco' ('samo' meaning 'summer'). Some authorities do suggest an Anglo-Saxon origin incorporating the personal name 'Hemman' coupled with a Saxon word for bend or hook. The British (or Celtic) origin has, perhaps, a slightly better ring to it. Like so many other names Hemyock has been spelt a number of ways over the centuries, including 'Hamihoc' in the Domesday Book of 1086, 'Hemioch', 'Hemmiac' and many others.

Alexanderhayes (a farm now known as Middle Mackham) was first noted as 'Alysandrehayes' in 1423, becoming 'Alexandrehayes', and is associated with the family of William Alexander.

Culm Davy (or Davey) was 'Comba' in the Domesday Book changing to 'Cumbe Wydeworth' in 1281 then 'Combe Davi' in 1285 and 'Columbdavid' by 1577. A William de Wideword (of Widworthy) held the manor in 1198, the David coming from a later Wideworth (Wydeworth) David. Comba or cumb means a narrow valley in Old English (borrowed from the Celtic 'cwm'). The modern spelling of Culm has obviously been influenced by the river.

Culm Pyne Barton (now Culm Pyne) was 'Colun' in the Domesday Book, becoming 'Colmpyn', named after its position near the Culm and from Herbert de Pynu who held the manor in 1242.

Mackham was 'Madecomb' in 1330 and 'Matcombe' in 1538, probably from a personal name 'Mada', hence Mada's Combe. Nearby Madford may have its origins from the same name.

Mountshayne has certainly been simplified over time. In 1330 it was 'Maundeuillesheghs', in 1359 'Maundesheghes', but by 1566 it had been modernised to 'Mounsheyes'. It is associated with Robert de Maundevill.

Symonsburrow (Simonsburrow) has also seen many changes ranging from 'Simundesbergha' in 1190 to 'Symondesborough Corner' in 1566. It means the 'beorg' or hill/burial place of Sigemund.

Many of Hemyock's farms and other properties have taken the names of individuals and families:

Browning's Farm: from William Browninge, 1610.
Buncombe's Cottage: from Thomas Bunkombe, 1699.
Churchill's: from John Churchyll, 1524.
Clements' Farm: from John and William Clements, 1814 and 1817.
Crocker's Farm: from Radulphus le Crokker, 1330.
Ellis' Farm: from John Ellis, 1657.
Goodall's Farm: from John Goodhale, 1524.
Hartnell's Farm: from John Hartknoll, 1672.
Jewell's Farm: from a Jewell (Juell) recorded in 1672.
Lemon's Hill: from Margaret Lemon and Thomas Leaman, 1633 and 1636.
Lugg's Cottages (now just Lugg's Cottage): from the Lugg family, 1692 onw.
Pike's Cottages: from the Pike family, 1636 onw.
Potter's farm: from John Pottere, 1333.
Toogood's Cottage: from William Toogood, 1583.
Blackaller Farm: probably from Walter de Blakeallre, 1244.

Some people may have taken their name from the place where they lived. For example, Robert atte Burgh came from Burrow Hill Farm in 1333, Coombeshead Farm was the home of Walter de Cumbeshead in 1244, and John atte More lived at Moorhayes Farm.

Other historic names in the parish include:

Ashculm(e), which was Aysshcomb in 1330 and was Aishecombe by 1566. It means 'Ashtree combe' and is another name where the 'combe' element has been altered to 'culm' in more recent centuries.
Castle Hill, which was Castell Mote in 1566.
Combe Hill, which was Culmehill in 1605 – an example where 'culm' has been changed to 'combe' rather than the reverse. It means hill by the Culm.

Conigar Farm (Cunniger in 1667), which comes from the Middle English 'coneygarth', meaning rabbit warren.
Culmbridge Farm, which is recorded as Columbrugg in 1281 and means bridge by the Culm.
Deepsellick Farm, which was Deepsellacke in 1624 and may come from an Old-English word 'sigan' meaning to fall, drip, etc. 'Sellack' could mean a slow-moving, sluggish stream.
Holcombe House, which comes from Holcombe Wood in 1566 indicating a 'hollow valley'.
Madford, which was Madresford in 1281 (see Mackham).
Millhayes, which was Millheghes in 1330, Myllehayes in 1566, and is associated with Robert atte Mulle, 1333.
Newton Farm, which was recorded as Newton in 1566.
Oxenpark Farm, which was Oxenparke Wood in 1566, and Pounds House, which was 'the Pounde' in 1566.
Shuttleton Farm, which was Sheteldoune in 1566 and Shittledon in 1583. The first element here probably comes from the Old English 'scytel' meaning 'dung'.
Tedburrow Farm and Westown, which were Tedborough and Weston (West Farm) respectively in 1566.
Windsor Farm, which was formerly Wynsore in Elizabethan days, the name deriving from a personal name coupled with 'ora', a 'bank'.

So much historical information can be gleaned from place-names. The antiquity of farm names and the names of their occupiers give a glimpse of the rich history of Hemyock.

In 1201 an event took place at Forde Abbey, near Chard, that was to have a great influence on the development, especially agriculturally, of our parish. A dozen monks were selected, with the workman Gregory at their head, to build an abbey on the boundary of Dunkeswell and Hemyock. This was on land close to the Madford River given by Lord William Brewer. It was, like Forde, a Cistercian foundation and being agriculturally progressive, was to shape the pattern of our local farms for centuries to come. The outline of their salmon ponds can still be seen and the first fulling mill (for processing woollen goods) in Devon was built on the Madford River.

Over the following centuries a great deal of farmland was bequeathed to the abbey which in turn became very powerful. Frequent disputes took place between the abbot and surrounding landlords, mostly over grazing rights for cattle. Mention should be made of one such incident between the Abbot of Dunkeswell and William de Asthorp, the lord of the manor, in July 1383. William had seized '12 oxen, 18 cows, 20 boretti and boriculi, 21 juvencae and 200 sheep of either sex' from the manors of Bolham and Biwode (Bywood). He took the stock for 'services and customs in arrears' and delivered them to the Bishop of Exeter's manor at Crediton where they were impounded. The Abbot of Dunkeswell, with 58 men from Hemyock and the surrounding villages, assembled his force at Broadhembury and then rode to the manor of Kynwordlegh, broke into the pound, assaulted and beat William's bailiffs and servants, then took and drove away all of the animals. Needless to say a court case followed. The abbey continued to function until February 1539 when it surrendered to King Henry VIII, at the Dissolution.

Several names of Hemyock inhabitants survive from the 16th century. One such list of names is contained in what is known as the Dynham Survey of 1566. Lord Dynham, who owned the Manor of Hemyock, together with many others, was the High Treasurer of England and when he died in 1501 the various manors passed to his four sisters. Eventually one quarter of the lands came into the possession of Henry Compton who had the whole estate surveyed. The abstracted list, with the name/location of their farms (where known) is shown opposite.

It is interesting to note the variation in the spelling of names that occur even within one list. It is not unusual to find several different spellings of the same surname in documents of this period, such as wills and inventories.

During the 1600s, the inhabitants of Hemyock took quite an active part in the Civil War. In common with many of the cloth-producing villages of the Culm Valley, Hemyock was almost completely united against the Crown. When King Charles I summoned East Devon to appear on a posse, 53 inhabitants of Culmstock, 43 from Clayhidon and 29 from Hemyock, refused to attend. In March 1644 a large insurrection against the King broke out here and the first thing they did was to seize Hemyock Castle. The events that followed are described in the chapter on Hemyock Castle.

Towards the end of the Civil War an outbreak of plague hit the county; at first affecting mainly the soldiers, and then, inevitably, spreading to the civilian population. In Hemyock it made its appearance on 1 June 1646 and continued until 14 August. On that date, when the burial of Marke Wardover took place, the end of the outbreak was remarked upon briefly in the Parish Registers as 'last in ye infection'. During those ten fateful weeks 47 of our villagers died, including no less than five in one particular family, the Penns. At this time a state of absolute panic must have gripped the parishioners, for on 14 July we read the rather poignant entry: 'Marks, Elizabeth, daughter in law to Gregory Blakemore and she deceased as the said Blakemore said and how hee heed up in the dung [sic]'. Gregory must have been so frightened that he buried his son's wife in a dung heap! She was later re-buried in the churchyard.

The history and lives of the people of Hemyock over the centuries were obviously closely involved with Hemyock Castle, the church and of course the village itself. In the chapters ahead we will learn more of this community and the lives of its members, beginning with a tour of the village itself.

Abstracted from Lord Dynham's Survey of 1566

Edmund Whitt	
John St. Clere	Jackey & Aishcombe (Ashculme)
John Calome	Bubbehayne
Richard Blewet	Symonsborough
Isabella Bowreman	Tuttburglefeld (Tedburrow)
William Kyne	
Peter Lyllyscone	Strowfeld (not far from the Catherine Wheel)
John Boodie	Aishcombe
John Tilend	Aishcombe
John Prounz	Symonsborough
Emma Wheton	Hemyoktowne
Henry Hurtenall	Ham
Peter Hollewaye	Allerhayne (in west of parish?)
George Cadberye	Netherplace
Christopher Knoleman	Longecroft & Shereparke
John Baylye	Barnesland
Elizabeth Rydgewaye	Monnsheyes (Mountshayne in Hemyock Town)
James Bowreman	
William Gredie	Myllehays (Millhays)
Richard Duvenell	near Hemyock Castle
Dorothy Gredie	Fishersmeade (near Holcombe?)
Nicholas Sowthewood	Crondehille
Isabella Knowlman	
Thomas Acote	of Hydon
James Harwoode	all the Castle of Hemyock
Henry Walrond	
John Scaddon	Sheteldowne (Shuttleton)
Elizabeth Smith	Chelsehayes
Johanne Barneville	Tedborough
Peter Manley	Newton
John Lyddon	Bakescroft
Richard Streate	Higher Oxenparke-land (Oxenparke)
Richard Bowreman	Grovemede
Stephen Risedon	Pennecrosse (Pencross)
Walter Horrewood	Shyteldon (Shuttleton)
Thomas Reynell	Cottage next to the pound
Thomas Roger	Borough, Sellake (Borough Hill & Sellick)
Humphrey Pen	Tetteborough (Tedburrow)
John Pen	Cottage in Hemyock Town & Oxenpark area)
Elizabeth Carnicote	Aishcombe
John Shakle	Merechaunthayes
John Buteston	Okerford (Culmbridge area)
James Moore	Simounesborough (Symonsburrow)
William Gervis	Cookhayes
John Podinge	Hetherland
John Gredy	Bubhayne & Tedborough
John Horewood	Grene Parke

CHAPTER THREE

The Village & Its People

 **M**uch of the story of Hemyock has been captured on postcards and through photographs, and this chapter is aimed at conveying something of the past century through visual reminders. But first a brief word about the days before the arrival of the camera.

The development of the village from Saxon days through the medieval period to the 17th century was closely linked with Hemyock Castle and the Parish Church. There are, within the parish, buildings of considerable antiquity, some of which were manor houses and which, with the passage of time, became farmhouses. Properties such as Mountshayne, Culmbridge, Whitehall, Culm Davy Farm, Alexanderhayes (now Middle Mackham) and others date back hundreds of years, although in the village centre itself few buildings of any great age remain. One reason for this situation was a fire which took place in 1693. Some idea of the scale of the event can be gleaned from the records known as the 'Devon Sessions Rolls' which contain an entry for the 'Midsummer' 1693 period entitled 'Hemyock Fire' and record details of property destroyed or damaged as follows:

2 June 1693. Mr. Rich. Forst, three dwelling houses 73 foot long and 20 foot wide, beside barnes and stable and other out-houses, loss amount – £150.0s.
Humphrey Moses, 3 dwelling houses 97 foot long and 20 foot wide – £93.10s.
Robert Borrow, 1 dwelling house 31 foot long and 20 foot wide – £30.0s.
Amboras Sarle, 1 dwelling house 32 foot long and 20 foot wide – £30.0s.
John Dalling, 1 dwelling house 33 foot long and 14 foot wide – £10.0s.
John Baillif, 1 dwelling house 18 foot square – £15.0s.
Jeremiah Petters, 2 dwelling houses 54 foot long and 19 foot wide, besides out-houses – £60.0s.

John Kelland, 1 dwelling house 36 foot long and 18 foot wide, besides out-houses – £35.0s.
John Scadding, 2 dwelling houses 43 foot long and 22 foot wide, besides barnes, stables and other out-houses – £150.0s.
Susana Mercy, 1 dwelling house 29 foot long, 19 foot wide – £30.0s.
The Church House, 21 foot long, 20 foot wide – £25.0s.
John Somerhaies, 8 dwelling houses, besides barnes, stables, stalles, linidges [sic] and other out-houses – £396.0s.

	Total is –	*£1024.10s.*
	goods –	*£690.10s.*

(Certified by)
John Baker, William Morgan   *Carpenters*
Hugh Morgan, Lawrence Manfild   *Masons*

THE DAMAGE OF LOSS OF GOODS

John Turke	*£30.0s.*
Barnard Hodge	*£15.0s.*
John Scadding	*£250.0s.*
John Kelland	*£20.0s.*
Samuel Clarke	*£5.0s.*
John Somerhayes	*£100.0s.*
John Bayley	*£10.0s.*
John Dulling	*£1.0s.*
Humphrey Moses	*£30.0s.*
Ezikiah Borrow	*£4.0s.*
Thomas Borrow	*£1.0s.*
Mary Moore	*£1.0s.*
Robert Borrow	*£20.0s.*
Ambrose Searle	*£5.0s.*
James Clarke	*£3.0s.*
Nicholas Wood	*£15.0s.*
Susana Masy	*£3.0s.*
Elizabeth Moore	*£3.0s.*
Aaron Scadding	*£3.0s.*
Joan Clarke	*£1.0s.*
Parish Goods	*£10.0s.*
Total is	*£690.10s.*

394   HEMYOCK HUNDRED.

HEMYOCK, or *Hemiock*, is a considerable village, which gives name to this hundred, and is pleasantly situated on the south side of the river Culm, in the picturesque valley, near *Culmbridge*, 5 miles S. of Wellington, and 9 miles N.E. of Collumpton. Its parish is in Wellington Union, and comprises the hamlet and chapelry of CULM-DAVY, on the opposite acclivities of the valley, adjoining the lofty Black Down Hills and the borders of Somersetshire. It also includes *Millhays*, *Westown*, and many scattered houses; and contains 1222 inhabitants, and 5437A. 2R. 15P. of land, belonging to many freeholders. Mrs. E. P. Simcoe is the largest proprietor, and also lady of the *manor of Hemyock*, which was part of the demesne of the crown at Domesday Survey, but was soon afterwards possessed by the ancient family of Hidon, who had a *Castle* here, which was used as a garrison and prison by the Parliamentarians in the seventeenth century. There are still some remains of four of the towers and a gateway of this castle, which passed, with the manor, from the Hidons to the Dinhams, and was purchased by the late General Simcoe. The manor of *Culm Davy* is vested in the devisees under the will of the late Henry Pook, Esq., and was formerly held by the Widworthy, Wogan, Corbett, Bowerman, and other families. *Hemyock Church* (St. Mary,) is a large and handsome structure, with a tower and five bells. It was rebuilt in 1846-'7, at a great expense, by subscription and rates, aided by grants from the Incorporated and the Exeter Diocesan Societies. It has 1592 sittings, but the old fabric had only about 1340. The latter had a chantry, founded by Peter Uvedale, and endowed with £10 per annum. The *rectory*, valued in K.B. at £32. 0s. 7½d., and in 1831 at £844, with the curacy of Culm-Davy annexed to it, is in the patronage of Edward Wm. Leyborne Popham, Esq., of Littlecote, Wiltshire, and in the incumbency of the Rev. Francis Warre, LL.B., of Cheddon-Fitzpaine, Somersetshire. The Rectory House is a good thatched residence, embowered in trees, and the glebe comprises about 100A. here, and 20A. at Culm-Davy, where there is an ancient *Chapel*, with ninety sittings and a bell turret. In Hemyock are two recently erected chapels, belonging to *Baptists* and *Wesleyans*. The tithes were commuted, in 1842-'3, for £700 per annum. The poor parishioners have 10A. of land, called Hurcombe, purchased in 1651 with £100, left by Peter Holway and other donors. They have also two yearly rent-charges, viz., 20s., left by *Charles Ford*, in the 25th of Elizabeth, out of Strood and Kean's meadows; and 5s., left by *Nicholas Lacke*, out of land at Dunkeswell. *Nicholas Marke*, at an early period, charged Ashcombe estate with the yearly payment of £5 for apprenticing poor children. This parish has a share of *Waldron's Charity* for schooling poor children, as noticed with Clayhidon.

Babb Mark, wheelwgt. & vict. Star	Waldron Philip, gentleman
Baker C. cooper, &c	Walker John, shopkeeper & tailor
Bennett Wm. gent. *Pounds*	Wood Francis, butcher
Bowerman James, gent., and James,	Wood Henry, gent. *Rosemount Hs*
jun., assistnt. overseer, *Culmbridge*	Wood Thos. R. mason & vict. New Inn
Cross Rev Robert (Baptist)	FARMERS. (* are Owners.)
Embrow Robert, carpenter	Bennett Frederick, *Newton*
FisherRev Chas. Forrest, curate, *Recty*	*Bowerman Jas. sen. *Culmbridge*
Fry Robert, parish clerk, *Post-office*	*Braddick —, *Ashdown*
Hine Jas. and Walker Wm. tailors	*Farrant Edward, *New-house*
Hine John, shoemaker	*Farrant John, *Tedborrow*
Hine John, jun. shopkeeper	*Farrant Robert, *Westown*
Masey James and Thomas, butchers	*Hine Thos. (maltster,) *Culmbridge*
Parsey John, blacksmith	Lane Frederick, *Lower Westown*
SpurwayWm.Hy.,Esq.*Culm-DavyHs*	Lock John ‖ Lutley Edward, jun.
Lutley Edward, sen. *Westown*	*Townsend Jas. & Jno. *Whitehall*
*Lutley Thos. (miller,) *Whitehall*	*Troake James, *Lemonshill*
*Mauley Henry (maltster,) *Millhays*	Tuck James, *Hemyock Castle*
Marks Wm. *Great Simonsbro'*	POST *from Wellington.*

Above: *Extract from* White's Directory, *1850.*

These details were copied from the original document by J. Manfield and published in *Devon Notes and Queries* some years ago. Mr Manfield pointed out that it was an exact copy but that the total was incorrect. One wonders if the 17th-century officials noted the error. It is interesting to compare the names of individuals who suffered at the hands of this fire with those listed in the Devon Hearth Tax Return of 1674, 19 years previously. Only one person, Aaron Scadding, is mentioned in both the Hearth Tax Return and the Sessions Roll but a number of the family names such as Kelland, Clarke, Moore, Serle and Hodge appear in both sets of records.

The Hearth Tax was levied from May 1662 until 1689 for each hearth in a property. Exempt from payment were those in receipt of poor relief and those who lived in properties worth less than 20 shillings per annum (who as such did not pay parish rates). Charitable institutions such as schools and almshouses were exempt as were industrial hearths (except bakers' ovens and smiths' forges). The tax,

paid by the occupier, was two shillings on each hearth. Some of the properties detailed in the 'fire' document were surely taxable. It may well be, of course, that the properties affected by the fire had changed hands since 1674 or had been built after that date. Another possibility is that the individuals listed in the Sessions were owners rather than tenants.

Like most other villages the population of Hemyock has changed continuously over the centuries. In the Hearth Tax Return of 1674, for example, out of some 120 names only a few would be familiar to the people of Hemyock today; names such as Cload, Holway, Lutley, Farrent, Prinn (Pring), Ackland, Cole, Hine, Pike, Grenslade and Wide (17th-century spellings). As names changed over the centuries so did the population numbers. There was a steady build-up during the 17th and 18th centuries with the biggest increases coming in the late 1700s and early 1800s. In 1801 the population of Hemyock was just over 1000 reaching 1228 by 1831. During the rest of the 19th century the census returns indicate that there was not a great change until the closing decade when, in 1891, the population was 877. Obviously this was a century of much social change which contributed to the decline. In the early 1900s there was a not a great deal of change; in 1931, for example, the population of the parish stood at 857, only 30 less than 1891. After the Second World War there was a gradual increase, greatly influenced by the physical growth of the village. This was accelerated particularly after the 1970s, since which time newly-built estates have had quite an impact. This is the year of the 2001 census, and an educated guess would put the population of Hemyock at over 2000.

One interesting way of learning something about the village, from the middle 1800s through to recent times, is by studying directories such as *White's* and *Kelly's*. Usually such directories give a potted history of the parish with details of population. Farmers, tradesmen and professional people are listed, together with some private residents though not all. *White's* of 1850 entry for Hemyock and *Kelly's* Hemyock entry for 1935 are reproduced here. It is interesting to compare the two but it must be borne in mind that the directories do not give the whole picture because normally only people who could afford to pay for their entry were included!

The commercial section of *Kelly's* covers a wide spectrum. Apart from the doctor, two dentists, a visiting solicitor, sports clubs and farmers there are numerous other commercial entries. Competition must have been fierce in those days with three cycle agents and three motor engineers. There are still two garages in the village; what was Alfred Wide's is now 'Hemyock Motors' run by Andrew and Geoff Perry, and Stanley Doble's garage still bears the name 'Dobles Garage' but has been owned for some 20 years by David Graham with his son Paul also in the business.

Further perusal of *Kelly's* reveals that Hemyock boasted a printer, a ladies' outfitter, four grocers, a butcher, a boot repairer, plus carpenters, a thatcher, wheelwright, blacksmith, even a rabbit trapper and several builders as there still are today. The name Hart is synonymous with building in Hemyock. *Kelly's* lists George Hart, John Hart and Walter Hart as builders. Today there are three separate Hart building concerns. Of Dennis Hart & Son, Dennis is now retired and his son Stephen manages the business. This branch of the Harts came to Hemyock from Honiton in 1702 and have stayed here ever since. There are also Richard Hart and Derek Hart who run independent family building businesses. Old Hemyock families such as the Harts, Prings, Dobles, Clists, etc. have intermarried over the years and many share common ancestors.

A most important entry in the 1935 *Kelly's* is the Post Office and newsagents, then run by Mrs Ellen Morgan. Fortunately Hemyock still has its Post Office which has been run for many years by Alex and Selina Eltringham. Before them were Percy and Hilda Sanders. The telephone number of the Post Office in 1935 was 'No. 1'. In 1935 there was a sub-branch of the Midland Bank Ltd and a Lloyds Bank agency, both long since departed from the village.

Over the last 50 years the commercial nature of Hemyock, along with other villages, has changed completely. With the increased ownership of motor cars and affluence in general, has come the movement of businesses to local towns. Hemyock is within a ten-mile radius of four towns where the

shops have multiplied and the range of goods on offer has increased dramatically. Already in the 1930s representatives from two grocers in Wellington, the Co-op and Bakers' stores, were cycling to Hemyock to take orders for groceries which were delivered two days later. Soon afterwards Messrs Soundy and Wakefield were bringing clothing and draperies by van from Tiverton and calling on houses in the village. These mobile tradespeople excepted, the village remained largely self sufficient until the Second World War. The traders existed because the goods which they produced were always in demand. Changing fashions, as we now understand them, and the pressure of advertising as it is today, had yet to appear. The *Kelly's* entry illustrates what a diversity of trades and businesses existed in Hemyock in the 1930s. The milk factory was a ready source of employment and the farmers had a reliable market for their milk, eggs and rabbits, so there was sufficient money in circulation to maintain all of these businesses. There was a degree of social cohesiveness within the community and as a village we are the poorer for having lost these entrepreneurs.

Although we have far fewer shops in Hemyock today we are still more fortunate than many villages. Besides the still busy Post Office which is also a newsagency and grocery store, there is a 'Spar' store where one can shop until 10p.m., 364 days a year. It has been run by Christine Stepney since the death of her husband David. There are two 'unisex' hairdressers, the Catherine Wheel, the two garages referred to earlier, a takeaway food establishment at Brook House and a financial advisory service (Two Counties) located at Halifax House, where there has been a Halifax agency for many years. Many services are provided by businesses and individuals based at home or on the small industrial estate. The builders and carpenters are very well represented and there are new services that would have somewhat baffled the Hemyockians of 1935; among them television engineers, computer experts and other high-tec specialists. With the recent loss of the Hemyock Milk Factory there is only one substantial commercial site, Brookridge Timber, which is located on the edge of the village.

Left: Two pages from George Clist's account book, listing journeys with his hearse for the years 1852–53. Details are given of where the coffin came from, the churchyard to which it was taken, the distance in miles, whether the palls were used and the cost. Some ten years later two of his children had managed to write their names on the bottom of the book.

HEMYOCK is a parish and village on the south bank of the river Culm, and terminus of the Culm Vale branch of the Great Western railway from Tiverton junction, opened in 1875; it is 5 miles from Wellington (Somerset), 12 east from Tiverton, 10 north from Honiton, and 10 south-west from Taunton, in the Tiverton division of the county, hundred of Hemyock, petty sessional division of Cullompton, rural district of Culmstock, county court district of Wellington (Somerset), rural deanery of Cullompton and archdeaconry and diocese of Exeter. The river Culm flows through the parish, and is noted for the quantity and excellence of its trout. The church of St. Mary, restored and enlarged in 1847 by the addition of a north aisle, is a large building of stone in the Early English and Decorated styles, consisting of chancel, nave, aisles, transept, south porch and an embattled western tower containing a clock and 6 bells: there is a screen between the chancel and north aisle: the font consists of a Norman basin on a shaft of Perpendicular date: there are 700 sittings. The register dates from the year 1635. The living is a rectory, with the chapelry of Culm-Davey annexed, net yearly income £500, including 10 acres of glebe, with residence, in the gift of Hugh Leyborne Popham esq. and held since 1927 by the Rev. Leslie Gilbert Ketchley M.A. of Keble College, Oxford, hon. C.F. In the churchyard is a granite cross erected in 1920 by public subscription as a memorial to 20 men connected with the parish who fell in the Great War, 1914-18. There are Baptist and Methodist chapels. A cemetery of about half an acre in extent was opened in 1901, and is under the control of the Parish Council. In this parish was the cream and butter factory of the Culm Valley Dairy Company Limited, the oldest of its kind in England, which was burnt down in 1923; the site is now occupied by the model factory of Wilts United Dairies Ltd. devoted to the manufacture of dried milk. An important market for live stock is held here every first and third Monday in the month, and is well attended. There are charities to the amount of about £29, the principal being Walrond's of £5, Land's of £12, and the Second Poor Fund of £31 5s. annually. There are the remains of a castle, formerly belonging to the Eldon family, who occupied it until the reign of Edward I. when it passed to the Dynhams, and was divided between the four sisters of Sir John Dynham 6th Baron Dynham K.G. and treasurer of England; in 1642 it was captured by the Royalists under John, 1st Baron Poulett, and eventually dismantled; portions of four of the towers and the gatehouse, a structure of flint, with part of the moat, still remain, but are fast falling to decay. Mrs. Barton, who is lady of the manor, William Edwards esq. John Clist esq. J.P. and Mrs. Lutley are the principal landowners. The soil is clayey; subsoil, various. The crops are wheat, oats and barley, but principally dairy and pasture. The area is 5,901 acres; the population in 1931 of the civil parish was 857, and of the ecclesiastical parish, 785.

The hamlet and chapelry of CULM-DAVEY, 1¼ miles north, is in this parish. The chapel here, about 1¼ miles from the village of Hemyock, is an ancient building of flint stone, with sittings for 60 persons. The old manor house, now occupied as a farmhouse by Mrs. Lutley, retains some ancient stone and plaster work.

Post, M. O., T. & T. E. D. Office. Letters through Cullompton

Railway Station (G. W)

Western National Omnibus Co. Ltd. service through, to Taunton & Seaton, daily

PRIVATE RESIDENTS.

(For T N's see general list of Private Residents at end of book.)

Ashland James, Rokeby
Agar Ralph, Cheritons
Barton Mrs. Castle cottage
Barton Reginald, Sunny Croft
Bell Victor, Tedburrow house
Beard Mrs. Parsonage
Clarke Albert, Tedburrow house
Clist John J.P. Mountlands
Edmondson Ronald Ernest, Dixcroft
... Florence Romaine, Culm Davey house
... Charles, Woodlands
Graves Robert, Rosemount
Griffin John Lysaght, Sandhurst
... Thomas, Culm Bridge house
... Neville J. Hemyock place
Ketchley Rev. Leslie Gilbert M.A., hon. C.F. (rector), Rectory
Lutley Mrs. Whitehall
Lutley Saml. Panlee
... Frank, Fircroft
Mitchell Sidney Chas. Kellands
Persons Frank Stanley, Windlehurst
... William, Pencross house
... Mrs. Elworthy
... Alfred, Orpington house
... Howard, Wyndham
... Miss E. The Fernery

COMMERCIAL.

Early closing day, Thursday.
Marked thus † farm 150 acres or over.

...nd Wilfred Hart, farmer, Mill...
...e William John, printer, Station road. T N 20
...b Eva M. (Miss), ladies' outfitter, ...tion rd
...d Charles, cycle agent
...y Wm. seed mer. Egypt ho
...mford Harry, smallholder, ...wahaath
...ick Charles John, grocer
...r William, dairyman, Tedburrow
...r Wm. farmer, Higher Mackham
...ery (Edgar Lawrence, clerk to the Burial Authority)
...t Chas. Clifford, blacksmith
...a Geo. farmer, Oxonpark
...a Jn. farmer, Mount...ayne
...Reginald. farmer, Lemons hill
...Chas. Bernard, farmer, Goodalls
...Rd. farmer, Goodalls farm
...Clara (Mrs.), cycle agt. Station rd
...Fly-fishing Association
...Leonard Chas. farmer, ...
...Merlin, farmer, Tanhouse

Doble Alfd. farmer, Upper Madford
Doble John, farmer, Culm bridge
Doble Stanley James, motor engineer & cycle agent, Station road
Drake Wm. Hy. butcher. T N 10
†Edwards Wm. farmer, Chapel farm
Evans Edward, cattle dealer, Castle hill
Farmer Jas. farmer, Clements farm
Farrant Edwd. L.D.S. dental surgn. (surgery)
Farrant Jn. farmer, Newhouse
Farrant Thos. frmr. Higher Ashculm
Farrant Wm. farmer, Westown
Forbear Alice (Mrs.), frmr. Mackham
Goldsworthy Florence Amy (Mrs.), smallholder, Straight Ash
Granger John, rabbit trapper & dealer, Cornhill
Granger Sidney, farmer, Deep Sellick
Greenslade Fredk. farmer, Sidwells
Griffin John Lysaght M.R.C.S.Eng., L.R.C.P.Lond. physcn. & surgn. Sandhurst. T N 6
Griffin W. farmer, Luggs farm
Hall Frank, cattle dlr
Hall William, motor engineer, cycle agent, ironmonger, saddler & boot & shoe dealer, Station road
Hart Geo. bldr
Hart Jas. farmer, Ellises farm
Hart Jn. builder, contractor & house decorator, Station road
Hart Walter, builder
Hartnell Fredk. Jas. farmer, Conegar farm
Hemyock Bowling Club (H. L. Wide, hon. treas.), Station rd
Hemyock Lawn Tennis Club
Hill Thos. farmer, Jewells farm
Hine Thomas William, miller (water), Culm mills. T N 22
Hookway Wm. carpntr. Whitehall
Howard Chas. Alvan, farmer, Thorne pk
Howe Edmnd. farmer, Holingarth, Station rd
†Howe Jas. farmer, Burrow hill
Hutchings Sidney, farmer, Higher Culme Pyne
Huth Sydney F., M.R.C.S.Eng., L.R.C.P.Lond. physcn. & surgn. & medical officer & public vaccinator (surgery)
James Albt. farmer, Holcombe
James Harold Wltr. sanitary inspector & road surveyor, Verdancott
James Regnld. F. grocer, Station rd. T N 2
Jenkins Ernest Hy. boot repr
Kemp Thomas, farmer
Lawrence Edgar, clerk to the Parish Council & to the Burial Authority, Ashculme farm

Lawrence Saml. farmer, Ashculme
Lee-Michell & Co. solctrs. (attend mons. fortnightly), High st
Lloyds Bank Ltd. (agency) (open mon. & fri.); head office, 71 Lombard st. London E C 3
Lowman James, smith, Whitehall
Midland Bank Ltd. (sub-branch to Wellington) (open mon. 10 a.m. to 3 p.m.; fri. 1 to 3.30 p.m.), Cornhill; head office, Poultry, London E C 2
Morgan Ellen (Mrs.), newsagt. & sub-postmistress, Post office. T N 1
Oxenham T. E. A. P. dentist (attends sat)
Parish Hall (H. W. James, sec)
Parsons Ernest Hy. farmer, Simonsborough
Payne Wm. farmer, Castle farm
Pooley Rd. farmer, Pound
Pring Fredk. farmer, Byes farm
Pring Dennis Jn. farmer, Westhayes
Railway Hotel (Clarence Radford)
Redwood William, farmer, Little Simonsburgh
Reed Hy. farmer, Culm Bridge frm
Salter Frank, wheelwright, Station rd
Salter Jn. thatcher
Salter Wm. Jas. farmer, Springside
Small George & Sons Ltd. coal mers
Smith Fanny (Mrs.), smallholder, Riverside, Whitehall
Stradling Jn. baker
Strawbridge Rd. Hine, bldr
Summers Chas. farmer, Alexander hayes
Symons Rt. farmer, Wheatmoor
Talbot Thos. Hy. farmer, Ashculme
Tancock Frank, farmer, Bodhaine
Thomas Emily (Miss), farmer, Culm Davey
Vean Marjorie (Miss), farmer, Pithayne
Webber Wltr. Jas. grocer
White Thos. Carter, farmer, Culm Pyne Barton
Wide Alfred & Co. proprietors of Orpington garage, agricultural implement agents, motor engineers, & garage, & egg & game merchants. T A "Wide, Hemyock;" T N Hemyock 3. See Advt. index
Wide F. E. & Son, fire, life & genl. insur. agts. Sherwood
Wide H. & Co. grocers
Wilts United Dairies Ltd. (R. E. Edmondson, mngr.), dried milk mfrs. T A "Factory, Hemyock;" T N Wellington 52
Wood Rd. farmer, Windsor
Wright J. farmer, Hill farm
Wyatt John, farmer, Black Aller

Left: *At the bottom of Cornhill with Mr Hall's saddlery, later to become the butcher's shop. Note the oil lamp by the bridge.*

Right: *An early postcard view of the Square in Hemyock. In the foreground is the Hemyock Pump erected in 1902. On the left is the Star Inn which burnt down in 1928.*

The old Saw Mill yard c.1891–93. This circular saw was driven by a portable steam engine, as opposed to a traction engine which moved under its own power. This engine was hauled by a horse and the shafts are visible in front of the smoke box. The chimney was hinged to fold horizontally, laying in the 'U' bracket above the valve chest allowing the engine to be stored or moved to other locations for thrashing, etc. The two poles (centre) are for making a ramp to the frame of the bench, enabling logs to be winched up for cutting. On the left is a long-handled shovel for removing sawdust. The engine driver, wearing the watch chain (believed to be Charlie Blackmore), has a shovel to feed the engine with sawdust, and leaning against the rear wheel is a long-handled rake for clearing out the fire box. His right hand is on the regulator, cranked at 90 degrees, ready to go. George Barton (1823–93) is standing by the front of the engine. George Barton junr (1865–1912) is standing on the saw bench.

Left: *In the Square where Broadway is now. The smithy can be seen on the left with a range of horse-drawn implements on display; from the left front, a horse rake, a pair of mowing machines and what would appear to be some drags beyond.*

Below: *Looking up Castle Hill. The Church Sunday School is on the left.*

Left: *Looking down the High Street towards the Pump. The cottages have climbing roses against their walls. Behind the Pump there is farm machinery on display in front of the smithy.*

Right: *The Square before 1900 with the original water pump. The coffee shop window is on the left, the cottages that were burnt down in the centre, then A. Wide's original shop and on the right Hides' shop always known as 'Up Steps'.*

Left: *An early view of the Square from the top of the church tower. Both public houses, The Star (which later burnt down) and the Catherine Wheel, were joined together and are on the right.*

Below: *The Square, where the thatched cottages have been replaced by the brick-built Orpington House and the old Post Office. A range of farm machinery is on display outside the smithy.*

Below: *Looking up the High Street to Mr Carrick's shop, where the windows are elaborately dressed with oil-lamps on the left and a tiered display on the right. Inside the shop, boots, buckets and jugs, etc. were hung from many hooks in the ceiling.*

Below left: *From the church tower, 1990s. The small white building (left, recently demolished) was the Midland Bank agency office. The centre property was a shop, which was last used as a butcher's. It is now a private house.*

Below right: *From Station Road towards Millhayes. Note the smoke from the factory chimney. Dobles Garage is now just beyond the terrace of houses (left). A field on the right, part of Hollingarth Farm, has been fenced into building plots, each sold for £50 before 1939.*

Left: *Looking from Culmbridge Road towards Fore Street. The top of the roof of the Baptist Chapel can be seen on the left. The present Post Office is part of the cottage with the tall chimney.*

Below left: *Looking towards Culmbridge Mill.*

Below: *Station Road before Castle Park was built, c.1950s.*

Henry and Victress Trickey outside their home in Culmbridge Road, 1920s.

Left: *Evelyn Alford of 'Mrs Alford up the steps' fame, outside her shop which stocked everything from groceries to collar studs. The shop has gone but the premises, 'Brook House', are now a food takeaway and B&B.*

Below: *Looking towards the Square from Cornhill. Note the oil street lamp by the bridge and the horse's collar outside the saddlery on the right. Beyond the Pump is a pile of flint where the cottages were burnt down c.1920.*

Mr and Mrs Webber's mobile fish-and-chip van in Hemyock Square, c.1972.

Hemyock Square as it is today.

Above: *One of Redwood's buses going through the floods at Millhayes.*

Above right: *A group looking at the aftermath of the floods at the corner by Hemyock Motors. Left to right: Martin Pring, Ruby Mather, Phyllis Salter, Sam Mather with Bob Lowman on the right. The buildings in the background housed Alfred Wide & Co's egg-packing station.*

Right: *Reg Hart in a snowdrift with a milk can at the top of Pencross Hill, 1963.*

Above: *Flooding by Hemyock Motors before Castle Park was built.*

Above right: *A snow scene at the lower end of Station Road, 1963.*

Right: *A modern winter view, looking down Prowses towards Pencross.*

LOCAL TRANSPORT

Obviously one of the most important changes in village life was the increasing use of motor transport for travelling, not only privately owned motor cars but coaches and buses. The story of one Hemyock business, Redwood's Coaches, gives a good picture of how public service transport developed in our village. In 1933 Walter J. Redwood sold his green-grocery business in Paulton, Somerset, and purchased a cycle-repair and car-hire business in Hemyock, from a Charles Bird. The small garage was located behind Rose Cottage in Fore Street.

By 1937 the garage was too cramped so Walter Redwood rented a house at Broadway and built another garage at the rear. It is now part of Hart's building yard. Mr Redwood started a bus service to and from Taunton that ran on Saturdays and Tuesdays. The last service would leave Taunton at 10p.m. thus enabling people to go to the theatre, etc. Because of licensing restrictions this service had to run via the back lanes as Western National held the licenses for the more populated areas. In 1945 a similar service was commenced to Wellington on the same route on Wednesdays and Fridays. Walter Redwood bought his first bus, a Chevrolet, in 1933. Parcel storage was on the roof, access being by a metal ladder strapped to the rear. The bus was driven by belts which slipped on the hills and people often had to walk and push. This bus was used for a school contract, via Madford, to Hemyock School.

During 1940 the Government requisitioned buses to convey workers to build aerodromes at Trickey Warren, Dunkeswell and Smeatharpe, later used by Allied airforces. A Government permit had to be obtained to buy a larger vehicle and a Bedford 32-seater was purchased. This had wooden seats, was painted brown and was parked at Hemyock Castle. During the war years Redwood's taxis were used in the morning, with the seats removed, to carry school meals from Culmstock Central Canteen to local schools including Ashill, Clayhidon and Hockworthy (all of which have long since closed). As garaging was becoming increasingly difficult Walter Redwood bought a plot of ground at Churchill's, in the High Street, and built a brick garage in which to maintain and park the larger vehicles.

After the war, although petrol was rationed, people wanted to make trips to the seaside and other places further afield. To cater for this new interest Mr Redwood purchased two more Bedford 29-seater luxury coaches and then, in the 1960s, 33- and 41-seater secondhand coaches were purchased and

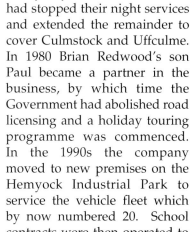

One of Redwood's early coaches, a 29-seater Bedford Duple Vista (Royal Blue) used from 1945 and pictured here at a rally.

more private hire taken on including Wellington School. Brian Redwood took over the business from his father and private hire contracts continued to build up including one with Queen's College in Taunton. Eventually, the business took over Doble and Shires Coaches of Taunton. The Redwood fleet had now extended to eight coaches and three taxis. In the 1970s Western National withdrew all bus services from the Culm Valley. By this time Redwoods had stopped their night services and extended the remainder to cover Culmstock and Uffculme. In 1980 Brian Redwood's son Paul became a partner in the business, by which time the Government had abolished road licensing and a holiday touring programme was commenced. In the 1990s the company moved to new premises on the Hemyock Industrial Park to service the vehicle fleet which by now numbered 20. School contracts were then operated to Uffculme, Honiton, Tiverton and Wiveliscombe but the bus services had to be withdrawn owing to competition from other companies and falling passenger numbers (due in the main to the fact that most families in the village now own at least one car if not more).

Redwoods Coaches are now to be seen all over the country – and Europe. It gives one quite a feeling to be hundreds of miles from Hemyock and suddenly see a coach passing by bearing the legend 'Redwoods of Hemyock, Devon' – a far cry from the small garage business of 1933! Hemyock is fortunate now to have several general buses providing daily services to local towns such as Wellington, Taunton and Honiton, even to the South Coast. Many rural communities in the county, in fact nationwide, have absolutely no access to public transport at all.

WIND & WEATHER

Whether travelling by bus, coach, car, bicycle, horse or merely on foot, the weather plays a vital role and over the centuries records show that Hemyock has experienced considerable extremes of climate. These may get worse with global warming; perhaps in the coming years flooding will become an ever greater problem – only time will tell. No doubt the television cameras will record everything for posterity. In the 1960s, however, when Hemyock experienced severe snow storms that cut off the village and flash floods that swept through the parish, it was the late Edgar Lowman who was on hand to record the events with his camera. Included opposite are a few of the photographs taken by Edgar nearly 40 years ago picturing Hemyock under siege from the weather.

Whit Monday Friendly Society Parade in the Square, complete with their banner, early 1900s. The Society was one of thousands throughout the country that, in return for weekly contributions, provided benefits for its members who suffered hardship through illness, accident or death. These 'clubs' played an essential part in our villages in the days before Welfare State provision. Hemyock's club was a branch of the Rational Friendly Society. Several of the men are wearing badges of office.

Above: *Culmstock Silver Band at a Whit Monday Friendly Society celebration in the early 1900s.*

Left: *A post-parade Friendly Society dinner in the school, June 1906. Among the decorations are a number of posters with messages such as: 'The Flowing Tide is With Us', 'Unity is Strength' and 'Bear Ye One Another's Burden', together with the Union Flag and the Rational Societies' emblem.*

SPECIAL EVENTS

Like most active villages Hemyock has always had something going on; fêtes and carnivals, sports days, fund-raising events for good causes. The people of the village have always been very generous whether raising money for local projects, or the Devon Air Ambulance, Cancer Research, People in Romania, Africa and India – the list is endless. Naturally all these activities require organisers and committees; where would we be without our committees? Fortunately committees have a habit of being photographed and a selection of such pictures is shown here. One of Hemyock's most famous landmarks, the Pump, was largely brought about by the efforts of the Coronation Committee pictured in all their splendour in 1902. The Pump was erected to commemorate the reign of Queen Victoria, the Coronation of Edward VII and the end of the Boer War. The sentiments inscribed on the Pump were particularly apt at a time when the British love of the monarchy and Empire was at a peak. They inspired the poet of the Blackdown Hills, Mr A.B. Blackmore, to write the following poem. It first appeared in *The Field* magazine in 1968, then in a small book of poetry entitled *The Bells of Kentisbeare and other Poems*. It reads:

Cissie Granger with maids of honour, left to right: Doris Bird, Marjorie Webber, Doris Ayres and Dora Bale.

HEMYOCK PUMP

The village pump in Hemyock Square,
(a fine ornate cast-iron affair)
Was builded there in nineteen-two,
Long before me or maybe you.

Lonely it stands, and long since dry,
While motor-cars go rushing by,
And no-one ever stops to heed
The words it bears for all to read.

'Fear God', it says, 'Honor the King';
Five simple words, but how they ring
Across the years, reminding us,
As we stand waiting for the bus,

That people, sixty years ago,
Were not (as now) ashamed to show
Allegiance both to Church and Crown;
Long live the pump in Hemyock town!

Mr Blackmore might well have found the community in 2001 even less willing to show their allegiances than they were in 1968. One village tradition that continues to this day is the gathering around the Pump at midnight, the linking of hands and the singing of 'Auld Lang Syne' on New Year's Eve. Many of the revellers have usually come from the Catherine Wheel and are in excellent voice, or think they are! One modern problem, however, is that very few people know the words of the song. Such is progress.

One of the events that has played a big part in village life is the Hemyock carnival. The date of the very first carnival is not known but it was certainly quite an event according to a 1930 advertisement. Not only was there a traditional procession around the village but additional events on the Recreation Ground. These included a 'grand boxing display', something that one would be unlikely to see nowadays with the lack of interest in that 'noble art'. Jazz and the 'Broadway Five Orchestra' were enjoyed by all. Prizes were numerous and, as ever with these carnivals, the event was in aid of a good cause, on this occasion the Wellington and Taunton Hospitals and the Hemyock Nursing Association.

In 1933 the first ever Hemyock carnival queen was crowned. She was Cissie Granger (later to marry and become Cissie Gunn). A local newspaper described her as 'a young lady of charming disposition, who worthily upheld the dignity of her regal position'. The newspaper then went on to describe the carnival procession itself:

THE PROCESSION

A novel tableau was a decorated car, so arranged that it was a very fine representation of H.M. Yacht Britannia. It was Mr. W. Griffiths' entry and the sailors were Messrs. K. Hole, H. Hole and R. Griffiths. The 'Unhappy Home', was demonstrated by Messrs. W.H. Agar and R. Quick on Mr Summers' lorry; and 'Wealth and Beauty' was represented by the snow-white plumes of a swan of exaggerated proportions, arranged on Mr. S. Lutley's car. Miss Molly Lutley was the gay young rider. Another attractive tableau was 'The Christmas Party' [with] Winnie Bird, Betty Bird, Stanley Tancock, Bryan Drake and Billie Grabham... obviously enjoying the fun of riding on Mr. Salter's lorry, and of having so much to remind them of the rapid approach of Christmas. Mrs Tancock arranged the tableau. Mr. W. James entered the 'Churchstanton

The Coronation Committee, by the newly erected Hemyock Pump on 14 August 1902. The inscription on the shield reads 'In Commemoration of the Glorious Reign of VICTORIA, the Coronation of EDWARD VII and restoration of Peace in SOUTH AFRICA, 1902, Fear God and Honor the King'.
Inset: A memorial card to Queen Victoria, 1901.

Coronation Committee, 1911. 1. ?, 2. Jack Salter,
3. Robert Graves, 4. Alfred Wide, 5. Revd de B. Forbes,
6. Mr Hall (Church Sexton), 7. Mr Tait, 8. Mr Pickard,
9. Mr Brain (Baptist Minister), 10. ?, 11. Frank Hall (butcher),
12. ?, 13. Mr Lutley, 14. ?, 15. Edwin Wide, 16. Mr Baxter,
17. ?, 18. Bennie Parsons, 19. Tom Lowman, 20. ?,
21. George Hart, 22. ?, 23. John Hart, 24. Mr Cload.

Coronation Lunch Committee, 1937. Left to right, back: John (Jack) Granger, Clarence Radford, Mr Howard, Mr Symons, Walter Redwood, Frank Tancock, John Hart, Stan Symons; front: Bill Drake, Jim Doble, Revd L. Ketchley, Mr Strawbridge, Sonny Farmer.

Above: *The entire Coronation Committee of 1937 outside the Parish Hall.*

Left: *Dancing through the street at the Coronation celebrations in the village in 1953. Early leaders in the dance are Thelma Lowry and Mrs Pike, June Bradbury and Mary Salter, Barbara and Les Bowden, Mrs Netherway and Marjory Webber, Barbara Hole and Michael Pike, and Mrs Reed followed by a large part of the population of Hemyock.*

❧ Hemyock Carnival ❧
1977–1995

Clockwise from above:

1st prize in the 1987 carnival. Left to right, back: Doreen Moores, Hilary Cole, Debbie Scoble, Sarah Scoble, Rita Hooper; front: Steve Moores, Derrick Parsons (driving tractor), and Spencer Moores.

Left to right: Neil Hawkins, Tom Young, Jim Hawkins, Phillip Hawkins, Adrian Lowman – 1977.

Carnival float, 1984, featuring 'Crocker's Lot'. Left to right: Barbara Bowden, Barbara Churchill and caveman, Jim Hawkins.

David Graham, proprietor of Doble's Garage, with a vehicle from his Second World War collection.

Hemyock Surgery's float, 1988, with Dr John Griffin in a white coat preparing to operate, Dr Jonathan Meads, Dr Donald McLintock dressed as a very fetching staff nurse, holding a giant hypodermic syringe, with a number of patients, and Mrs Christine Meads disguised as Mrs Thatcher looking on.

Opposite page, top to bottom:

First revived carnival, November 1977, with Richard Young as the king and Stephanie Edmonds as the queen, Nicola Lowman as the princess and Susie Batten, Penny Weymouth, Lynette Shere and Sandra Allen as attendants.

Carnival, 1995. The Hemyock School and PTA entry, 'Tutankhamun and his followers'.

Cyril Finch's steam roller which made many appearances in carnival processions.

Carnival float, 1989. Left to right: Barbara Churchill, Barbara Bowden, a young evacuee, Les Bowden, Jim Hawkins and John Churchill.

Ropers', a reminder of the Wild West. The Wellington South Street Centenary Band (conductor Mr. W. Walters) and the Wellington Fire Brigade under Captain Eno, were also in the procession... Individual masqueraders were:- Raymond Casely (Robin Hood), Bill Casely (Jester), Mrs James, Churchstanton (Carnival Follies), Mrs Norman (Pirate), Mrs H. Bale (Decorated Pram), Leslie Smith (Tramp), Mrs A. Baker (Farm Labourer), Mrs V. Bale (Autumn), Mr. T.L. Edwards (Scarecrow), Miss Burrows (Cat).

Children obviously played a big part in the carnival procession, and some of the young prize winners included Christine Lowman (Powder Puff), George Bale (Corn Field), Phylis Trickey (Chinese Girl) and Cecil Lowman (Bedtime). Ah! Happy Days.

The war years unfortunately brought an end to the Hemyock carnival, as it did so many things and there was no carnival in the village until 1977. As in the 1930s the enthusiasm and effort of organisers and participants alike ensured that there was a successful carnival for the next 21 years. The selection of photographs in this book of the event over the years gives an idea of the hard work and imagination put into floats and costumes and of the organisation involved every year. Sadly the last Hemyock carnival was held in 1998. There was no lack of ideas for the event itself but lack of man- and womanpower made it impossible to go ahead. Perhaps the carnival has become a victim of modern society; many families have both husband and wife working and just do not have the time to become involved. But who knows; perhaps the situation may change in the years ahead and the Hemyock carnival will be revived once more?

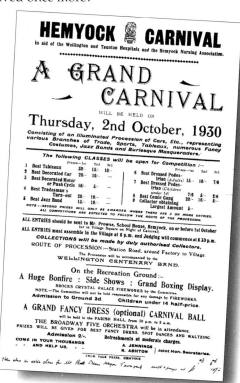

Laying the foundation stone for Hemyock Parish Hall in 1927. On the right is the Revd de Burgh Forbes. And on his right Mr Jim Hart who built the hall. A time capsule was placed beside this stone at the time. The Revd Forbes was remembered when the smaller of the rooms in the building was named 'The Forbes Lounge'.

Mention was made earlier about the Hemyock Recreation Ground which is located alongside the Parish Hall. This area was set aside shortly after the First World War. At a Parish Meeting in March 1919, it was decided not only to erect a Memorial Cross to the 'Men and Lads' who had lost their lives in or through the Great War, but it was also hoped that it would also be possible to commemorate the victory of the Allies by acquiring a 'Village Green' or 'Recreation Ground'. Contributions had been sought within the parish for both projects and the village did get its War Memorial and Recreation Ground. Something of the story is set out in a notice, signed by the Revd John de B. Forbes, Rector of Hemyock and Chairman of the Hemyock Recreation Ground Committee.

The Hemyock Parish Hall is probably one of the finest in Devon. It is well appointed, well maintained and very well used. Every conceivable use is made of the building: playgroups, concerts, public meetings, musical shows, flower shows, a Saturday market, dance class, aerobics and much, much more. The success of the hall owes a great deal to generations of people who have served on, or are still part of the Parish Hall Committee: Edgar Lowman, Roy Barton, Dennis Hart, Robin and

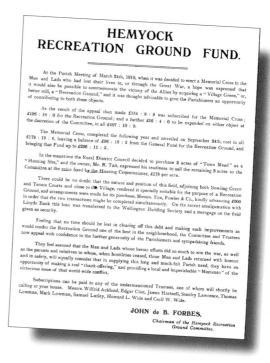

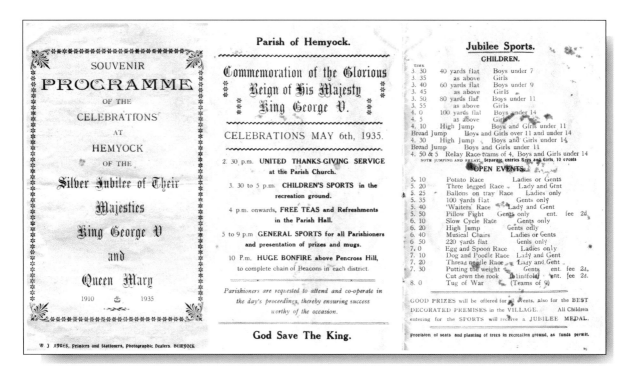

Top right: *Fund-raising notice for the Recreation Ground.*
Above: *'Souvenir' programme for the Silver Jubilee celebrations of King George V and Queen Mary, 1935.*

Heather Stallard, Dennis Gubb, and so many more too numerous to name. As was said earlier, 'where would we be without our committees?'

Jubilees, Coronations and similar significant dates were always a good excuse for planned celebrations. Obviously over the years hundreds of events have taken place in Hemyock and the collection of photographs here and elsewhere in the book can only scratch the surface of village social activities. We have also included in this chapter a small selection of photographs of Hemyockians past and present, families and individuals who were, and still are part of the ongoing story of the parish.

Naturally the millennium brought about its own share of events and projects. One such project was the eye-catching 'WELCOME TO HEMYOCK' sign. Situated at the top of Pencross Hill the sign greets visitors who enter the village from the north on the road from Wellington. The whole idea was the brainchild of the 'Hemyock Party Club' Committee consisting of Dennis Gubb (Chairman), Pam Gubb, Les Bowden (Treasurer), Barbara Bowden, John Hooper, Rita Hooper (Secretary), Derek Brooks, Ruth Brooks, John Churchill and Barbara Churchill. Money collected from people during the Party Club's annual carol-singing round the village in 1999 was pledged for a village sign. The idea was developed into a dual-aspect seat on the back of the sign enabling people to sit and admire the wonderful views down the Culm Valley and as far as Dartmoor. Local people and organisations gave freely of their time, materials, money and use of facilities. Uffculme Environmental, the Hemyock Parish Council, Brookridge Timber and Scoble Plant Hire all made contributions, together with a number of local people giving local stone for the structure. Martin Pring, of Pring & Son Carpenters and Joiners, selected, prepared and fitted two seats made of local chestnut. The polished granite tablet, measuring 4 feet by 2 feet, has engraved inlaid lettering. Each corner of the tablet is embellished with natural coloured acorns and oak leaves. It was sand blasted to ensure a grand appearance that will last for years. The tablet was prepared by the award-winning monumental mason Daniel Howsham of Lowestoft. On the back of the structure are two small plaques reading 'Donated by Hemyock Party Club and the people of the village' and 'Supported by Uffculme Environmental in partnership with Viridor'. The joint efforts of Bob Wigley and Wil Pike, of the Devon County Council and South West Highways, helped in the build up and preparation of the site. The official unveiling took place on Friday 20 October 2000 and was performed by retired local doctor, John Griffin, who was born and bred in Hemyock. This project is a wonderful example of initiative and community spirit and we can be certain that the people of Hemyock and its visitors will be able to enjoy the sign, the seats and the views for generations to come.

✃ VE Day Anniversary, 1995 ✃

Top to bottom:
St Mary's book stall with Chris and Shirley Dracott, Revd Tony Grosse and Alec Smith.

Jim and Mary Hawkins at their stall.

Claude Caple in the 'communications' tent. Many are the occasions when Claude has been responsible for the setting up of the public-address systems for Hemyock events.

❧ Women's Groups ❧

Left: *WI parish hall clock presentation. Left to right, back: the Misses Finch, Naish, Le Fevre, Lutley, Lutley, Lowman, Hole, ?, South, Fuller, Farrant, Bennett; middle: Guppy, Clist, Board, Ackland, Clatworthy, Priestman, Edwards, Doble, Warren, Woodman, Farrant, Baker, Webber, Evans; front: Willey, True, Shere, Hallam, Lowry, Netherway, Salter, Burgess, Pike, Cork, Hutchings.* (Courtesy of Express & Echo)

Right: *WI show: 'Fashions through the Ages', 1950s.*
Left to right, back: Joan Lutley, ?, Mary Netherway, Emily Salter, Barbara Hole, Mrs Naish, Lilly Guppy; middle: Marion Lowman, Mollie Lutley, Mary Rich, Marjory Webber, Alice Clark, Elsie Board, ?; front: Joan Hannaford, Mrs Bennett, Evelyn Pike, ?.

Left: *The last meeting of the Hemyock Royal British Legion Branch (Women's Section), 1988. Left to right, back: Dorothy Howsom, Sarah Lowman, Edna Dunn, Elvira Dunn, Phyll Kallaway, Dorothy Gammon (partly hidden), Dora Fuller, Mary Payne; front: Vera Gard, Mrs Hutchings, Mrs Clarke, Sarah Bale and Margaret Lowman.*

Right: *Another new generation of Hemyockians pictured with their proud mothers at a Hemyock baby show, c.1949/50. The proud mothers include Mrs Joan Lawrence with John sitting in the front row right and also Mrs Granger, Mrs Higgins, Mrs Salter, Mrs Pursey, Mrs Still and Mrs King.*

❧ Family Gatherings ❧

Left: *The Hawkins family, 1897. John and Elizabeth Hawkins with their family. Left to right, back: Emily, Harry, Bessie; front: Grace sitting between her parents.*

Below: *The Barton family at Castle Cottage c. 1920. Left to right: Lydia Jane, Reginald and Mabel Dora (née Russell).*

Below right: *Eli and Lily Clist at Churchill's Farm. Jack Granger is standing in the road and the other lady is Granny Granger.*

Below: *The Northam family, c.1920. Left to right, standing: Olive, Frank, Ivy, Ciss, William, Charles, Gwen, Nancy; seated: George, Gwen, 'Granny', May.*

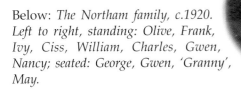

Right: *A wedding group, c.1920, following the marriage of Lily Granger and Eli Clist. The small girl standing in the front and to the left wearing boots is Cissie Granger. The bride is in the white dress in the front row and her groom is standing behind her.*

✍ Hemyock People ✍

Left: *Charlie Choke at work making a horseshoe in his blacksmith's shop. These premises were behind Fore Street.*

Below far left: *Gerald Pring, carpenter, in 1973, surrounded by the tools of his craft. For generations his family have been carpenters. His son Martin continues the family tradition and also runs an undertaking firm, Culm Valley Funeral Services, with his partner Lynne Isaac.*

Below centre: *Ronald Doble, a builder, in 1973, who began his career as a carpenter and wheelwright.*

Below right: *Norman Lowman, c.1973, working in Doble's Garage in his days as a mechanic. Norman is now retired. One of his great loves is gardening and his floral decorations in Station Road are a joy to behold. He is also an enthusiastic photographer.*

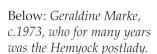

Bottom right: *Stanley Doble in his garage in the village which sold bicycles, motorbikes and radios. The motor-car trade became the most important part of the business. He retired over 20 years ago but the garage, taken over by David Graham, is still known as 'Doble's'.*

Below: *Geraldine Marke, c.1973, who for many years was the Hemyock postlady.*

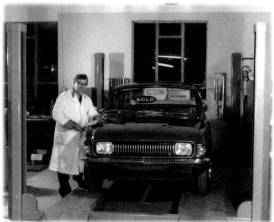

Left: *Jack Granger, c.1930.*

Below: *John Hawkins seen near Pencross returning home after a day's work.*

Right: *Margaret Mitchell at work in Hemyock Post Office where staff dress up and enter into the spirit of carnivals and Christmas.*

Below: *Dennis Hart, c.1973, whose family first came to Hemyock in 1702. Dennis' son, Steve, now runs the family business.*

Bottom left: *Lilian and David Fensom on VE Jubilee Day, who met on Cilla Black's television show 'Blind Date' in October 1993. Love blossomed and after a civil wedding at Tiverton on 5 February 1994 their marriage was blessed at St Mary's Church, Hemyock. Cilla Black attended the wedding, which was filmed for television. It was a very hectic day for Hemyock when the village was taken over by an army of TV cameramen, technicians and hundreds of onlookers.*

Bottom right: *Brian Clist and son Julian gathering weather data for Hemyock. Brian's officially-recognised weather station is used for gathering a wide range of information relating to rainfall, air movement, humidity, sunshine, etc.*

An early postcard view of St Mary's Parish Church, prior to the erection of the War Memorial in 1920. Note the iron railings which were removed in later years.

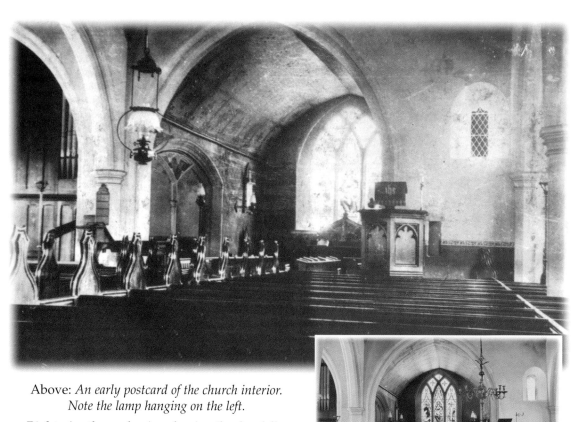

Above: *An early postcard of the church interior. Note the lamp hanging on the left.*

Right: *Another early view showing the chandelier which was originally purchased in 1773 at a cost of £5 and was later moved to its present position in the centre of the chancel arch.*

CHAPTER FOUR

Village Churches & Chapels

There are now three active places of worship within the parish; St Mary's Parish Church, the chapel at Culm Davy (see Chapter Nine) and the Baptist Church. Until recent years there were also a Methodist Chapel, a Roman Catholic Chapel of Ease and a Community Church that met in the Parish Hall. Unfortunately the Methodist Chapel was forced to close owing to the small size of the congregations. The Roman Catholic Chapel of Ease also closed in 1996 and the Community Church moved to different premises in Wellington in the same year because the Parish Hall could no longer accommodate the congregations.

The oldest place of worship in the village is St Mary's. There are no written records relating to the church until 1268 but there is evidence at the base of the existing tower that there was a substantial building on the site by the early 1100s. There are still Norman arches inside on the north-west and south sides dating to that period. At that time the church was probably in the shape of a cross with a central tower. Changes took place in about the year 1200 when the basic plan of the church as it is today came into being.

A new nave was built which was separated from its aisles by five arches resting on marble columns. These arcades were subsequently removed in 1768, but a re-used capital, base and shafts were incorporated in the font.

In 1275 the advowson (the right to present a clergyman to the benefice) can be traced to Sir John de Hydone who was lord of the manor at that time. The relationship between the manor and church was always close and in the 13th century, from 1267–83, members of the de Hydone family were rectors of Hemyock.

The tower was raised in the early Middle Ages and a vestry added, but one of the most important changes took place around 1330 with the construc-tion of a short outer south aisle. This was the Chantry Chapel of St Katherine founded by Sir Peter de Uvedale and his wife Margaret (a de Hydone by birth). There is a reference in the Hemyock Parish Records in respect of the chantry which (translated from the Latin) reads:

Perpetual Chantry of the chapel of the Parish Church of Hemyock, built in honour of the blessed Virgin Katherine commonly called the Chantry of Colmbrygge (Columbrygge).

The variations of Columbrygge refer to the present-day Culmbridge on the edge of Hemyock. Further changes in the church took place in 1768 when the inner south aisle was absorbed into the nave, and the north arcade and what had been the outer south arcade were rebuilt. Until about 1700 the tower had been crowned with a spire which was then replaced with a 'little steeple'. The present parapet of the tower dates to 1767 but the steeple has long gone.

The most dramatic changes to St Mary's took place between June 1846 and July 1847 when the Victorians undertook a 'restoration'. The Victorians were very fond of 'restoring' parish churches all over England, not always to the best effect. The cost of Hemyock's restoration was £900. The architect was a Richard Carver of Taunton and the contractor William Lacock of Chard. The south aisle was extended westwards, the north aisle widened and the south porch re-positioned. In addi-tion the pulpit, gallery, seating and floor were renewed. A north chancel aisle separated from the chancel by a stone screen was added.

When St Mary's re-opened after these renovations in 1847, the first sermon was preached by the Revd Henry Addington Simcoe, son of General John Graves Simcoe. It is believed that the General's widow, Elizabeth, may have contributed to the restoration of the church. Two of the Simcoe daughters made their own contribution to the church with the coloured glass in the east window of the south aisle, which may well have been of their own

ᴄᴏ Hemyock ᴏᴄ
Bellringers

Left: *Postcard of the bellringers with the Bishop of Exeter in 1908 for the reopening of the bells.*

Right: *Bellringers, c.1949, at the time of Revd L. Ketchley's departure as Rector of Hemyock and the arrival of Revd Stamp. Left to right, back: Les Morrell, Dennis Hart, Donald Salter (in RAF uniform), Joe Thomas, Brian Small; front: Revd Ketchley, Charles Trim, Leslie Hart, Michael Pike, Revd Stamp, Ernest Symons.*

Left: *A later group of ringers. Left to right: Les White, Les Morrell, Len Mutter, Dennis Hart, Les Hart, Bert Hill, Revd Stamp, Tom Bright, Michael Pike, Leonard Netherway.*

Below: *Ringers in the bell tower, 1970. Left to right: Len Mutter, Les White, Tom Bright, Martin Pring, Royston Perrott, Les Morrell, Alan Watson, Fred Perrott.*

Below left: *Refurbished bells outside St Mary's in 1983 prior to being rehung in the tower.*

design. The Misses Simcoe also designed some of the windows of Dunkeswell Abbey Church and had a flair for this type of artistry. The glass in the south chancel window is in memory of Revd Popham who was Rector of Hemyock from 1873–96. It is by Alexander Gibbs of London and was given to the church by Revd Popham's mother.

The font has quite a complicated background as set out in a short history of St Mary's by Robert Sherlock. It appears that a new font was introduced in 1200 when the church was rebuilt. It was made of marble and consisted of a square bowl resting on five columns and a square base. This was replaced in the 1400s by an octagonal font but when the alterations of 1768 took place the bowl of the earlier font was discovered and re-set on the 15th-century base. When the 1846 alterations were being carried out the remains of the marble arcades were discovered and used in replacement of the 15th-century section of the font.

There are many other features of interest within the church including the chandelier that dates to 1773–4, and a parish chest bearing the names of R. Fry and S. Farrant, dated 1820. There are also a number of monuments. These include wall monuments in the chancel to Alexander Rayner MD (a physician of Bath who died on 18 September 1746), Elizabeth Rayner (wife of Edward Rayner, who died on 17 June 1769), and Edward Rayner MA (Rector of Hemyock from 1739 until his death on 2 March 1775).

The second wall monument is to the Revd John Land, Rector of Hemyock from 1775 until his death on 17 April 1817. There are also 17th-century floor slabs commemorating members of the Waldron and Clode families but these have now been covered. On the west wall are two tablets, the first referring to:

An account of money and lands given to the poor of Hemyock. Charles Ford Esq., gave 20s. to be paid yearly to the Poor House keepers of this parish out of his lands called Strouds and Keens meadow for ever. An estate called Holcombe purchased with money given to the poor now in the hands of Feoffees in value about £5 per annum for ever. Nicholas Lack gave to the poor house keepers of this parish 5s. per annum to be paid out of his lands at Dunkeswell yearly for ever. Thomas Moore gave £5 the interest of it to the poor for ever.

Robert Farrant, Richard Gill, Wardens 1773.

The east window which contains glass by John Hardman of Birmingham given by Revd Edward Popham in 1876.

The second tablet also records a generous bequest:
Mary Waldron late of Honiton, spinster, gave by will £110 to purchase lands, the rents and profits thereof to be expended in teaching five poor children in each of the parishes of Hemyock and Clayhidon to read.

Samuel Farrant, Aaron Broom, wardens 1834.

In the church is a board setting out the names of individuals with responsibilities within the church and parish from the 17th to the 20th century. Firstly the Parish Clerks of Hemyock are given:

John Peter	1609–1611
Peter Manley	until 1644
William Gervis	In 1672
John Serle	In 1694–1731
Isaac Manley	1731–1776
Robert Manley	1776 until at least 1805
William Fry	In 1808 & until 1835 or 6
Robert Fry	1805 or 6 until 1865
John Hart	1865–1874
John Hine	1874–1888
William Hall	1888–1937

Then come the 'Dogwhippers or Sextons of Hemyock':

Josiah Wide	In 1697 until 1699 or 1700
Isaac Bull	1699 or 1700 until at least 1708
Moses Clark	In 1725 until 1742
John Hart	1743–1772
Joseph Manley	1772–1776
Robert Hart	1776–1777
John Hart	1777–1785
Robert Hart	1785–1809
Thomas Wood	1809–1819
Mary Wood	1819 until at least 1825
Robert Wood	In 1827–1844
Robert Wood	1844–1882
Barnett Wood	1883–1896

In that excellent book, *The Parish Chest*, by W.E. Tate, the function of a 'dog-whipper' is described:

An important subordinate of the wardens was the dog-whipper, whose duty it was to preserve order amongst the canine attendants at church, and sometimes amongst the children too.

Another extremely vital role in the life of the village and its church is that of the bellringers. Sadly many parish churches are without either bells or ringers today but Hemyock is fortunate in having both. It is known that by 1552 St Mary's had five bells in the tower. A sixth bell was put on a separate frame above the existing installation, a wooden frame dating from 1767. The 1767 frame is believed to have replaced one that hung the bells on two levels, suggesting perhaps that the earlier bells had been purchased over a period of time. By 1904 the ringers of the day felt that all was not well and in 1906 a decision was made to rehang the bells. The contract to do the job was won by Harry Stokes of Woodbury (see *The Book of Woodbury*). He built a cast-iron frame resting on large oak beams which carried the weight and thrust of the bells down to the thicker walls in the clock room. The treble was again hung in a separate frame above the second and third, with the ends bearing directly into the walls. It is the latter frame that caused concern in recent times.

There were no major problems for some time but by 1979 the ringers were again saying that the 'go' of the bells was worsening so in 1983 the bells were rehung on modern bearings by John Taylor & Co of Loughborough at a cost of £8025. This makes an interesting comparison with the cost of rehanging in 1906 which was £200.13s.6d. When the bells were rehung in 1983 they were tuned as a peal for the first time.

The treble bell weighs 5cwt and was cast in 1858 by Warners of London. It had been ordered by the churchwardens of the day who hoped to collect subscriptions for it. One warden, James Bowerman, cancelled the order because he thought the subscriptions were coming in far too slowly. The other

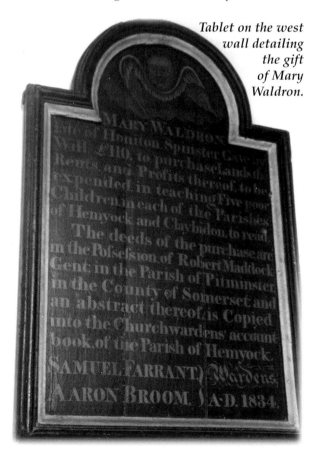

Tablet on the west wall detailing the gift of Mary Waldron.

warden, Edward Lutley, promptly paid the deficit himself and all was well. The second bell was cast by Thomas Bilbie at Cullompton in 1811 (whose family cast bells in Devon and Somerset for three generations). The bell has the standard Bilbie marking on the shoulder. The third, the Enigma Bell, is the oldest of the peal dating to 1624. It bears no founder's name or information but such decoration as there is on the shoulder is similar to that known to have been cast by Thomas Pennington of Exeter. There are a number of initials which may have been those of people in the village who had subscribed to the cost. The initials are R.L., C.S., H.G., H.H., I.M., H.B., W.K., I.K., W.G., E.T., P.M. The fourth bell, carrying the motto 'Draw near to God', weighs 10cwt and was recast by Warners of London in 1858. The original was cast by Pennington in 1621. The fifth bell weighs 14cwt and was recast in 1821 in Cullompton. Like the second bell, it bears the signs of the old method of tuning by chipping around the mouth. On the shoulder friezes are impressions of halfpenny and penny coins of 1807. It had been recast at least twice before, in 1703 and 1776. The bell bears the motto, 'True Hearts and Sound Bottoms'. This, as far as is known, is unique on the bells of Britain. The tenor bell, cast in 1860 by Warners of London, is a recasting of the previous tenor and as there are records of the Hemyock tenor being recast in 1793 and 1621 it is possible that some of the metal of this bell was at least 400 years old. The old bell was taken to London in 1860 by train from Wellington. It left Hemyock at 19cwt, 1qtr., 17lb. Its present weight, after retuning, is 17cwt, 3.2lb. The motto on this bell is typical of tenors across the country and common in Devon and Somerset: 'I to the church the living call and unto death do summon all'. (The details of the history of the bells has been drawn from a booklet *True Hearts and Sound Bottoms* by Brian Samuels, long-standing Hemyock bellringer and holder of the office of 'Steeple Keeper'.)

A recent addition to the church is an oak screen with etched glass panels situated at the rear of the building under the west gallery leading from the church to the tower room or ringing chamber. This screen was erected in 2000 as part of the millennium-celebrations.

The church clock has an interesting history. It was purchased in 1747 from a clockmaker in Honiton and has had the occasional problem. In 1948, for example, the minute hand stuck at 11.20. Roy Barton, who was home on leave from the RAF, repaired the fault and the clock kept going for another 50 years. When the millennium drew near it was decided to electrify the clock and Peter Reed was commissioned by the Parochial Church Council to replace the original antique weight system with the lighter weights required for the electrification – an undertaking that required considerable skill and much hard work.

Before 1813 there was only a wall on the south

side of the churchyard. On the west side was a hedge and there was a fence to the north. The present wall and entrance gates date to 1813. The churchyard was closed for burials in 1901. From that date village burials took place in the cemetery on the Culmstock Road. Within the churchyard there is a magnificent yew tree of some antiquity which, in what is always a beautifully kept churchyard, stands as a symbol of what is so delightful about English parish churches and their surroundings.

There are nearly 40 gravestones standing with a number of fragmented monuments. Some of the inscriptions are reasonably clear but earlier ones are quite weathered and not easy to decipher. The majority of the stones date to the 19th century but several to the 18th century. The earliest dates to 1755 and relates to the burial of 'John Blackmore, son of (?) Richard and Mary Blackmore of Clehidon [sic] who died on 9th. December, 1755 aged (25?) years'. Richard Blackmore of ? (undecipherable), aged 67, and one other individual are all buried in the same plot. Another 18th-century burial plot is that of Sarah, wife of John Farrant of Culmpine, who died on 22 November 1796 aged 42. The monument also records the burials of other members of the Farrant family including Mark who died in 180?, aged 87; Robert of Culmpine who died on 24 March 1843, aged 50; his wife Anne who died on 16 April 1875, aged 84; and finally John Farrant of Culmpine House who died on 27 March 1807, age unknown. The latter was probably Sarah's husband. The inscription relating to John makes reference to the Hemyock troop of Volunteer Yeomanry although some of the inscription is unreadable. Presumably John was a member of that Corps. The Farrant family also figure on another monument of the 1700s. There was Robert Farrant of Lemonshill who died on 30 December 1784, aged 45, his wife Betty and several other members of his family, probably children, who are also mentioned on the same spot.

The names of other families who are buried and remembered in the churchyard include White, Hart, Cook, Hannaford, Lowry, Selley, Flay, Graves, Wood, Clist, Morgan, Hembrow, Barton, Lutley, Purchase, Bowerman, Cload, Manley, Hine, Jackson, Fry, Gill, Salter, Thomas, Ewins, Spark and Valentine. Some of these names go back centuries in the parish. It is interesting how widely the descendants of these and other Hemyock families have spread around the world. One has only to examine the church visitors' book to realise how far people have come to visit their ancestral village and in some cases the graves of their ancestors and distant kinfolk. The growth of interest in genealogy in recent years has been quite staggering.

There is another, extremely important memorial alongside the churchyard, the Hemyock War Memorial which stands on the site of the old church house which was demolished in 1886. There had

The Flower Festival in St Mary's Church, c.1995. The display was the result of a great deal of skill and hard work by the local ladies of Hemyock.

been a church house on the site certainly in the 17th century. The original was probably destroyed in the fire that devastated the centre of Hemyock in 1693 and was rebuilt. Over the years there have been various artists' impressions of what this part of the village must have looked like before 1886. The War Memorial, which was unveiled by Edward Lutley in 1920, commemorates the men of Hemyock who gave their lives in the two world wars and later active service overseas. Their names are:

1914–1918

C. Boyland
H. Browning
S. Clist
P. Farrant
S.G. Forbear
W.J. Fussell
J. Griffin
J.H. Hall
E. Hill
H. Lowman
G. Hold
J.A. Lutley
T.E. Lutley
E. Moore
W.H. North
W. Ridgeway
H. Rowsell
A. Vincent
P. Wide
W. Wide

1939–1945

J.A. Elmes
R.T. Hine
H.R. Pooley
R.J. Small

Malaya 1956

B.R. Mathews

St Mary's Church Choir, c.1960. Left to right, back: Patricia Fuller, Joyce Clapp, Ann Turner,
Margaret Llewellyn-Jones, John Northam, Sid Turner, Leslie Purcell, Francis Bustard, Susan Pring,
Brenda Pring, Monica Bright, Janice Fuller, Sheila Marke;
seated: Mr Farmer, C.J. Hannaford, Frances Hart, Revd W. Llewellyn-Jones, Ron Cork, Ray Clapp, Mr J. Hart;
front: Ian McCulloch, Gary Still, Richard McCulloch, Geoffrey Casely, David Llewellyn-Jones,
Martin Pring, Gordon Hold, Brian Middleton.

St Mary's Church Choir in the early 1990s.
Left to right, back: Revd Tony Grosse, Polly Eden, Rebekah Bawler, Peter Reed, Olive Goodman,
David Palmer, Janice Bawler, Joan Lawrence; front: Stuart Summers, Betty Petch.

Revd Anthony Grosse (now retired) pictured during the delivery of one of his absorbing sermons, c.1973.

A few feet from the War Memorial and within the church wall is a small rose garden created as a 'Garden of Peace' in 1995, 50 years after the end of the Second World War.

The Parish Registers which record births, marriages and deaths within the parish, provide us with invaluable historical information. Hemyock's Registers date from 1635 although records of a few odd years prior to that date are found in the Bishop's Transcripts, dating back to 1602. The records are available for study at the Devon Record Office but bound transcribed copies are also to be found in the West Country Studies Library in Exeter, also in the care of the Rector of Hemyock. Unfortunately the index has many omissions. The Registers did not always confine themselves to the routine of birth, marriage and death. Events of local importance would often be noted. For example, the Registers record a number of names and events: 'In ye year 1646 from June ye first to June ye last day of the same moneth [sic] died in the inffectious [sic] Disease in ye Towne, 57 people died in the infection'. Then:

March 4th. Anno Dni 1655. Shettledon watter Lake was brought in to Hemiocke Towne att ye charge of John Every of Wootonglanvell in the Countie of Dorsett, Esq. And Directed by ye advice of John Kelland mercer.

In 1691 another entry deals with a local problem:

September 9th. 1691. Memorandum that the bridge near the church called Matthew Bridge fell to decay. In my time and Upon a meeting of the parish it could not be proved the Bridge was to be repaired at the charge of the rector but I freely gave a tree and he was set up att [sic] the parish charge.
Witness our hands
Peter Fisher, Rector,
William Wilmutton, his mark
John Wide, his mark
Way Wardens for ye year

On occasions burial entries would be enlarged upon by the incumbent to give the cause of death: '1790 4th. October Thomas Cordwent killed by the fall of a horse', and '1793, 16th. June John Thomas killed by waggon wheels'. Even in the 18th century the roads and lanes could be dangerous.

Incumbents of Hemyock

1267   Thomas de Hydone
1274   Symon de Hydone
1283   Master Ralph
1321   Sir Henry de Whitely
1321   Sir Thomas de Whitely
1341   Sir William de Hokham
1361   Sir Ralph de Duelonde
1378   Master William Trevellys
1382   Master William Graundone
1384   Sir Richard Spicer
John Whattecomb (date not recorded)
1395   William Rothewell
Sir John Halsanger (date not recorded)
1429   Sir John Wynford
1461   Robert Trevethen
1473   Master Oliver Dynham
1473   Master William Bradely
1475   John Windoner
1493   Henry Prows
1525   Master William Moyne
1549   John Swayne
Thomas Clapham (date not recorded)
1587   Anthony Bonde
1619   Roger Kelly
1643   Robert Chapline
1689   Peter Fisher
1739   Edward Rayner
1775   John Land
1817   James Sparrow
1829   Francis Warre
1854   Francis John Kitson
1873   Edward Leybourne Popham
1896   John de Burgh Forbes
1927   Leslie G. Ketchley
1949   Harold W.T. Stamp
1958   William Llewellyn-Jones
1973   Anthony C.B. Grosse
The Revd Grosse retired in 1996 and the present Rector of Hemyock is Margaret Cameron.

For some years now the Rector of Hemyock, in common with many other clergymen throughout the country, has a responsibility for more than one parish. The Rector of Hemyock covers the parish of Hemyock, which includes the chapel at Culm Davy and the neighbouring parishes of Clayhidon and Culmstock. Obviously life can be extremely busy for the rector of the village and a busy schedule of services alone can lead to mad dashes from one place of worship to another. Many parishioners remember encountering Tony Grosse racing around the lanes in a style that would have made him an excellent rally driver. Fortunately Hemyock has attracted several retired clergymen to the village and they are available to help the rector out now and then.

Outside St Joseph's Roman Catholic Chapel (now demolished), Golden Jubilee, 1989. Left to right: Roman Catholic Bishop of Exeter, the Rt Revd Christopher Budd, Betty and Bill Granger and Father Terence Perkins.

ROMAN CATHOLICS

Roman Catholics in the parish had to travel elsewhere to worship until 1939. In August of that year a Roman Catholic Chapel of Ease, St Joseph's, was established in Station Road opposite Doble's Garage, in the month before the outbreak of the Second World War. St Joseph's came about as a result of the generosity of a Mrs Reynolds, the widow of a lawyer, who took up residence in Station Road in 1936/7. There was a clause in the contract relating to her property that stated that Mass was to be celebrated every fortnight in the living room. Two years later Mrs Reynolds purchased a plot of land next to her bungalow and had a chapel built in memory of her late husband. The priest was a Father Bouchier of Cullompton, who, on retirement, ended his days in Hemyock. Unfortunately St Joseph's was closed in February 1996 and subsequently demolished. So once again local Catholics had to go elsewhere. Mention should be made, however, of Mrs Peggy Granger and her husband Bill who for 39 years looked after the building with considerable love and dedication.

QUAKERS

Nonconformity played a great part in the history of worship in Hemyock with both Methodists and Baptists being catered for, but first a mention of the Quakers. The Quakers, formerly known as the Religious Society of Friends, were founded by George Fox in the 1640s. Although they did not have a regular meeting place in Hemyock, they may have met in one of their dwelling houses, or the later ones could have attended the Quaker Meeting House at Spicelands near Culmstock. We are not sure how many of them lived in our parish but they invariably had an influence on the neighbourhood that exceeded their numerical strength. From their family names it would appear that most of them lived in Culm

Davy, the hamlet to the north-west of the village of Hemyock, which, being close to Culmstock, was very much involved in the production of wool. Wool merchants from Europe came to the Culm Valley to trade; these men brought with them the latest ideas concerning religious development. It is thought that one of the reasons for the importance of Puritanism locally, and later Nonconformity, stems from these merchants. Some of the Quakers who lived in the parish and who are listed in the records with the following details:

Isaac Ackland, a poor labouring man, husband of Eleanor. They had 4 children, Mary born 1693, Isaac born 1695, Jane born 1697 and Eleanor born 1700.

Ann Ackland married Nicholas Sommers of Uffculme in October 1706.

Bridget Ackland married William Calway of Holcombe Rogus in May 1706.

Peter Holway, a thatcher, married Susanna Lutley, widow of Uffculme, on 30 June 1692. Peter was buried in 1718 and Susanna in 1730.

James Holway, Peter's son, was buried at Spicelands on 10 November 1692.

Mary Manly was buried in May 1712.

Dorothy Ramster was buried in 1701.

Frances Ramster, daughter of John, married William Southwood of Uffculme in 1688.

Joan Ramster was fined for not attending the Anglican Church in 1682.

John Ramster was buried in 1700, aged about 80. Another John was buried in 1716, as were Prudence in 1703 and William in 1701.

John Read, husband of Joan, was buried in 1696 and Joan herself in 1696.

Thomas Salter was convicted both in the spring and autumn of 1680, of being at conventicles in Cullompton. (A conventicle was a secret, illegal religious meeting and in these cases probably meant Quaker Meetings.)

Joseph Smith was buried in October 1701.

Robert Smith's daughter Ann married Thomas Hayle of Wellington in October 1706 also at Spicelands,

Elizabeth Clist, daughter of John Clist, married Charles Fry in 1695. (Elizabeth was probably a widow when she married Charles because she had previously married a Daniel Browne in 1685, – if it was the same lady.)

Another of John Clist's daughters, Mary, married Robert Webber in 1693, also at Spicelands.

There are frequent references to both the Cadbury and Fry families in the Parish Registers from this period and later both of these Quaker families moved from Hemyock and achieved fame and prosperity in the manufacture of chocolate. There may have been no tangible Quaker building in Hemyock but these families had a substantial influence on the future development of the village.

METHODISTS

Like the Milk Factory, the Methodist Church has in recent years become part of the rich history of Hemyock after its closure as a result of decisions taken at national level. All that remains at the present time in the case of the Methodist Church is a rapidly decaying empty shell. For almost 200 years there had been a Methodist presence in the village, and for most of this time before the union of the various branches of Methodism in the 1930s, it was the Wesleyan section that flourished in Hemyock.

In 1820 Benjamin Wood obtained a licence from the Bishop of Exeter to enable him to hold Wesleyan services in his farmhouse in the hamlet of Ashculm. Such consent was at this stage required in order for Nonconformist worship to take place legally and to become a Nonconformist required a strong measure of will-power at that time. Those who did not declare themselves members of the Anglican Church were barred from most professions; they could not go to university but they could engage in trade and at this many of them excelled and prospered. In subsequent years the entrepreneurial spirit of the Nonconformist families was to have a great influence on the development of the parish.

The Wesleyans flourished and after 18 years were able to build their own chapel in the centre of Hemyock at a cost of £242.6s.4d. This was financed in a number of ways: a public subscription raised over £107, and there was an interest-free loan of £15 as well as other loans at five per cent interest. Interestingly, not all the gifts were in cash. John and Henry Wood gave 'a load of stones on the spot' and James and Euphemie Parfitt, from Willand, gave a bible and hymn book. When the building was opened in November 1838, there were 14 members:

Samuel Lamble	William Bennett
Agnes Bennett	Robert Wood
Elizabeth Wood	Mary Eales
Thomas Macey	William Lee
Sarah Grabham	John Perryman
Mary Ann Fry	Dorothy Manly
Elizabeth Clist	Samuel Farrant

Chapel membership grew quite rapidly, and by March 1840 there were 34 members with a further ten 'on trial'. In March 1842 55 members were listed. The gallery was added to the interior of the chapel in 1840 at a cost of £40.

The early Wesleyan chapels were arranged in groups known collectively as Circuits. From the mid 1800s Hemyock was in the Wellington Circuit, which included chapels at Dunkeswell, Hemyock, Wellington, Milverton and Wiveliscombe. Most of the services were conducted by local preachers, who were trained but not ordained, and to enable these preachers to travel around the circuit horses had to

be hired; complaints are recorded that the 'Methodists did not get the best horses'.

It was necessary to recruit fresh members to train as local preachers. In 1887 two members of the Hemyock congregation were approached, Samuel Farrant and John Clist (both founders of the Milk Factory). Mr Farrant's response is not known but Mr Clist declined the invitation saying 'that he had neither the time, ability or disposition for the work'.

In 1895, when a schoolroom was built adjoining the chapel, there was an undercurrent of Anglican/ Methodist dissension in the parish. A few years earlier the old Parish House which had served as a house for poor people and the village school was demolished (before the new village school was built in the 1870s). An acrimonious dispute took place as to why the Anglicans should have kept the financial proceeds. Subsequently the election of the Board of Managers of the new school became a Church versus Chapel affair, which culminated in the Nonconformists refusing to pay the 'educational part' of their local rates. In turn they had some of their property seized for what was termed the non-payment of 'Church Rates'. At this time the Wesleyans proposed that the Sunday School could be used as an alternative school but this was not pursued. In 1927, however, the head of the village school rented the Sunday School for use as an extra classroom, an arrangement that continued for over 30 years.

The Methodist Church continued to play an important role in the life of the village, albeit an independent one. The idea of Anglican and Nonconformist co-operation was still a distant dream, and gradually the Baptists and Methodists would close their respective chapels to join the other denomination for special services. Much later, well after the Second World War, the Anglicans and the Nonconformist churches began, occasionally, to co-operate in joint worship; Christian unity is a very slow process! Until the 1960s the membership

The Methodist Chapel in the High Street on a wintry day in the 1960s.

After Harvest Festival at the
Wesleyan (Methodist) Chapel, 1962.

remained at about 50 but for various reasons the church failed to attract the younger generation and the membership grew increasingly older. In 1989 it was suggested that the building be closed down and it almost was, but as a last resort it was agreed to meet for worship every fortnight and this arrangement continued until the mid 1990s, the surviving congregation still managing to meet its financial requirements. When the congregation fell to about eight, the church was finally closed down and the building then put up for sale by tender.

The Parish Council established a need for the building for community use, commissioned an appraisal to see if it was a financially viable proposition and then put in a tender. This was in fact the highest offer but it failed to obtain the property. The building was sold privately and although the new owner eventually obtained permission to convert it to a dwelling it still remains empty.

BAPTISTS

In December 1695 the Parish Registers mention that 'Walter Wyatt was buryed behind the Church, being an Anabaptist'. After the Reformation the Anabaptists developed an extreme form of Protestantism in so far as they did not believe in infant baptism but insisted on adult baptism. At that time if you did not conform to Anglican doctrine then you could not be buried with those who did; therefore, on death, you had to be buried on the north side of the churchyard (behind the church), removed from your fellow parishioners.

In the late 1600s there were both Quakers and Anabaptists in the village, with the latter later becoming Baptists. By the 1830s eight people were meeting in a house on the site of the old Post Office in the Square, owned by Christopher Baker who was a cooper. The object of the house meeting was:

... to worship the Great God of Heaven and Earth by prayer and praise and to make known the way of salvation for fallen men by Jesus Christ, the bible to be read and remarked upon.

In March 1831 an application was submitted to the Bishop of Exeter for a licence for religious worship. The Wesleyans had obtained such a licence three years previously enabling them to worship at Ashculme (now Ashculm). By 1832 the need for a chapel was being discussed but the Hemyock group remained an offshoot of the Baptist Church at Prescott in nearby Culmstock. It is of interest that in November 1832 a meeting was held 'around the bed of Mrs Clist' to talk over the matter of the Church. Present were Jane Hine, Anne Searle, Dorothy Manley, Samuel Clist junr, Samuel Clist senr, Richard Searle and Alex Henderson. It was proposed 'that as we might be commencing what should last for ages to come, the foundation of our rules should be drawn from the Word of God'. Further meetings were held in January and March 1833, when the Baptists were still holding their services in Samuel Clist's house with Alex Henderson as the pastor. In 1834 the membership list was as follows:

Female	Male
Jane Hine	Alex Henderson
Anne Searle	Richard Searle
Mary Henderson	Samuel Clist
Anne Furze	William Hart
Elizabeth Manley	
Dorothy Manley (suspended)	
Elizabeth Manfield	

Because the Baptists did not believe in infant baptism ('infant sprinkling' as they called it) their children were excluded from the Parish Registers 'till a more liberal plan be provided by civil authority'. (In fact this took place in 1837 when national registration of births, marriages and deaths became law.)

The following births are recorded in the Baptist records:

Name	Parents	D. of Birth
John Coles	Ann & William	13/3/1831
Pass ? Henderson	Mary & Alex	25/1/1834
William Coles	Ann & William	28/1/1834
Robert Coles	" "	24/7/1837

A meeting at Rosemary Lane in Clayhidon began on 25 November 1833 in the house of George Redwood and for the very first time a sermon was preached there. According to records 'he appears to have been acceptable'.

At last the first corner-stone of the first Baptist chapel in Hemyock was laid on 11 June 1838; this building no longer exists but it was in the High Street next to Rosemount and a stable. There appears to have been no formal opening of the building but by 1840 it was in regular use for services. Before the baptistry was built baptisms took place in the open air, in St Margaret's Stream (which flows to the east of Castle Hill and subsequently between our Parish Church and Hemyock Castle). A few details of the inside of the chapel are known. The entrance was on the north side of the building, a box pulpit was on the south and on the western side 'between an old fashioned family pew' was the baptistry.

National events were recognised and remembered. For example, in March 1832 a fast appointed by the King was kept and 60 people met at 7a.m. to pray that the cholera epidemic that was sweeping across the whole of Europe would abate. On another occasion the freeing of slaves in British Colonies was celebrated.

The Baptist set of rules drawn up in Hemyock were strictly adhered to. On a number of occasions members were suspended for being drunk, for swearing, for attending the village 'Club' processions and for visiting friends on Sundays. A society that is bound together by rules becomes a strong group and in Hemyock the Baptist congregation increased rapidly. By January 1862 the first chapel was not large enough and there was discussion about building a larger one. By 1864, a friend, Mr Lock, had given a piece of ground in the village upon which the new place of worship could be built. In July 1864 the foundation stone of the new building was laid by a Mr James Brown of Torquay, after which 'about 300 partook of Tea given by ladies of the congregation... under the cooling shade of the apple trees in Mr. W. Drake's orchard'.

The new Chapel and School Room was opened for public worship in October 1865. Two spacious tents were erected in nearby fields, one for the preaching and the other for the dinner and tea. On the morning of the opening the weather was fine but later in the day it rained.

An account of the proceedings reads: 'Hemyock was soon deluged by vehicles of all descriptions conveying friends all anxious to hear the great preacher of the age.' It is fortunate that the vehicles were horse-drawn, for such a 'deluge' in modern Hemyock might well have presented a slight traffic problem. The preacher was the Revd C.H. Spurgeon, from the Metropolitan Tabernacle in London, perhaps the best Baptist preacher of his day. The tent was 'full to overflowing' long before he arrived; it was estimated that about 2000 people attended in the morning and 3000 in the afternoon.

The new building was designed to accommodate 300 people and was built by a local builder, Mr James Hart, at a cost of £617. The old chapel had been sold to a Mr Thomas Walker for £12. For some time afterwards it was used as a temperance house through the efforts of Mr James Wright and 'it was opened some evenings for the young as a sort of reading room and for games, and a cup of coffee could also be purchased.' Later it was sold to Mr Manley of Millhayes who, in turn, exchanged it for an adjacent piece of land owned by Mr Bowerman. Eventually, having been used as a 'trap house' and stable for many years, it was demolished in the 1960s to enable a new bungalow to be built. The church, opened in 1865, is still flourishing and the local Baptists continue to exercise a considerable influence in our community. One of the best-known pastors in recent years was Ron Cassell who retired in 1992. At the time of writing the pastor is Michael Jarrett.

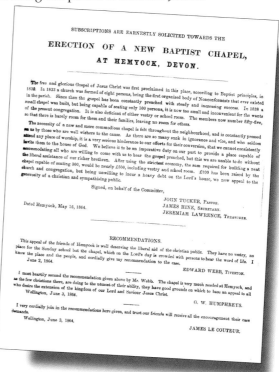

Copy of a subscription appeal, dated 1864, to raise funds for the erection of a new Baptist chapel.

East Gateway, Hemyock Castle, Devon.
Sketched on the spot, July 17, 1851.

North side of the Moat and ruins of Hemyock Castle, in the county of Devon.
Coloured on the spot, August 5, 1851.

Sketches courtesy of the West Country Studies Library.

CHAPTER FIVE

Hemyock Castle

Over the years a number of individuals, including General Simcoe one-time owner of Hemyock Castle, have suggested that the building might have Roman origins. There is no evidence to support the idea that a Roman building existed on the site but the discovery of iron slag, dated to the 1st century AD, in the core of the front wall of the castle, does give some food for thought. There were some iron workings in the vicinity during the 1st century, either Roman or Romano/British, and the resultant iron slag utilised when the castle walls were constructed centuries later. We will probably never know. We do know that the origins of the castle lie at least as far back as the 12th century when the de Hydon (also Hidon, Hydone, etc.) family were lords of the manor, during the reign of Richard I (1159–99). There was a Richard de Hydon of Hemyock and it is probable that he or his son Sir John de Hydon built a manor house in Hemyock. The present house at Hemyock contains the hall built by the de Hydons as part of their manor house although this has been much altered over the centuries. Between two chimneys in the present building there is a bay of ancient timbers that formed part of the old hall. The timbers are partly blackened by the smoke of the open fire which would have heated the open hall all those centuries ago.

The de Hydons were patrons of the churches in both Hemyock and Clayhidon and between 1267 and 1283 were rectors in the village. After the death of the last male de Hydon, Richard, Hemyock passed to his daughter Margaret. In 1292 Margaret married into yet another family with Norman origins, the Dynhams (Dinham, Dyneham, etc.). In fact, she had three husbands in all, her third being Sir Peter de Uvedale with whom she founded and endowed a perpetual chantry in Hemyock Parish Church dedicated to the Virgin Saint Katherine. The Chantry Chapel was made by adding a south aisle to the

church. Sir Peter Uvedale died in 1336 and was buried under the floor of the chapel as was his wife some years later. All that now remains of the building is the piscina where the Holy Water would have been kept and the wall by the Psalm Board. One presumes that the remains of the Uvedales still lie beneath Hemyock Church.

By 1380 Hemyock Manor had passed to Sir William Asthorpe. Asthorpe had married Margaret Dynham who descended from Margaret Hydon and her first husband Sir Joyce de Dynham. It was on 5 November 1380 that Richard II gave permission to Sir William and Margaret Asthorpe to fortify and crenellate their manor house at Hemyock:

The King, to all whom it may concern, greeting, Know ye, that, of our special favour, we have for ourselves and our heirs, granted and given special licence to our trusty and well-beloved William Asthorpe, soldier, and Margaret his wife that they be permitted to fortify and crenellate their Manor House of Hemyock with a wall of stone and flint; we further give permission to the said William and Margaret, and their heirs, to occupy the house so fortified and crenellated for ever, without let or hindrance either from ourselves, our heirs, our justices of the peace, our esquires, our lieutenants, or any other whether our bailiffs or other officers whatsoever. In witness whereof etc. Given by the King at Northampton, 5th. November by a brief and under our private seal.

Kings only granted licences to loyal men to establish law and order on their behalf. In medieval times civil disturbances were common; in fact there was a peasants' revolt in Devon in 1382. Trouble could raise its head at any time. In any event the now fortified manor house/castle was in a key position. To give an idea of what sort of castle was constructed by the Asthorpes it is simpler to quote from *Hemyock Castle* written by Margaret Sheppard, its present owner:

The castle built appears to have been similar in design to other medieval castles of the period like Bodiam in Sussex. A curtain wall with nine or ten towers was

Above: *An early postcard of the castle ruins and church.*

Right: *Renovations under way to the gatehouse, 1980s.*

Left: *Early postcard view of the castle outbuildings and stables, with the main house in the background.*

built roughly in a rectangle to enclose a cobbled yard and the Manor House and outbuildings. Two taller towers guarded the entrance and around the outside of the curtain wall flowed the moat fed by the nearby stream and natural springs. The curtain wall was between four and six feet thick, the rubble and stone core was faced by the local chert stone (like flint) that was quarried from the tops of the nearby Blackdown Hills which surround the valley of Hemyock.

The round towers were at least 40 feet high, had walls up to six feet thick and stood out proud from the 22-feet high curtain walls. The stone facing of the curtain walls and towers appears to have been rendered with plaster to make them difficult to scale, and then they were lime-washed. The Asthorpe's castle with its gleaming white towers and walls dwarfing every other building in the valley must have given quite a surprise to travellers as they came over the hills towards Hemyock.

The two entrance towers of the Gatehouse had no ground level entrances unlike the other towers which seem to have archway entrances closed by wooden doors. Slots which held the wooden door posts have been found in all save the Gatehouse Towers. The top row of larger log holes in the Southern gatehouse tower indicates where the wooden beams supporting the floor were inserted, suggesting that this tower was perhaps used to house prisoners who were lowered down from above. (It would have been impossible to have an underground dungeon in Hemyock as the water table is high and it would have flooded.)

The curtain walls and towers were topped with crenellations and the towers probably had conical roofs. Entrance to the castle was over a drawbridge spanning

the moat and under the archway between the two towers of the gatehouse. Between these towers was a portcullis which could be lowered to keep out unwanted visitors. At the outer end of the drawbridge, across the moat, stood the guardhouses, restricting entrance over the drawbridge. The drawbridge would have been supported by chains fixed to strong wooden beams fitted into the holes each side of the archway.

Doubtless Hemyock Castle was quite a formidable structure!

Little is known of its story following the deaths of William and Margaret Asthorpe. It remained one of the many Dynham estates but was more likely to have been occupied by one of the family stewards than by any of the Dynhams themselves. The centuries seem to have passed the castle by. The last Dynham died in 1509 and by the end of the century Hemyock and the castle had passed on to Sir John Popham, the Lord Chief Justice in Elizabethan times. Popham had quite an interesting track-record. He was responsible for sentencing the Earl of Essex and Sir Walter Raleigh to death, even giving evidence against Raleigh. He also sentenced Mary Queen of Scots and Guy Fawkes. He was clearly a pretty ruthless individual who often acquired property by very dubious means. He once acquitted a Willmers Darrell, despite overwhelming evidence to the contrary, of burning his illegitimate new-born baby to death. After his acquittal Darrell gave Popham a property, Lytelcote.

Hemyock Castle played a small but interesting role in the Civil War. The war broke out in 1642 at which time the Popham family still owned the

Michaelmas Fayre at Hemyock Castle, 27 September 1986. Left to right: Phyllis Fleming, Joan Austin, Meg Palmer, Beryl Smith, Joan Lutley, Ted Wassink, Charlotte Whitby, Phyllis Kallaway (in stocks), Betty Wassink, David Palmer.

stronghold and most of Hemyock. The family supported Parliament rather than King Charles I and the castle was garrisoned for the Parliamentarians and used to house Royalist prisoners.

In March 1644 (1643 by some calendars and contemporary accounts) a large insurrection against the King broke out in Hemyock and Parliamentary troops under Major Butler were sent from Lyme to assist. On arrival at Hemyock they were attacked by the Royalist Major Carne who was killed. On 9 March Royalist forces commanded by Lord Poulett, Sir John Berkeley, Sir Richard Cholmondely and Colonel Blewitt headed for Hemyock to deal with the matter and seize the castle. The Royalists took the 'town' forcing the 'rebels' into the stronghold. The following morning the Parliamentary forces surrendered the castle. Inside were 200 prisoners, 10 officers and 80 horses. The Parliamentary prisoners were 'bound up like rogues' and taken to Exeter along with the 80 horses and a great store of arms. Three of the ringleaders were hanged in front of the castle by the Royalists who refused to let their families cut the bodies down.

The old castle gate, c.1900, with George Barton.

The Parliamentary Commander at Lyme, Colonel John Ware, wrote of the 'siege' in his journal:

March 4th
Several messages come out of Devonshire to inform us the country was in arms and desired assistance of the Council of War at Lyme of horse and ammunition. By general consent was granted Major Butler Commander in Chief and some other captains sent out with him. They advanced to Hemyock where they were set upon by Major Carne who lost his life and divers of his soldiers.

March 5th/6th
The enemy drew out of their garrison at Axminster and Colyton, Chard, Exeter, Taunton and Bridgwater what forces they could to fall upon Hemyock.

March 9th
To divert their besieging of Hemyock, we fell upon Collinton with 300 men and took that town besides divers persons of note and were advancing to the relief of Hemyock but met with ill news of our officers being surprised which hindered us and caused us to retreat to Stedcombe House.

One of the Royalist prisoners being held at Hemyock was the Revd James Burnard the Vicar of Awliscombe and Upottery. Apparently he was known to be a strong supporter of Charles I which led to a Parliamentary troop of horse riding to his vicarage and taking him into custody for drunkenness and incontinency. It would seem he was possibly guilty of the first allegation but the second was based on a rumour that he had a woman friend in Honiton who had borne him a child, a 'kept' woman. He spent the next few years at Canonsleigh in Burlescombe where he was given refuge after his release from Hemyock.

After the restoration of the monarchy it is said Charles II ordered that Hemyock Castle be 'slighted' although it is not clear if these orders were carried out or, if they were, how much damage was actually done. Nearly 100 years later there were still substantial remains of Hemyock Castle. In 1755 Dean Milles, a well-known historian, was collecting material for his proposed book the *History of Devon*. (Milles was the father of a Jeremiah Milles who went to school with, and was a close friend of General Simcoe.) The Dean sent off questionaires to the clergy of Devon seeking information about their parishes and the people who lived there. The Rector of Hemyock at the time, Edward Rayner, wrote of the castle in his reply to Dean Milles' request:

The Gateway with a tower on each side, was standing in my time; but the upper part of it being much gone to decay, it was later pulled down. However, about 40 feet of the 2 towers and the arch between them are still remaining. Besides these there is nothing of the old Buildings to be seen but the Foundation of the Walls and the Ruins of the Round Towers that stood at the Angles of the castle. It was surrounded by a moat, filled I suppose by the stream of the water that runs close by it.

The castle had passed from the hands of the Pophams to the Every family towards the end of the 17th century. The Everys took measures to improve the supply of water to Hemyock by bringing a leat down the hill from Shuttleton (south of the village). The stream that had fed the moat was diverted to the course it takes now which allowed the moat in front of the guardhouse and eastern side of the property to be filled in, thus enabling a farmyard to be formed. It was around this period in the castle's history that it began to be referred to as 'Castle Farm'.

At the turn of the 18th and 19th centuries the castle and the lordship of the manor of Hemyock was purchased by General John Graves Simcoe (see Chapter Eighteen). The General and his family never took up residence at Hemyock Castle, having their own substantial home at Wolford Lodge near Dunkeswell. Castle Farm as it was called, stayed in Simcoe hands until it was sold in 1869.

One of the principal tenants of the farm during the mid-19th century was a farmer, James Tuck, and his family. In the 1841 census Tuck, aged 50, his wife Mary, 45, and the eight Tuck children were living there. They had two 15-year-old servants Jane Fry and Charles Morgan. During these mid-Victorian years the castle was visited on several occasions by Peter Orlando Hutchinson of Sidmouth, a diarist and watercolourist (see *Travels in Victorian Devon*, Devon Books). He visited Hemyock Castle on 17 July 1851 describing the state of the remains of the castle at that time. His diary for that date contains the following:

Went with Mr. Heineken over to Hemyock from Sidmouth, to try and find Hemyock Castle, not having been aware till lately, that the remains of a Norman Castle existed in the neighbourhood... The area within the outer walls and the tower is now an orchard… There are stony mounds, overgrown with grass about the orchard; and these are seemingly the remains of former erections now ruined. It is strange that none of the county histories make any particular mention of this castle. I heard of it only by chance.

Poor Hemyock Castle was neglected in more ways than one, although at least one historical work on Devon, *Magna Britannia Devon* (1822) did contain some reference to it. Hutchinson returned again in August and commented in his diary:

If I had Hemyock Castle I would soon make a pretty place of it. I would clean away the ugly and dirty farm buildings, and the mass of apple trees by which it is choked up; and repair and restore the towers and battlements of the castle itself. I am surprised that the owner should neglect it so much.

The owner at the time of Hutchinson's visit was General Simcoe's surviving son Revd Henry Addington Simcoe. Simcoe's widow Elizabeth Posthuma had died in 1850. It is interesting that in the years prior to her death Mrs Simcoe had spent a great deal of money on the restoration of Dunkeswell Parish Church and probably also Hemyock Church, as well as the building of a new church at Dunkeswell Abbey and other philanthropic projects, yet she appears to have invested little or nothing on Castle Farm. Her late husband would have dearly loved to have undertaken some restoration of the property had he lived, so it is a little sad that his plans for the castle were not carried through by either his wife or son. One possibility is that by the middle of the century the Simcoe coffers were under great pressure and work on Castle Farm was not a priority. Perhaps, however, some small effort was made by the Simcoes to improve the castle. In an item in *Devon and Cornwall Notes and Queries* (1928/9) the writer comments that at Hemyock he had been informed that the granite doorway had been brought from Cornwall by one of the Simcoes. This is a possibility because Henry Addington Simcoe was the parish priest at Egloskerry in Cornwall, very well placed to lay his hands on some granite for this purpose. Perhaps one day an enthusiast will make a study of the splendid doorway, which is still in situ, and ascertain the origin of the granite used.

Hemyock Castle seems to have had a fascination for Peter Orlando Hutchinson because he was back there again in July 1865. His diary entry says it all: 'We thought that the remains did not look in so good a condition as at our last visit 13 or 14 years ago.' In 1869 General Simcoe's grandson Captain John Kennaway Simcoe put Castle Farm and other properties in Hemyock up for auction (see Chapter Eighteen).

The Barton family of Hemyock purchased Castle Farm and farmed the land until early in the 20th century. The Pring family then became tenants, to be followed by the Paynes. Whilst the Paynes were living at the castle, the old thatched roof which had adorned the house for many years was replaced with slate. The Redwood family also lived at the castle for a short period when the Paynes were in residence. The Paynes were followed by the Ticehursts and when they left the fields were spilt from the farm and the farmhouse was sold as a private dwelling.

Hemyock Castle was not entirely ignored by historians, professional or otherwise. The *Exeter and Plymouth Gazette* for 26 June 1873, for example, reported that the Exeter Naturalists Club and Archaeological Society held their first field meeting of 1873 at Hemyock. The newspaper item reads:

The members numbering about twenty left Exeter by the 12.25 train and at Tiverton Junction conveyances were in readiness, in which they journeyed to Hemyock, a distance of seven miles. The drive was a most enjoyable one, the route being through a park-like road, magnificent elms bordering it on either side. The weather, at starting looked rather ominous, but shortly after the start from Tiverton Junction it cleared up, and throughout the day the elements were favourable. On arrival at Hemyock the members were there joined by the Right Worshipful the Mayor of Exeter (C.J. Follett Esq) and some of the residents of the neighbourhood, partook of luncheon at the Star Inn. The host, Mr. Babb, catered for his guests in excellent style, and the manner in which he provided for them reflects the greatest credit upon a country establishment with such comparatively small resources.

After a hearty lunch the members of the society held their business in the schoolroom adjoining the inn after which the secretary of the day read a paper on 'Hemyock Castle'. No doubt after this the society

THE BOOK OF HEMYOCK

Castle gateway and granite doorway to the house, 2000.

members took the opportunity to see what they could of the castle remains. (Had the society chosen to visit Hemyock after 1876 they would have had the benefit of travelling to the village by rail following the opening of the Culm Valley Railway in that year.)

In 1983 came the beginnings of a significant change to Hemyock Castle with the arrival of the Sheppard family, Captain William Sheppard OBE, RN (Bill), his wife Phyllis and their daughter Dr Margaret Sheppard. Over the years the Sheppards undertook a programme of restoration and renovation, helped by a grant from English Heritage. Towers were cleared of their ivy covering and carefully restored by skilled craftsmen. Much clearance of undergrowth revealed the remains of the curtain walls and their towers. Many artifacts were discovered including cannon balls and a musket ball embedded in a wall dating to the siege during the Civil War.

Limited excavations in 1989 were carried out by the Exeter Museums Archaeological Field Unit which revealed fragments of a wall which was taken to be possible evidence of an interval tower along the suggested western curtain wall of the castle. During these and other excavations and other work on the castle site extremely useful remains came to light which helped to tell the building's story. These items included parts of medieval roof tiles and louvres (chimneys), a fragment of a 'Rouen' jug of the 12th or 13th century, as well as the aforementioned cannon and musket balls. Perhaps the most interesting pottery finds were fragments of a 16th-century 'Bellamin' jug from Frechen in Germany and fragments of a jug originating in Portugal. These items were of high quality and hint at relatively affluent owners. Samples of pottery found at Hemyock Castle dating to the period after the Civil War were not of foreign origin and of lesser quality, indicating a different social status perhaps of the castle's occupants at that time.

In 1999 a geophysical survey was carried out at Hemyock Castle by the Archaeometry Branch of the Ancient Monuments Laboratory of English Heritage. The principal object of the survey was to locate stone wall foundations of the castle using techniques no doubt familiar to readers who have watched the television programme 'Time Team'. The conclusions of the survey are too detailed to outline here but do give some indication as to the course of the western curtain wall and the suggestion of a second entrance or interval tower.

Today Hemyock Castle is a privately-owned Scheduled Ancient Monument open to the public on Bank Holiday Mondays or at other times by appointment, and there is an Interpretation Centre telling the story of the castle and its occupants over the centuries. In addition some outbuildings have been converted into holiday cottages which have proved extremely popular over the years with people who enjoy historical surroundings. Guests have included descendants of the Tuck family who were tenants back in the mid-19th century.

Various events have been staged at Hemyock Castle in recent times including a medieval 'Fayre', and on the weekend of 25–26 June 1994 there was an exciting visit by members of the Sealed Knot Society, 'Colonel Wardlaw's Dragoons' (*see page 12*). This event was organised by the Hemyock Carnival Committee. The soldiers, together with their wives, camp followers, etc., camped at the castle for a weekend and gave demonstrations of drill firing of volleys and other military activities. One poor soldier tried to desert but was tracked down having a crafty pint of ale in the local tavern. He was deprived of his ale and duly punished.

From medieval manor house, to castle, farm and private dwelling with holiday accommodation, Hemyock Castle has been witness to substantial change over the centuries; but of necessity it has had to move with the times. One treasure that has been retained at the castle is an ancient cider press that was used for so many years to produce an excellent local draught. Unfortunately Captain Sheppard and his wife are no longer with us but their daughter still lives at what is one of Hemyock's most important historical sites and she is confident that there is still much to be discovered about the castle's history.

Are there legends associated with Hemyock Castle? One story asserts that there is a secret tunnel linking the castle with the ruins of Dunkeswell Abbey just a few miles to the south, but no one has found it – yet!

Right: *Looking down into one of the towers under repair in the 1980s with Gerald Lane who worked on the masonry of the buildings.*

CHAPTER SIX

The Milk Factory

The Hemyock Milk Factory is now just a memory, but it is a memory that will remain in the minds of the many village people who have had connections, in various ways, with the enterprise. A massive oak tree grows from a very small acorn, eventually to either blow down, or to be cut down. The development of the Milk Factory in our village mirrors this analogy, from the very small beginnings on a local farm at Mountshayne some 125 years ago. It moved to its permanent site at Millhayes about ten years later and continued to expand dramatically over the next 115 years. The factory experienced several changes in ownership and a number of different dairy products along the way, before being sacrificed and cut down at the political whim of the huge national company that eventually owned it. The whole site that had been occupied by the factory was purchased by a developer and the entire working area has been razed – nothing remains, just an open space, as is the case with the site of the adjoining railway station.

At present an eerie silence pervades the whole area, a complete contrast to the regular noisy comings and goings of the railway engines, the clanking of milk churns and the constant hiss of steam that came from the milk factory in its heyday. One of the great virtues of Hemyock is that it is adept at reacting to changing circumstances. Just as our forefathers developed a factory when they spotted an industrial need in the 1870s, so today when this demand has gone, yet another need is being addressed. A development of a mixture of houses, light industry, and increased leisure facilities is planned.

The story of this almost unique, very successful factory has to be told but first it is essential that we understand the agricultural background that led to its formation. Climatic conditions in the West Country have for many hundreds of years been very favourable for grassland production and this

invariably lead to the eventual formation of many small family farms, whose traditional success lay in their ability to produce a range of agricultural products. Our ancestors were fiercely independent, largely puritan during the Civil War of the mid-17th century and with an increasingly Nonconformist population in the centuries that followed. The production of wool from the 16th to the early-19th century brought great wealth to the area and allowed the rapid spread of new political and religious ideas from the continent, especially Holland, along with the wool that was traded. Hemyock, with neighbouring villages, would have had knowledge of the latest agricultural practices and, being free of a resident powerful lord of the manor, could have exploited them to the full. The trade in wool declined after the Napoleonic Wars and quite quickly our small family farmers diversified into keeping sheep, bred primarily for meat; into the production of flax (many local farms had their 'retting pits', so essential in the production of the fibre); into pigs; and, more importantly, into beef and milk production.

Before the arrival of the railway, liquid milk could not be transported to towns and cities because it went sour before it could be drunk. The milk was converted on the farm to butter and cheese and taken either to a local market or sold to a local merchant. After 1850 two significant changes took place in English society. For the first time more of the population lived in our towns and cities than lived in the countryside. Consequently the demand for food in these urban centres increased dramatically. Secondly, the railways spread almost everywhere and this meant that food could be transported easily and quickly to even the remotest parts of the kingdom. In 1876 the railway line from Hemyock to Tiverton Junction was opened, giving access to the main railway system throughout the country. At the same time an agricultural depression had taken place, farmers were receiving ever-lower prices for their products and a feeling of general despair prevailed.

Looking back it seems so obvious that the conditions were just right for an entrepreneur to combine the marketing of local agricultural products and to utilise the railway system to distribute them to the ready markets that existed in towns. Had we been living then would we have spotted the opportunity? In late 1885 three of the largest milk producers in Hemyock, Messrs John Clist, Samuel Farrant and Edward Lutley, met at the house of Mr James Wide who was the main butter buyer in the village. The object of the meeting was to discuss their problems and to find a way of producing butter of unvarying quality and to market it effectively. The problem with butter production until then was that because it was produced on small individual farms there was no way that it could be quality controlled. From this meeting and from several others that followed in quick succession, the origin of the company that they started, the Culm Valley Dairy Co. (CVDC) can be traced.

Early in 1886 Mr Clist and Mr Lutley travelled to Lord Vernon's estate in Derbyshire to look at a factory where butter was produced mechanically. They found that the butter produced there, being of a regular composition, was both easy to sell and commanded a higher price. The drawback to the method's adoption in Hemyock was the apparent necessity of delivering milk to the factory twice daily and the subsequent disposal of the by-product of the process, skimmed milk.

Unlike the farms in Derbyshire, our local farms were small and the roads on the Blackdown Hills were of poor quality, making a double delivery of milk to a central factory almost impossible. It was suggested that milk from the evening and morning milkings might be mixed and a double delivery to the factory avoided. A lengthy correspondence with various authorities, both in England and on the continent, concerning this problem offered little encouragement. The difficulty seemed likely to prove fatal to the local farmers' plans but having gone so far with the project and faced with the prospect of the local market for butter collapsing, the four men reputedly said 'let us try'.

The original deed of partnership survives, and shows that the initial capital for the venture was £3000. The partners were equal in all respects. There was to be a meeting of the Directors each month. Were any of them to die one quarter of the capital could be withdrawn, no individual partner could spend more than £5 of the company's money without the unanimous consent of the others, and finally, no partner was to subscribe or become associated with any similar business. Such complete involvement in the proposed enterprise went a long way to ensure the success of the embryonic company. Additionally the four men came from families who had lived in the village for many generations. They were all friends as we have seen, and large amounts of their personal money were tied up in their new venture. Their total commitment cannot be

emphasised too much. The decision to start the business must have been in each case a joint family one, because they all had young children and all their assets would have been lost had the business failed.

From the start the new factory, known simply as 'The Milk Factory', was set up at Mountshayne, John Clist's farm. Traces of the original tanks and cellars, the shafting and wheels that transmitted the power to the machinery and the milk reception platform remain visible.

To mechanically separate cream (from which the butter was made) from milk, a Laval cream separator was installed by Mr Stenner of Tiverton and driven by a steam engine. The first milk was received at Mountshayne on 16 May 1886 and for the first time ever the cream was produced from both evening and morning milk combined. The experiment was a risk but one worth taking; this was the very first time that cream mechanically separated from mixed milk had ever been achieved on a factory scale. Very quickly neighbouring farmers started sending their milk to Mountshayne. Some indication of the meteoric expansion of the amount of milk being processed is illustrated in the table below. The figures relate to the amount of milk processed during the month of May (a peak month) for the following years:

1886	3000 gallons	1890	100000 gallons
1887	17000 gallons	1891	120000 gallons
1888	36000 gallons	1892	150000 gallons
1889	47000 gallons	1893	180000 gallons

Milk was being taken to Hemyock from well outside the area initially envisaged when the factory was planned. We have records of one farmer who was bringing his milk from Oake, in Somerset, at least ten miles away. We can only speculate as to whether such an expansion in milk production had any influence upon the business decisions about local farming practices. There is no evidence that any amalgamation of farms took place. However, it does appear that the traditional Red Devon cow was crossed with a more prolific dairy breed from Somerset, probably a shorthorn type. Older farmers still talk of a 'milky Devon breed' of cow that was in existence at this time. It had a 'mealy appearance, with a basically red coat and white hairs intermixed'.

We can safely assume that the increase in milk supplies in the Culm Valley came from a change from a mixed beef/dairy animal, to a more specifically dairy type of cow. This was coupled with an increase in milk yields from each cow – as a result of scientific improvements in animal nutrition (by the use of oil seed cake) and in grass production through the use of artificial fertilisers.

The Culm Valley Dairy Company was only interested in the fat content of the milk (4 per cent of the total amount) because butter was made from cream and it took ten gallons of milk (45 litres) to provide enough cream to produce 1lb of butter (450 grams). The liquid that remained (skimmed milk) was of no direct use to the factory. However, it contained all the proteins that were in the original milk and other solids too and thus was ideal for feeding to pigs and calves. Farmers who brought their milk to Mountshayne could either wait for it to be processed and then take the separated milk back to their farms, or they could sell it to the Culm Valley Dairy Company, which had its own piggery at Mountshayne for fattening pigs.

Once again, the design of this piggery was innovative. It was situated 100 yards from and 20 feet lower than Mountshayne. The skimmed milk flowed to the piggery through a pipe, straight into the pigs' feeding troughs. This was an excellent labour-saving idea involving no manual lifting in the process. (The churns in use at the time held 17 gallons and weighed 70kgs when full and they were very awkward to empty.) For many years there had been a few pigs on every farm in the area where mixed farming predominated and every farmer kept a variety of animals. The success of the milk factory meant that much more milk was being produced locally which in turn meant that many more pigs could be kept. There was even a pig market at Millhayes. In his book *The Blackmore Country* (1906), F.J. Snell wrote:

It is impossible to forget that Hemyock is a famous mart (market) for pigs. The whole district is piggy and the sleek black animal with the curly tail is as highly respected in life and in death, as his congener in that porcine paradise Erin.

Fortunately, the village outlook was such in those days that no one complained about the smell from this multitude of pigs!

Between 1886 and 1891 the premises of Mountshayne were much improved by the installation of a new steam engine which could drive three Laval separators. The venture became more successful and many farmers from neighbouring parishes brought their milk to Hemyock. As the Culm Valley Dairy Company only required the cream in the milk to manufacture butter, it was logical to start small depots that could separate the cream in local villages. The problem of unnecessary transport was eased, because only the cream had to be brought to Mountshayne to be turned into butter. The first of these satellite depots was started in Culmstock in 1888. Here water-power from the river Culm was harnessed to drive two separators, one of which was adjusted to produce extra-thick cream, which was sold separately in small cloam jugs and pots and sent all over the country by the local train. In April 1888 another branch was opened in Clayhidon. This one also used water-power. It had been a separate company, the Upper Culm Valley Dairy Co., with its own

directors and a capital of £438. We know that in 1889 it made a profit of £65 of which £21 was distributed as a dividend. Subsequently, it was taken over by the Culm Valley Dairy Company.

In January 1889 a depot was set up at Ruggin, West Buckland. With the co-operation of Viscount Sidmouth, a new brick-and-iron building was constructed at Rawridge in Upottery. Uffculme was the next village to have its own collecting depot (at Leigh). At this site separators worked on a different principle than that employed by the Laval models and we know that they were driven by a turbine wheel of the 'Little Giant' type. Some time later, a branch was opened in Dunkeswell. Finally, in November 1890, a depot was built at Pitminster, with the four Hemyock Culm Valley Dairy Company Directors together with five local farmers as local Directors. This branch was financed by 60 shares at £5 each of which £4 was paid up at the time. The period between 1888 and late 1889 must have been a very active one for the company's four founders. It should be remembered that they were primarily farmers who clearly learnt the methods of big business very quickly. At the same time we must realise that this was taking place in the late-Victorian era when entrepreneurial skills developed apace throughout the country.

At all of the depots the milk had to be delivered before 7a.m. On arrival it was weighed and its fat content determined. It was quickly found that the compositional quality of the milk varied from farm to farm and the milk was paid for according to the amount of butterfat that it contained. The cream from the depots was taken to Hemyock daily, allowed to ripen, then made into butter mechanically, each butter churn producing 300lbs (136 kgs) of butter at one time. The advertising material of the Culm Valley Dairy Company laid great stress on the fact that the product was untouched by human hand during manufacture and was uniform in shape, flavour and quality. It was despatched from Hemyock by rail to all parts of the country. Eton and several Oxford colleges were large customers.

With the rapid expansion of the company some difficulties arose. Obviously expansion at this rate must have strained its capital resources. On 1 January 1889 the firm was converted to a limited liability company and its capital increased to £10 000 (half being paid up). Some additional Directors were appointed – mainly local farmers but also with some provision merchants from Birmingham and Manchester.

The details of the new company make very interesting reading. Records of the time stated that:

The objectives are to purchase of Messrs. Clist, Farrant, Lutley and Wide, the business of butter and cream manufacturers and merchants, milk dealers and general dairy factors carried on by them in partnership under the style of the Culm Valley Dairy Co., at Hemyock, Culmstock and Clayhidon.

The entrance to the factory when it was the Culm Valley Dairy Co. There were two houses on the left, both of which were subsequently demolished to make way for the office block and the yard beyond. The railway lines on the right ran into the factory.

Reference is also made to an agreement for the new company to carry on the business of:

> *... butter, cream and cheese manufacturers and merchants, pig breeders and dealers, ham and bacon curers and merchants, ice manufacturers, poultry keepers, dealers and merchants, condensed milk, electric light and power producers.*

Perhaps the ideals of these four farmers were a little premature but what a vision they had for the future of their company!

It soon became apparent that the premises at Mountshayne were not large enough to deal with the ever-increasing supplies of milk and in 1897 the factory was moved to Millhayes, about one mile away. Millhayes boasted an ideal position for such a factory. It was beside the river Culm so power could be utilised easily, although a steam engine was always in use as well. The river was well suited to carry unwanted waste materials away from the butter and cheese manufacturing processes! Anti-pollution laws had not even been thought of in those days and it is said that the trout between Hemyock and Culmstock reached a very large size!

A very important feature of the Millhayes site was that it was at the head of the Culm Valley Railway line and the line was actually continued across the road into the factory itself, thus facilitating easy distribution both inwards and outwards. The building at Millhayes had been a corn mill before being extended for use as a milk factory and there is strong historical evidence that before its use as an animal feed mill it had been a cloth mill. The Culm Valley Dairy Company capitalised on this too. They realised that in order to produce milk of a good quality, it was necessary to feed the cows well, so the grain milling side continued and the feed stuffs sold to the farmers at the same time as they delivered their milk. Coal and other necessaries could also be purchased. The piggery at Mountshayne was retained, and it was necessary to actually transport the skimmed milk from Millhayes to that site.

In addition to butter production, the new premises allowed other products to be developed, the most obvious one being cheddar cheese. Details of one day's operation for 26 October 1897 survive to illustrate how the whole process had become much more industrial and scientific than the small-scale cheese-making operations that had taken place on most farms before this date:

58 gallons mixed milk, temperature 85 degrees F
2.5 quarts starter-heated rennet 20 sec   9.55a.m.
19½ drops rennet added, stirred for 5 mins
coagulated in 13 mins cut at   10.50a.m.
Turned on steam for scalding   11.25a.m.
Reached 102 degrees F at   12.00p.m
Left to settle until   1.00p.m.
Whey run off   1.15p.m.
Put on cooler   1.25p.m.
Covered and pressed with 56lbs Weights.
Turned and piled one end of cooler   1.45p.m.
Cut and tied in 2 bundles   2.30p.m.
Turned into dry clothes   3.00p.m.
Ditto   3.30p.m.
Ditto   4.00p.m.
Ground at   4.40p.m.
Put in vats   5.00p.m.
24oz. salt added

71lbs curd obtained

The 58 gallons of milk resulted in 71lbs of curd and presumably eventually 60lbs of cheese. Several annual reports of the Culm Valley Dairy Company survive. One from 1913 is typical and illustrates the progress that had been made since the company had been formed over a quarter of a century before. It is also the last report to be issued prior to the outbreak of the First World War. The accounts showed a profit of £683.3s.6d. (£683.17), an average for the pre-war years. During the war profits of £1102 (in 1914) and £1039 (in 1915) were recorded. A dividend of 10 per cent was declared (free of income tax) and this amounted to £500. The business involved the whole village and a worker's bonus scheme had been in operation for a number of years. Some 2.5 per cent of the net profit was distributed to the employees. In 1913 this amounted to £13.17s.0d. (£13.85p). Without doubt this was a reflection of the liberal political views of the Managing Directors and must have had the effect of producing a remarkable family feeling in the factory.

As so often happens it was not the actual amount of money to be given away that was important but that the workers had a financial share in the success of the venture. Labour relations were extremely good throughout the history of the Culm Valley Dairy Company. Local Directors worked alongside the men and the whole unit realised that it was to their mutual benefit that the entire factory was run smoothly.

A partial breakdown of the accounts illustrates how conditions have changed over the last 90 years. The expenditure shows that:

Wages and directors' fees were	£1170
Coal	£156
Rent, rates and taxes	£162
Horse hire	£238

On the credit side of the accounts the size of the operation is shown – 123 607lbs (over 56 000kgs) of 'Farmers' Butter' was produced. This returned a gross profit of £129 and the net profit was ¼d. per lb. Additionally 80 760lbs of 'Colonial Butter' was imported. This was blended with some of the English butter to give a profit of £84 from the operation. The corn mill was still running and it purchased grain at a cost of £8294, from which a profit of £328 was made on its resale to local farmers. It is significant that the corn-milling operation contributed no less than 50 per cent of the company's total profit.

The accounts survive for the Dunkeswell Branch and show that a profit of £52 was made. The depot purchased 29 644 gallons of milk at a cost of £602 from which it manufactured 11 857lbs of butter, which realised £722. One man was employed at Dunkeswell and he worked for 310 days per year at a wage of two shillings a day (10p). A horse was hired for 1s.6d. (7½p) a day. The separator there was obviously oil-driven, as the purchase of petroleum amounted to £10 during that year. By examining the year 1913 in some detail we are able to see how a hard-working group of people was able to produce a reasonable profit for both the local farmers and the Culm Valley Dairy Company. At the same time a very useful source of local employment was created.

By the middle of the First World War a rapid change was taking place in the dairy industry. Wartime conditions meant that the diet of the nation was changing. In the dairy industry, margarine, a new competitor for butter, appeared and rapidly gained a large share of the market. Margarine was made from vegetable oils and was cheap. As the war continued, milk, along with other farm produce, became increasingly expensive. Naturally butter became more expensive too. Not only this, but the market for liquid milk in the cities was rapidly expanding in both volume and price. This meant that the Culm Valley Dairy Company could not pay its farmer suppliers as much for their milk as the larger dairies that bought milk for liquid consumption. On 15 September 1916, the Directors of the Culm Valley Dairy Company sent a letter to their shareholders. It stated that they recommended that the company should be sold to the very much larger group, the United Dairies Ltd of London. This was in effect an early example of a business take-over. It is understood that United Dairies let it be known that had their proposals been rejected, they would have constructed their own factory on the other side of the river. In actual fact the terms for the purchase were quite generous. For each Culm Valley Dairy Company £5 share, United Dairies offered £9. In their letter the Culm Valley Dairy Company Managing Directors (two of whom by that time had their own sons on the board) pointed out that they had been in business together for 30 years. Rather poignantly, they added: 'naturally the time has very nearly arrived when they must be capable of less energy'! The initial stage in the development of Hemyock's almost unique milk industry was over. No longer would local families control the destiny of the company but the factory would continue to expand with the injection of fresh capital that was readily available from the United Dairies Group.

The main factory block that remained until the demolition of the entire site in 2000 was built in 1920–21. From the time of the take-over until 1920, milk which was surplus to the liquid requirements of the London market was made into cheese. After the construction of the new buildings, a large proportion of the milk was converted into condensed milk, which left Hemyock in tins, this being almost the only way that milk could be kept fresh for a long period of time in the days before refrigeration was readily available.

In 1923 a disastrous fire destroyed most of the original building, including the office, the butter-making plant and the packing room. Rebuilding took place quickly, but the butter-making side of the business was finally lost. In its place facilities for dealing with the transportation of milk to London in glass-lined railway tankers were expanded. An engine-driven winch, which could operate a cable that extended into the railway station, via a large capstan, pulled the empty wagons from the Great Western Railway railhead across the road and into the factory. These tankers then underwent sterilisation by steam, quite a noisy process, before being filled with milk. The tankers, when full, were allowed to run by means of gravity back into the railway station with a worker attempting to control the speed by manually pushing down on the large brake handle. Whilst this operation was going on two men were on the main road equipped with large red discs to control the traffic. Rather surprisingly there was never an accident on the milk factory's private lines. This cannot be said of the Great Western Railway's side of the operation! On numerous occasions the railway staff succeeded in derailing the engine by not operating the simple points system correctly, thus allowing the engine to jump the rails with the necessity of getting a rail crane to put it back on the lines! The timing of the whole operation was precise. The milk tankers, up to five in number, were attached to the train that left Hemyock at 2.15p.m. They joined a complete milk train at Tiverton Junction and arrived at Wood Lane in London for distribution the following morning.

Demand for the milk was ever increasing but there was a physical limit to the number of cows that could be kept on local farms under the farming systems then practised. The old adage 'three acres to a cow' was not far from being true. Under these circumstances the only solution appeared to be by increasing the annual milk yield of the cows. What proved to be a brilliant idea was the formation of the Calf Club in Hemyock (see Chapter Eleven). The sons and daughters of the farmers were targeted and were provided with a heifer calf from a high-yielding breed which they had to carefully look after for a year, then either sell or buy back. In fact, all of the cattle remained on local farms and over a period of a few years the milk yield improved from about 500

Mr Hole with the first milk lorry. Note the horn on his left and the lights which appear to be oil-lit, c.1920.

In 1923 part of the factory was destroyed by a serious fire.

gallons a year per cow to double that figure. Consequently the factory increased its milk supply significantly from the same number of cattle. The 'mealy' Devon cross cows that previously figured prominently in our local landscape, were replaced by the brown and white Ayrshire breed. Over the years these Ayrshires have, in turn, been replaced by the ubiquitous black and white Friesians. The result of all of these changes was that the small collecting depots were closed and all of the milk from the surrounding district was taken to Hemyock. This operation was facilitated because a lorry, the first of many, was purchased to carry milk churns from the farms. The first lorry was a Trafford with solid rubber tyres. To protect the driver in bad weather, the windscreen was a tarpaulin, which could be raised or lowered. Even the type of milk churn in use was changed from the conical shaped one (*right*). These had two hinged handles on the side and were extremely difficult to wash and sterilise. The new cylindrical design first contained 12 gallons and later 10 gallons. These remained in use until churns were phased out some 40 years later. The cylindrical shape maximised the number of churns that could be loaded on to a lorry.

Bill Northam with an early milk churn that could hold 17 gallons of milk (75 litres) and weighed 210lbs (90kgs) when full.

For some reason, between 1922 and 1928, the factory was leased to J. Lyons and Co. who traded in Hemyock as Milkal Ltd and Dried Milk Products Ltd. During their occupancy the factory was altered again to produce milk powder. This was by means of the 'Milkal Spry Drying Process' and was the first time that milk had been dried commercially. Powdered milk continued to be produced here for another 50 years and the product must have been good because it was almost exclusively used in Mars bars and by the famous Cunard shipping line. Whilst Messrs Lyons remained in Hemyock they experimented with soft fruit production on the triangular area of land between the factory and Higher Millhayes. Apples, raspberries, loganberries, blackcurrants and damsons were all cultivated around the factory and the fruit made into jam. A well-known story from this time was authenticated by the workers who actually made the jam. They stated that wooden pips were added to the raspberry and loganberry jams!

By 1925–26 104 people worked in the factory. This number was augmented during the summer months, when milk production peaked, by unemployed workers from Wellington who were brought in to ensure that the dryers could operate 24 hours a day by means of three eight-hour shifts. This side of the business was expanded again in 1932. The final evaporation and milk drier was installed in 1956. The plant could then dry 1200 gallons of milk an hour and produce 70 tons of milk powder a week.

During the Second World War several research projects were carried on here. Original research on drying eggs was developed in Hemyock and parts of the milk-drying plant were used to see if it was a commercially viable operation. For two weeks the factory was used by the Ministry of Food to actually prove that it was feasible and subsequently the 'know-how' was sent to Australia and New Zealand. From these dominions thousands of tons of dried eggs came to England. A method of condensing apple juice was found and exploited. Imported maize came to Hemyock and was weighed out and packed. The most popular of all these developments must surely have been the production of thousands and thousands of 2oz (50grm) packets of mixed tea, milk powder and sugar which were made in Hemyock and despatched to our servicemen all over the world. Apparently these packs were most appreciated by our armed forces in the jungles of South-East Asia. When the Second World War ended ice-cream powder was made in Hemyock and proved to be enormously popular.

For the last 20 years of its life as a milk-factory, milk was collected from an area of 100 square miles in both Devon and Somerset. A fleet of 17 lorries based at Hemyock collected the milk from individual farms, each lorry making at least two journeys daily. From 1964 onwards the factory was as automatic as it was possible to be. A new milk reception block was designed and built entirely by the factory staff. This enabled 20 churns a minute to be handled by just two men. A remarkable innovation was incorporated in the design. A large churn storage area was created which meant that in future there would be no delay in re-loading the lorries with empty churns. In retrospect it seems unfortunate that this extremely sophisticated machinery was developed just when the use of the churn as a means of transporting milk was almost over. By the late 1960s an increasing number of farmers were installing their own bulk tanks to hold milk. This was collected by bulk milk tankers and taken to the dairy. Under these conditions it was not necessary to transport milk a short distance to a small factory. It made economic sense to take milk to larger factories nearer to the new motorways that were edging ever closer to the West

Factory staff in the 1930s.
Left to right back: Bert Head, Frank Browning, Tom Lowman, Mark Lowman, ?, Bill Northam,
Bert Bickle, George Northam, Frankie Masters, Dick Pooley, Reg Barton, Vic Bale;
3rd row: Sid Land, Jim Woodgate, ?, Bill Wotton, Percy Pike, Fred Trickey, Harry Towell, ?, Red Lowman,
Edgar Lowman, Bill Hutchings, Fred Cork, Ernie Best;
2nd row: ?, Ern Lowman, Eli Lowman, Tom Bright, W. Guppy, Bill Cload, Bill Casely, Bert Marks,
Percy Salter, Kath Curtis, ?, Chris Board, Bill Bennett, George Lowman, Bill Tricky, Jim Mitcham;
sitting: Jack Exton, Harry Summers, Bill Griffiths, Hazel Wide, Ted Hassan, Bill Hole, Mr Anderson,
Sam Lutley, Bill Miller, Queenie Pring, Jack Jennings, Edward Lutley, John Webber;
on the ground: ? Ayres, Elsie Bendle, Phyll Lowman, Beat Osmond, ?, Kit Pike, Gwen Bennett.

The social life of the factory workers was not neglected.
This is a Christmas party for the children of the employees in the old factory hall, c.1940.

Country. The age of rail transport was over and commercial haulage by road was the future for moving goods. A train of events had started which would be almost impossible to stop. The production of milk had become very profitable, too profitable perhaps. Cattle were kept under very intensive conditions. Farms were amalgamated into even larger units on the grounds of increased efficiency. But at what cost? For several years there were rumours about the future of the Hemyock factory. Eventually these rumours proved true and on 31 October 1975 Unigate Foods Ltd ceased production at Hemyock.

One of the reasons given for the closure was that the railway line was to be blocked close to Tiverton Junction, so that the M5 motorway, then under construction, could pass through without having to provide a road bridge to cross the railway line. It was obvious to local people that this type of decision must have been taken months, if not years before, and yet the removal of the rail link was given as an important reason for the closure of the milk factory. Instructions were sent from the head office that everything had to be removed from the site. All of the machinery so carefully maintained by dedicated

employees went, as did all the papers and records. The factory became an empty shell. A feeling of gloom spread over the whole village and over 100 people were made redundant. The social impact of enforced redundancy was sorely felt in a rural environment. To become unemployed as a result of a decision taken in a boardroom 100 miles away was difficult to understand, more especially because Hemyock was a very profitable part of Unigate.

Hemyock became strangely quiet. The hum of

Top: *The factory in its coal-burning days. A Renwick Wilton coal truck can be seen being unloaded. The cows in the picture could almost deliver their milk direct to the factory!*
Above: *Staff from the factory outside Taunton Station en route to London for the annual two-day 're-union' for long-service staff, 1957/8. Left to right: Percy Pike, W. Bradford, Bill Griffiths, Bill Miller, Jack Jennings, Bill Alway, Bill Trickey, Kit Pike, Harry Trickey, George Northam, ?, ?, Bill Cload, Ernie Hole.*

✑ *Factory Life* ✑

Left: *Mr L. Mutter with one day's supply of milk in five tankers ready to be taken to London.*

Below: *The first plant for sterilising milk churns before their re-use. These ten-gallon churns were emptied and upended on the receiving tank and were then placed inside the steam steriliser where they revolved in a clockwise direction. The man on the right is removing the clean churn ready for re-use. The churn lids went through the same process.*

Left: *Mr W. Miller at the controls of the milk powder plant.*

Above: *Mr Hassan, the motor engineer, by the garage for the lorries, c.1950s. A fleet of 14 Bedford lorries had just been purchased.*

Above right: *View of the milk reception bay with two older lorries.*

Right: *The dried milk powder was dispatched in these barrels made of plywood and known as 'Venestas' (from the name of the firm that made them).*

Top: *After the severe storm in 1963 it was several days before tractors could move and all day long farmers came from miles around with their milk. The station is on the right and a milk tanker has been pulled across the road to be filled with milk and sent to London. A delivery of bread has also just arrived.*

Left: *The milk reception platform after the storm.*

Below left: *Clearing snow from the rails beside the station in 1963 to enable the train to get through. The factory had converted to oil-fuelled boilers and the oil storage tanks can be seen in the background.*

Below: *Snow is cleared to allow access to the factory.*

✌ Demise of an Empire ✍

Top: *Aerial view of the milk factory taken about 30 years ago. The fields at the top of the photograph later became the Hollingarth housing estate. The factory was demolished in 2000.*

Above and left: *Scenes showing the demolition of the milk factory in the latter half of the year 2000. The last photograph was taken on 2 December 2000. What the village saw develop over more than a hundred years was reduced to rubble in a few months.*

A steeplejack inspects the old chimney.

the machinery, the clanking of chains against churns, the occasional hiss of escaping steam, the smoke from the tall chimney that told us the wind direction – all ceased. A 'For Sale' sign appeared outside the premises and guard dogs were introduced to make the place secure. Meetings between local councils, the local Member of Parliament and Government officials confirmed that the inevitable had happened. Significantly, after exactly six months the 'For Sale' sign was removed. Within a couple of days a letter was issued to all residents of Hemyock from Unigate Foods Ltd telling them that: 'As a result of the serious implications for the community of the closure of the milk factory, the directors proposed to re-open it as a development unit which could be used for research and testing purposes.' Very shortly afterwards the factory started to become active again. A great deal of expensive machinery was installed. Some Hemyock people were sent to Sweden and Swedish people came to Hemyock. Hemyockians began to be re-employed, all of whom were sworn to secrecy about the future of the factory. Eventually it was realised that 'research and testing' meant a full-scale factory again. More and more people discovered that a new butter substitute 'Gold' was to be manufactured in Hemyock based on a Swedish patent. In 1977 'Gold' was launched and 66 people were employed.

The reasons for the re-opening of the milk factory soon became apparent. Throughout 1976 butter prices in the UK had been rising rapidly and sales were falling, to the detriment of St Ivel's profit. At the same time margarine sales were increasing because it was cheaper. Unigate were looking worldwide to find alternative milk-based products and came across a low-fat spread developed and in production in Sweden. This product contained half the fat of butter; it was low in calories, high in protein and had the added advantage that it could be spread on bread straight from the refrigerator.

An agreement was drawn up with the Swedish company, which gave Unigate exclusive rights to produce the new product in the United Kingdom in exchange for paying royalties to the Swedish firm for the current and future product technology for a period of 15 years. Market research was carried out and the results were very encouraging. Shortly afterwards 'Gold' (the name for the new product) began to be produced in Hemyock. Initially it was launched in the South West but the sales were so good that very quickly it was sold throughout the United Kingdom. The following table illustrates the business' success:

Date	No. of Employees.	Details	Annual Tonnage
April			
1977	66		2500–3000
1978	116	National launch	8000–10000
1979	138		10000–20000
1981	150		36000
1986	250	Centenary year	40000
1988	300		48000
1994	212		52000

The number of employees was reduced between 1988 and 1994 as a result of the installation of automated machinery, thus increasing efficiency. Over the years the product range increased and such products as 'Low Fat Gold' and 'Utterly Butterly' appeared.

In 1999 the company decided to stop the production of these products in Hemyock and to relocate to Liverpool. It was rumoured that the move was a result of financial grants being offered to Unigate to move to Liverpool to solve a massive unemployment problem there. Whilst this objective was no doubt achieved, the irony is that it created an equal amount of unemployment in the South West!

Yet again Hemyock was in the same situation as it had been some 20 years previously – the factory was empty. More seriously we now knew that this really was the end of an era. Quickly any machinery that was of use was removed. Later a sale of what was salvageable took place and walls were knocked down and the roof opened to get the last of the machinery out. The building was left in a very sorry state, just the intangible memories of over a century of its existence lingering in the minds of those who had witnessed its development. The whole site, including the old railway station area, was advertised, but soon seemed, from an industrial viewpoint, to have no future; an alternative use would have to be found. After a while the site was sold to a firm of house builders – Bloor Homes. We have reason to believe that Hemyock was fortunate that such a development company bought the site. From the outset Bloor Homes have sought out the opinions of the parishioners and all through the many planning processes, for the first time ever, the Parish Council was involved and took part in the discussions. As this book is published, building is about to begin. The factory has been razed, just huge piles of rubble remaining. Some 35 homes will be built, an industrial development erected on the site of the old railway station, the factory 'hall' will be given to the Parish Council and recycling facilities and a BMX track for our young people will be provided. Generally villagers consider this scheme a suitable successor to the milk factory and one of which both our ancestors and the generations to come would approve.

A view of The Star Inn, 1908. On the left is Mrs Hawkins, grandmother to Mrs Evelyn Pike.
Mrs Hawkins who cooked lunches in The Star, is talking to a Mrs Quick. In the background are Mr
Luxton the ostler and Mr Denning who brought the Royal Mail from Cullompton to Hemyock.
The gentleman with the broad-brimmed hat was Vicar of Dunkeswell Abbey Church.

Above: *The Star and Railway Inns before the 1920s.*

Left: *The remains of The Star after a fire destroyed it in 1928.*

CHAPTER SEVEN

Village Inns

 Today there is only one inn in the village, the Catherine Wheel, but this has not always been the case. At one time, in fact up until the year 1928, there had been three, two of them, The Star and New Inn, alongside each other in the centre of the village, the third, the Culm Valley Hotel (known to some as the Culm Valley Railway Hotel), was at Millhayes near the milk factory.

The history of The Star and New Inn goes back to the 18th century whereas the Culm Valley Hotel was a comparative newcomer, opening some time after the arrival of the railway in 1876. The hotel was probably established by the end of the 19th century or in the early 1900s. To most local people of the day it was known as the 'Millhayes'. According to the account of one old Hemyock resident, the late Bill Griffiths, the principal customers of the Culm Valley Hotel were rabbit trappers but obviously they were not the only clientele with the milk factory being so near at hand. Apparently the licence for the inn was allowed to lapse when J. Lyons and Co. leased the milk factory (1922–28) and was not renewed because of opposition from 'non-drinkers'. The unlicensed premises were used for accommodating visitors to the factory during the J. Lyons era but after 1928 the Culm Valley Hotel was divided into two houses, Nos 1 and 2 Millhayes. Bill Griffiths lived in No.1 for many years and the Summers family in No.2.

Turning then to the story of the much more ancient Star and New Inns. The first written record of an inn in Hemyock is that of an unnamed hostelry in 1740. Details of early ale- or beerhouses and their proprietors can be found in Quarter Sessions records which are kept at the Devon Record Office. These records include Licensed Victualler Recognizances and Registers and cover the years 1552–1828. These records are far from complete so the fact that nothing can be found for Hemyock prior to 1740 does not necessarily mean that there was no tavern prior to that date. Records for many years are completely missing. The Recognizances referred to were bonds, sworn before two Justices, that the alehouse keeper or retailer of beer would maintain an orderly house. A surety (or sureties) was also required, usually in the sum of £10. Unfortunately inn names were not often shown prior to the latter half of the 18th century. The first time a Hemyock pub had its name recorded was in 1793 with the New Inn. 'New' tends to indicate that the premises had an earlier name or replaced a previous building.

Something of the history of both The Star and New Inns (later the Railway Hotel and then the Catherine Wheel) has been gleaned from documents in the possession of Ushers Brewery. One such document, an Indenture of 1844, for example, refers to:

... a messuage and tenement with its appurtenances then and therefore called or known by the name of Scaddings situate in the said parish of Hemyock in the County of Devon but which messuage or tenement was then and has been for many years converted into a public house or Inn called the New Inn.

Another Indenture (or Endenture) dated 25 March 1811 deals with a William Cooke of Hemiock (one of the various spellings of Hemyock) and Oliver Chard of Halse in the County of Somerset. Chard was to lease the New Inn for one year. What is interesting in the body of this document is the following passage which described the property:

All that Messuage or Dwelling House situate, lying and being within the town of Hemiock aforesaid which was some time since built on the ground and space in some part thereof whereon Messuage or dwelling house in the possession of Edmund Goodall and afterwards of John Saunders was burnt down heretofore in the possession of John Somerhouse deceased...

It was only after Oliver Chard became a Hemyock innkeeper that the name of The Star appeared in the

Quarter Session records, alongside that of the New Inn, in the year 1812. Were there two inns prior to this date or was this a new commercial enterprise? It should, perhaps, be pointed out at that this stage The Star and New Inn were literally joined together until the former was destroyed by fire in 1928. It is necessary to go back to another conflagration, the Hemyock fire of 1693, in the search for clues. An entry in the 'Devon Session Rolls, Midsummer 1693', which is entitled 'Hemyock Fire', lists a number of individuals and their properties together with what appear to be either a valuation of property destroyed by the fire or estimates for the cost of rebuilding or replacing property. Full details are given in Chapter Three but our particular interest here is in two individuals who lost their property in the fire. The first was John Scadding who owned two dwelling houses plus barns, outbuildings, etc., and the second was John Somerhaies, the owner of eight dwelling houses and other properties.

Is it possible that the John Scadding referred to in the 1844 Indenture was the individual whose name lead to the property being called 'Scaddings' (or perhaps that this was one of his descendants)? The Indenture of 1811 refers to property being built where earlier property, owned by John Somerhouse (deceased), had been. Could the 1693 John Somerhaies be the same man, or of the same family, whose surname changed with the passage of time?

There were several branches of the Scadding family in Hemyock in the closing years of the 18th century. The Hemyock Land Tax Return for 1780, for example, lists an Aaron Scadding (who was at Oxenpark), John Scadding, Richard Scadding, Charles Scadding (at Brownings), and William Scadding, so it is not impossible that the 1844 reference to Scaddings was linked with one of these gentlemen.

The fire in 1693 seems to have devastated the heart of Hemyock but the Sessions list does not mention an 'inn' as such. From this we can only speculate that an alehouse or inn arose out of the ashes of the fire when the centre of the village was rebuilt or that one or more of the dwelling houses rebuilt after the fire became an inn prior to 1740.

It is the Returns of Licensed Victualler Recognizances that really provide the first historical evidence as to the existence of the Hemyock taverns. As mentioned earlier the only extant records respecting Hemyock inns or alehouses date to 1740. In these documents the name of the village is spelt either Hemyock, Hemiock or Hemiok. For most years two licensees are named, although there are sometimes three or even four. This does not necessarily indicate two or more inns, as the licensees may have merely shared licences. Thus it is impossible to be certain whether or not a second inn was in existence prior to 1812 when The Star first appeared as an inn name.

These Returns are a good illustration of part of the social life of the village and as such details are given here of licensees and their sureties between 1740 and 1828 (some years are missing). In 1740 Roger Masey and Robert Manley were licensees, with a surety being provided by Yeoman Chris Clode. The 1754 licensees were Robert Gillard, Isaac Manley and Robert Manley, with sureties being provided by John Scadding, Robert Smith and Edward Lutley. From 1755–57 Isaac Manley was the licensee with his surety being given by Robert Manley (cordwainer). For licensees John Star, Robert Gillard and Robert Manley, the sureties were given by William Collings and Isaac Manley.

In 1758 Robert Gillard and Isaac and Robert Manley were still licensees, with one surety, given by John Saunders. Robert Gillard was a licensee with Isaac and Elizabeth Manley, and their sureties were given by William Morgan and John Saunders, both described as yeomen. In 1760 the situation was the same, although sureties came from William Bud, John Saunders and Isaac Manley. The following year, 1761, again saw the same state of affairs, but with an additional innkeeper, John Morgan. Sureties came from Francis Cridland, John Saunders, W. Saunders, I. Manley and Thomas Cridland. It seems highly unlikely that five sureties were required for one inn and it appears that 'I.' Manley (no doubt Isaac), a licensee himself, may have stood surety for his friend in the adjoining tavern – so perhaps a second inn did exist at this point.

From 1762–69 the licensees were Isaac Manley, John Saunders and John Morgan. For 1762 there was only one surety given – by James Bowerman: in 1763 there was again only a single surety, Robert Manley. In the succeeding years, this fell to Edward Lutley (a baker), Henry Wood, Paul Cooke and Clement Waldron – some familiar names from Hemyock's history.

The turn of the decade saw a change when George Clist joined John Saunders as one of the licensees, and from 1770–85 George Clist was always listed with either Thomas, John or Elizabeth Saunders. The sureties during this period came from George Collings, Thomas Burrow, Francis Dimmont (sometimes Dimont), William Hollis, Edward Lutley, Henry Jervis, Wm. Holway, Edward Webber, Tho. Spark, John Flea [sic] and Samuel Fry. Records for the years 1779, 1783 and 1786 are missing.

In 1787 and 1788 there was only one licensee listed, Samuel Mansfield, with John Southey giving the surety. No records are available until 1793 when Robert Manley became the only named licensee. This was the first year in which an inn name appeared in the records, the New Inn, and from this year until 1812 the situation did not change. There was always just one innkeeper named and one inn. Robert Manley was in situ until 1802 although 1796 is missing from the records. His sureties over these years were given by Henry Howett, Hezekiah Verman (?) and James Tapscott. From 1803 until 1811 the sole licensee was Lawrence Mansfield. The sureties for this period were given by several individuals, including Mansfield himself, Edward Lutley, William Redwood, George Clist, Edward Brice of Uffculme (sureties did not necessarily come from the same parish), John Lutley and Robert Blackmore.

In 1812, for the first time, the inn name 'Star Inn' appears in the records, so from hereon both The Star and New Inn are recorded as such in the Quarter Sessions records. In 1812 Lawrence Mansfield was recorded as licensee for the New Inn and Oliver Chard for The Star. Mansfield's sureties came from Robert Farrant and Robert Brown and Chard's came from Henry Spurway and Anthony Cordwent. Lawrence Mansfield and Oliver Chard remained in their taverns until 1817. Their sureties were given by Adrian Morgan, Henry Manley, Robert Willey and Joseph Poole, Edward Lutley, James Mansfield, John Haddon and George Shaddock.

From 1818 until 1828 James Townsend took over the New Inn and Oliver Chard remained at The Star. The only new name among those standing sureties over these years were Robert Fry and William Walker.

Running a public house during the 18th and 19th centuries was not a particularly lucrative proposition (some publicans might even argue that the same comment applies for the 20th and 21st centuries). Many innkeepers found it necessary to supplement their incomes by following other trades. In 1850, for example, *Whites Devon Directory* shows that the then licensees, Thomas Wood of the New Inn and Mark Babb of The Star, were a mason and wheelwright respectively. The Babb family remained at The Star for many years after this date.

An interesting event took place in 1828 that might throw some light on the alternative uses a public house/inn could be put to. A local man, Ralph Gillard, was involved in an accident that led to the amputation of one of the unfortunate fellow's legs. It would appear that the operation took place in The Star and the accounts for Hemyock's overseers of the poor explains all (or nearly all):

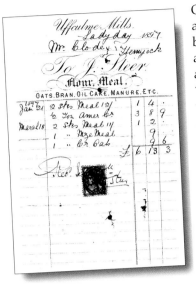

One can just visualise poor Gillard being plied with alcohol to act as an anaesthetic. As the 'op' took place in the inn, can we assume that James Moon was the innkeeper? If the 16s.10d. was purely for drink that was quite an intake at 1828 prices. Was Mr Blackmore the surgeon? Was the leg buried in the churchyard? That hardly seems likely. Whatever the answer to these questions it is clear that Ralph – and his leg – were very well looked after.

The Census Returns give some idea of the staff employed in the village inns, the 1871 census for Hemyock showing, for example, that John Cridland, the 22-year-old licensee, had a 46-year-old housekeeper from Clayhidon by the name of Mary Blackmore and that George and Sarah Babb of The Star employed a young girl of 13, Carolyn Wynn, as a barmaid/servant. Interestingly an Indenture of 1877 relating to the New Inn refers to John Cridland and Mary Blackmore as the licensees. Obviously Mary's status had changed since the 1871 census.

The documents kept by Usher's Brewery reveal that by 1899 the New Inn had been renamed the 'Railway'. This name no doubt reflects the impact of the Culm Valley Railway on Hemyock, although the exact date of this change of name is not known.

Ralph Gillard and James Moons expenses
    at the 'Star' — 16s.10d.
Paid when Ralph Gillard's leg
    was taken off — 11s.5d.
Coffin for Ralph Gillard's leg — 3s.0d.
Burying Ralph Gillard's leg — 1s.0d.
Attendance on Ralph Gillard — 5s.0d.
Paid Mr Blackmore for Ralph Gillard's
    leg — £2.0s.0d.
Paid Mrs Wood for attendance on Ralph
    Gillard — 7s.0d.
Two pairs of drawers for Ralph Gillard — 6s.2d.
Counterpane for Ralph Gillard — 4s.6d.

Top: *Receipt from Uffculme Mills for oats, meal, etc. to Mr Clode, a village publican, dated Lady Day 1897.*
Above: *Norton Brewery receipt for spirits, wines, etc.*

Top: *The result of a flash flood outside the Catherine Wheel, c.1963/4.*
Above: *Somerset cricketer Vic Marks pulling a pint after opening the renovated Catherine Wheel in 1983.*
On the left are Jane and Keith Root, the licensees at that time.

The Star and Railway continued quite happily together over the years although there must have been just a little bit of friendly rivalry now and then regarding trade and customers. Apparently for decades prior to the Second World War Hemyock tended to be a rather abstemious place so how these two pubs, plus the Culm Valley Hotel, made ends meet is something of a mystery. In 1928 the New Inn lost its close neighbour when fire destroyed The Star – any arguments that might have existed over custom were resolved as far as the Railway (ex New Inn) was concerned.

For many years Hemyock Market had been held on the land behind the adjoining village inns so things might not have been so bad financially as far as the licensees were concerned. Apparently the brewers who owned the New Inn in the 1930s paid £6 a year to Knowlman & Sons, the auctioneers of Culmstock, for a right of way from the market to the back of the inn premises. This was to allow users of the market, owned by Knowlmans, to enter the inn from the rear, and as Knowlmans were in the habit of giving their clients a 3d. token to spend in the pub this was a very convenient arrangement.

In the early 1950s the Railway was run by a George Vian who was succeeded by Donald Chidgey in 1955. It was on 1 July 1960, during his tenancy, that the pub name was changed yet again, to the 'Catherine Wheel'. No doubt this name was chosen because of the historical association of St Catherine with Hemyock Church, opposite the pub. In the 14th century a chantry, dedicated to the saint, was established in St Mary's Church. Probably the brewery or the licensee felt that the name would be highly appropriate. Traditionally St Catherine (or Katherine) was a virgin martyred at Alexandria during the 4th century. She had been tortured on a Catherine Wheel in an attempt to make her deny her faith and marry the Emperor Maxentious. The Catherine Wheel was adopted from the badge of the Knights of St Catherine of Mount Sinai, an order formed in the 11th century to protect pilgrims on their way to the Holy Sepulchre. So the Catherine Wheel depicted on the sign hanging outside Hemyock's only surviving pub has very ancient origins indeed.

In 1982 The Catherine Wheel was taken over by Keith and Jane Root who undertook a series of changes and improvements over the next decade. The changes ensured that the pub retained its role as one of the focal points of village life. When the Roots left the pub it was under new management for a short time before being taken over by a Hemyock man, Geoff Taylor.

The Catherine Wheel is still a 'traditional' style establishment with two bars, good food, a skittle alley and all of the accoutrements of an old English pub – which, bearing in mind its history stretching back over more than 260 years, seems only too appropriate.

The Catherine Wheel in 2000, seen from the churchyard of St Mary's.

A postcard view of the opening of the Culm Valley Light Railway in June 1876.

An early postcard view of Hemyock Station with the River Culm in the foreground.

CHAPTER EIGHT

The Culm Valley Railway

On 31 October 1975 a British Rail engineer's 'special' train left Hemyock, the last goods train to run on the line that had been in existence for nearly 100 years. The last passenger train ran on the line on 9 September 1963. The end had finally come for a Great Western Branch Line that had served the Culm Valley since 1876 – a service which all began with a young man named Arthur Cadlick Pain.

Pain was a man of West-Country origins although he was born in Battersea, London. After leaving his school, Winchester, he served an engineering pupil-lage under the Devon County Surveyor, then for a year worked with two engineers, one of whom, R.P. Brereton (then Chief Engineer for the Great Western Railway), had formerly been an assistant to Isambard Kingdom Brunel. One of Brunel's great achieve-ments was the construction of the Great Western Railway, part of which, the section from Taunton to Exeter, ran through the edge of the Blackdown Hills and entailed cutting a tunnel at White Ball. When this tunnel was under construction train services were extended to a temporary terminus at Beam Bridge near the Exeter Turnpike. The Taunton to Exeter stretch was opened on 1 May 1844, just 32 years before the light railway in the Culm Valley was opened only a short distance away over the hills.

In 1866 Pain decided to branch out on his own and spent a number of years overseas, returning to Devon in the early 1870s. A great enthusiast for the idea of light railways, he felt that the many rural industries nationwide would benefit from having access to light, simply built and designed railways filling the gaps left by main and branch lines. Deciding that an ideal location for such a line would be in the Culm Valley to run between Tiverton and Hemyock, Pain approached a Director of the Bristol and Exeter Railway, Henry S. Ellis. Pain's approach

fell on fertile ground. Ellis was enthusiastic and contacted a number of individuals who he thought might be interested in such a project. A series of meetings was held in the Culm Valley area to explain the plan and seek subscribers. The first such event was called by an Uffculme solicitor, Richard Bowerman, and was held at the George Inn, Uffculme, on 15 May 1872. The meeting was suc-cessful and a committee of 17 men was formed.

The first Directors of the Railway Company were elected at a public meeting in Uffculme in November 1872. They included Henry Samuel Ellis of Exeter who became Chairman; Charles John Follett, a solici-tor and Mayor of Exeter who was Deputy Chairman; William Furze, owner of the brewery at Uffculme; and Edward Lutley, a farmer and landowner of Hemyock. Immediately after this meeting the Directors got together at the Commercial Hotel in Uffculme and Arthur Pain was appointed as engi-neer. Brewery owner William Furze must have improved his personal profits with so many meetings being held at local licensed premises.

An approach had already been made by Pain to the Bristol and Exeter Railway to undertake the run-ning of the line and they agreed to do so under cer-tain conditions. It had also been agreed that the Bristol and Exeter Railway would have the opportu-nity to buy the completed line at a later date. So the Directors now pressed on with plans to get sub-scribers for the company. At a later meeting at The Star Inn, Hemyock, on 1 January 1873, there was con-siderable enthusiasm for the project and a resolution was carried to encourage further support throughout the district – a resolution celebrated, apparently, by a peal of bells from St Mary's Church opposite The Star. Interestingly the previous meeting in Hemyock had been in the New Inn adjacent to The Star. The Culm Valley Light Railway Co. liked to spread their custom.

Royal assent was required for the Culm Valley Light Railway Act and this was forthcoming on 15 May. A capital of £25 000 in £10 shares was authorised with powers to borrow a further £8000. In

An early postcard view looking towards Hemyock Station with Pencross Hill in the background.

A later postcard view showing the arrival of a passenger train at the station.

addition the company was given five years to build the railway. A prospectus was issued in September 1873 inviting subscriptions for shares. The number of shares on offer was 1100, and another 1400 shares had already been allocated to subscribers. Shareholders in the newly created company included the following gentlemen from Hemyock:

George Babb	Innkeeper (Star Inn)	1 share
George Barton	Yeoman	5 shares
George Clist	Farmer	1 share
Henry Ellis	Farmer	1 share
Edward Farrant	Yeoman of New House	10 shares
Elizabeth Farrant	Widow of Holcombe	1 share
John Farrant	Yeoman	10 shares
Edward Lutley	Merchant	33 shares
Edward Lutley j.	Miller	1 share
John Tucker	Yeoman	5 shares
James Wide	Storekeeper	1 share
John Wide	Storekeeper	1 share

Many familiar Hemyock names are on the list. It is not known if farmer Henry Ellis was related in any way to Henry Samuel Ellis of Exeter, the Director of the Bristol and Exeter Railway. Interestingly the list of shareholders at the time of the cessation of the Culm Valley Light Railway Co. (1880) included Mary Ann Ellis, a widow, of Ladbroke Grove Road in West London. As Henry Samuel Ellis died in 1878 this was probably his widow, and perhaps there was a link with the Hemyock farmer but it seems unlikely.

Work started on the construction of the line in the Spring of 1874 but progress proved to be much slower than anticipated. The first contractor blamed heavy rain, floods, etc., and in addition there were financial problems. In June 1875 Arthur Pain was given personal control of the operation but even then the problems continued, finance being just one of them. There was even a strike by men working at a ballast quarry in Craddock. Edward Lutley, who farmed at Whitehall, had wanted a station at Whitehall included in the construction for goods and passengers. That was not to be, although a halt was added some years later and he had to be content with a siding which was installed and operational when the line was opened in May 1876.

In January the Bristol and Exeter Railway was taken over by the Great Western Railway who proved to be a little less co-operative than the Bristol and Exeter. The various problems regarding the line and its construction were, however, slowly overcome. In January 1876 Colonel Yolland, an Inspector for the Board of Trade, inspected the line and listed a number of matters that required attention. On 20 May he inspected the line again and agreed that the line could be opened to the public subject to certain conditions, namely:

One engine only shall be in steam between Hemyock and Tiverton Junction.

The speed shall not exceed 15 m.p.h.
The weight of the engine shall not exceed 8 tons on each pair of wheels.

The Great Western Railway, running the line, agreed to these terms and the Culm Valley Light Railway was opened on 29 May 1876.

The great event was formally celebrated on Thursday 1 June and in Hemyock it was all done on a grand scale. The station had been bedecked with flags and bunting and a band of the Tiverton Volunteers was there to greet the inaugural train bringing the Directors and other dignitaries to Hemyock. A committee in the village, under the Chairmanship of Revd Popham, Rector of Hemyock, had arranged for a lunch in a marquee with seating for some 300 people. No doubt suitable liquid refreshments were available, perhaps provided by one of the shareholders, George Babb, proprietor of The Star. The celebrations were presided over by C.J. Follett who spoke of the hope that the railway might be 'an incentive to agriculture and it might improve the productive character of the valley'. Mr Follett also hoped that one day there would be a hostelry called 'The Culm Valley Terminus Railway Inn' (see Chapter Seven).

Obviously one of the main purposes of the Culm Valley Railway was to carry goods, but passengers were also of great importance and one hope was that travellers would wish to take 'excursions' on the line. Clearly they would require refreshments and a refreshment room was opened at Hemyock by a local man, Richard Hine. This venture did not last for long when expected numbers of day trippers on excursions did not materialise. The goods traffic was, however, as successful as had been hoped.

One commercial venture that was undertaken locally was the establishment of the Culm Davy Brickworks. The influential Follett family had lands in Culm Davy, between Whitehall and Hemyock. On that land they found clay deposits which they decided to utilise in brick-making. Two of the family, R.W.W. Follett and C.J. Follett, accordingly set up the Culm Davy Brickworks in September 1876. Clearly for such a venture access was required to the Culm Valley line by means of a siding. Plans were drawn up by Arthur Pain, and the siding, paid for by the Folletts, was built. This did not prove to be a profitable venture for either the railway or the brick company. The latter was incorporated in May 1880 as the Culm Davy Brick and Tile Co. Ltd but the project was so unsuccessful that the company was wound up in July 1881. To this day old unused Culm Davy bricks can be found in many Culm Davy and Hemyock homes.

Financial problems were mounting for the Culm Valley Light Railway Company and the Company was dissolved in November 1881. By this point, the Great Western Railway had already taken over the

Engine 1466 with a couple of admirers in the early 1960s.

Clearing the line of snow in 1963.

The last passenger train to leave Hemyock, 9 September 1963.

The last goods train to leave Hemyock, a diesel engine No. 8Z 80, pictured on 31 October 1975.

Above: *An excellent elevated view of the station in the 1950s. The track on the far left crossed the road and was used to deliver coal to the factory and to collect milk powder. The other track on the left only ran a few more feet into buffers. The track on the right crossed the road and was used for milk collection.*

Left: *Almost the same elevated view, this time of the remains of Hemyock Station in 1975. The station building had been demolished. The building seen on the right was once a café. The kissing gate in the foreground and the tracks have now long gone.*

Culm Valley line in August of the previous year. When the Culm Valley Light Railway Co. was dissolved shareholders received 11 shillings for each £10 invested.

In 1886 an event took place that was to have a considerable impact on the Culm Valley Line. In that year four local men, John Clist, Samuel Farrant, Edward Lutley and James Wide, founded the Culm Valley Dairy Company. The success story of that company is told in Chapter Six, and this company was to provide the Culm Valley Branch Line with much of its revenue for the foreseeable future. In 1906 another interesting commercial venture was undertaken in Hemyock by a James Yates. This gentleman set up in business as a coal merchant and quarryman, apparently quarrying stone from Coombe Hill, north of Hemyock. Initially this venture seems to have been reasonably successful and in 1911 Yates incorporated the Hemyock Stone and Coal Company Limited. By 1913, however, the business had obviously ceased to be financially viable and went into liquidation. Yates must have provided quite a bit of goods trade for the railway because in 1913 the Great Western Railway traffic figures for the line stated that goods traffic on the line had doubled since 1903 due almost entirely to 'other minerals' amounting to some 12 000 tons, no doubt assisted by Mr Yates' activities.

One of James Yates' employees had been the late Bill Griffiths. He remembered how the quarried stone was transported from the quarry to Hemyock Station by horse and cart. Apparently the carts had heavy beam brakes and could be heard from far off as they negotiated the steep Pencross Hill, down into Hemyock. Today, of course, it is not cart brakes that can be heard on the hill but the air brakes of huge modern lorries. Bill Griffiths' father was one of the engine drivers on the line in those days. He drove engine No. 1300, one of the 2-4-0 engines used by the GWR at that time.

In the early 1930s improvements were made to the Culm Valley Line and the stations. At Hemyock the carriage and engine sheds were removed and a longer run-round loop put in to enable newer GWR carriages to be utilised, and on 27 February 1933 Whitehall Halt was opened. In the 1930s passenger traffic was at its peak but freight was still the dominant factor and there were other 'goods' including livestock such as cattle and pigs from Hemyock Market.

The Second World War had a bad impact on the line with a steady decline in goods traffic; in fact by 1948 goods carried were at virtually the same level as they had been in 1879. During and after the war a limited number of passengers were still being carried which included schoolchildren heading for Tiverton School (including one of the authors of this book).

The Culm Valley Line was very much part of community life and on occasions would provide a service that was just a little out of the ordinary. Apparently the engine drivers were in the habit of giving coded signals on their whistles to advise the local school headmasters when the train was carrying one of the Schools Inspectors as a passenger, obviously before schools had their own telephones. Nowadays such warnings would be given in a far more sophisticated and technological fashion far beyond the wildest imaginings of those drivers or the headmasters they were tipping off.

Alas the writing was on the wall for the Culm Valley Branch Line. In the 1960s many changes were taking place on the railway system throughout the country. Small lines such as the Hemyock to Tiverton service were doomed. On 9 September 1963 the last passenger train left Hemyock to a sad if not tearful farewell from the local people. The line had carried passengers, be they 'day trippers' or local people, for nearly a century and it must have been an emotional day.

The next blow came in September 1965 when Hemyock was closed to all rail traffic except that relating to the milk factory. Despite the reduction in traffic, changes were made at Hemyock where the track was strengthened to take heavier locomotives. These included diesel hydraulic locomotives of Class 29 and later diesel electrics, Class 22. By now, however, it was only a matter of time.

The transportation of milk from the factory was transferred to road and the railway was now only being used to convey oil to the factory. Then Unigate, which owned the milk factory, announced that they were closing in October 1975. The fate of the Culm Valley Line was sealed. On 31 October 1975 a last 'special' train left Hemyock. By January 1977 all the rail track had been removed, just over 100 years after the Culm Valley Light Railway opened.

Ironically not long after the closure of the line the milk factory re-opened although it is unlikely that this factor would have saved the railway even if it had not already closed. Since then there have been mutterings about re-opening the Culm Valley Branch Line to take some of the heavy traffic off the roads but this could never be a realistic proposition.

There are small lines that have survived around the country including the West Somerset Railway, but such lines have only lasted because they became tourist attractions. It is possible, one supposes, that some extremely wealthy individual might hatch the idea to pay for the re-building of the Culm Valley Line purely as a tourist attraction, but would it not be better that the line is remembered for what it was, a small honest working railway serving Hemyock and the other communities of the Culm Valley?

Now, not only has the railway gone but the milk factory has also been demolished. It is to be replaced by housing and light industrial units. Such is progress. There are still many people in Hemyock who remember the railway and what it meant to the village but for those who have no such memories it would be worth climbing to one of the high viewpoints around the village, looking down into the valley and trying to imagine a sturdy little engine with its carriages and goods trucks chuffing along beside the curves of the River Culm and giving the occasional whistle to warn the local headmaster... or to get a cow off the line.

NOTES

We are grateful to Michael Messenger and his definitive book, The Culm Valley Light Railway, *for much of the information used in this chapter.*

A modern view of Culm Davy Chapel.

Rogation Day at Culm Davy Chapel, c.1960. The churchwardens on either side of the gateway are Mr 'Sonny' Farmer on the left and Mr Jack Hart on the right. David Llewellyn-Jones is on the steps followed by Susan Pring and Rita Salter, Janice Fuller is on her own, then come Joyce Clapp and Judith Hannaford, Margaret Llewellyn-Jones and Brenda Pring, C.J. Hannaford and Ray Clapp, Ron Cork on his own followed by Leslie Purcell, Gordon Leslie and Revd W. Llewellyn-Jones. The congregation included Christine Matthews, Cissy Lowman, Mrs Edwards and Mrs Salter.

CHAPTER NINE

Culm Davy

A particularly special day for the farm tenants in the manor of Culm Davey (today the spelling Davy is more usual) was 15 November 1611 – the day of the Court baron. The lord of the manor usually called two courts, a Court leet and a Court baron, both of which met at regular intervals. The occasion in question took place almost 400 years ago, some 70 years after the dissolution of Dunkeswell Abbey, only 30 since the Spanish Armada had sailed up the English Channel and three decades before the English Civil War – all events which would have had a profound effect on the lives of Culm Davy's inhabitants.

On the day of a Court leet or Court baron tenants had to present themselves at Whitehall, where the proceedings were held. The main purpose of the Court was to exact various forms of payment from the tenants which would go directly into the lord's hands. The first matter on the agenda in 1611 read:

... the tenantry here, namely Clement Cheriton, and his peers come and on oath present that on the death of Elizabeth Holwaye, widow and customary tenant that she is in mercy as to £3.

The name Cheriton still exists in the form of a house name, and the fields around would have been both enclosed and farmed by the Cheriton family, of whom Clement was a member. When a tenant died the lord of the manor was entitled to come and take the best cow from that person's estate as a heriot, but in practice the lord often chose to take cash instead and in this case elected to take £3. The next three items all concern another lady tenant who was unlucky enough to be 'presented' to the court for three shortcomings:

1. that the house of Margaret Westlake, widow, is in decay, namely the roof over the hall of the house... under the penalty of 3s.4d.
2. that the ditch of the said Margaret in the close (field) called Wigglesforde ought to be scoured (cleaned) before next Christmas under the penalty of 3s.4d.

3. and that one parcel of land of the said Margaret called Downcrofte is in decay, namely hedges and ditches, for which a day is given for them to be repaired before next Easter under the penalty of 3/-.

Today such misdemeanours may seem slight, but for the community of 1611 they were highly significant. Houses were built of cob or flint, with dry mortar, and without a roof the walls would quickly disappear; Margaret's house was still single storey because the decayed roof was over the 'hall' (main room) of the house. Most of Culm Davy stands on the side of a hill, so a blocked ditch could affect tenants living at a lower level – they would have either too much or too little water in their ditches. The 'decayed hedges' would affect other farmers as well. Hedges had to be kept in good repair especially in an area where there were a great many cattle and sheep, otherwise the animals could escape and damage the neighbour's crops.

An aerial view of Culm Davy House and grounds, believed to have been taken in the 1960s.

❧ Then & Now ❧

Below: *The view today taken from an almost identical position. The property on the left has been altered and the thatch removed. The yew tree still has pride of place but the other trees have gone and there are now telegraph poles in place.*

Above: *Chapel Mead, c.1918. Culm Davy Chapel can just be seen through the trees. The sheep belonged to Robert Lutley.*

Left: *Whitehall's railway halt today; the track has long gone but the remains of the halt platform can be seen on the left beyond the gate.*

Below: *A modern view of Whitehall Manor House.*

The third item concerns William Tooker who, it was reported, 'ought to hold the keys here for this year who gives to the Lord a fine of 2/- according to custom.' What were the keys for? Obviously their holder was acting as an agent of the lord of the manor and paying 2 shillings for the privilege on the basis that there was some profit to be made from the situation. It seems likely that these keys were those belonging to the village pound where roaming animals, waifs and strays, or the goods of any felons could be impounded by the lord of the manor and released only after a payment was made.

The meeting then moves to the fourth item on the agenda, where we read 'that Lawrence Aishe, son of Thomas Aishe, is aged 16 years and does not take an oath in the Assize of the King, therefore is distrained.' Four centuries ago Lawrence would have 'come of age' at 14, but obviously at 16 he was required to swear an oath, which he had failed to do. This may have been for religious reasons as there was a Quaker presence in Hemyock about this time. A Peter Holway, who was a thatcher, married Susanna Lutley in the late 1600s and was mentioned in Quaker records, as also was Lawrence Cadbury's family who subsequently became prominent Quakers. What is certain is that a strong Nonconformist element was beginning to develop in Hemyock and it may be that Lawrence Aishe would not swear an oath to the newly crowned first Stuart King, James I.

Another, probably more likely explanation for his shortcoming was that the statutory swearing was to do with military service in the local militia, which was a requirement of all males between certain ages.

The fifth item concerns the ancient, almost forgotten agricultural practice of using 'pannage' for pigs. Almost half of the Culm Davy Manor was still unenclosed at this time and was known as the Lord's Waste, or common land. It would have been well wooded and in the autumn there would be an abundance of acorns and beech mast, both of which made ideal food for pigs. Each autumn they were let loose on the common for several months, each farmer or pig owner paying the lord of manor 1½d. for each adult pig allowed to stray. A record of this practice provides a useful record of owners and their stock:

Clement Waldron	7½d.	5 pigs
William Tooker	1½d.	1 pig
James Holwaye	4½d.	3 pigs
Edmund Lutley	1½d.	1 pig
Laurence Cadburye	3d.	2 pigs
William Trigges	1d.	1 piglet
Robert Bowerman	3d.	2 pigs
Margaret Westlake	3d.	2 pigs
John Shebroke	3d.	2 pigs
Charles Bowerman	3d.	2 pigs
John Harrys	7½d.	5 pigs
Joan Goodale	3d.	2 pigs
Thomas Aishe	4½d.	3 pigs

Apart from most of the family names some deserve special mention. John Shebroke, Joan Goodale and Thomas Aishe were possibly connected with current farm names – Shoebrooks at Hemyock, Goodalls and Straight Ash at Culm Davy. Laurence Cadburye's family was later to move to Culmstock and subsequently found the world-famous chocolate firm.

The meeting then turned to the appointment of manorial officers for the coming year. Laurence Cadburye was elected Tithingman, William Tooker was to become the Reeve and Thomas Aishe and William Trigges were sworn as woodwards. These offices were held for one year and as their duties could be onerous they were not popular ones. The Tithingman, for example, had to keep the peace; in fact he was a predecessor of the village policeman. He had the advantage of knowing all the families in Culm Davy and could almost solve a problem before it had arisen. The Reeve was the agent for the lord, who in this case did not live locally, making the former's job all the more important. He looked after the husbandry of the manor, the hedges and ditches and most important of all the allocation of the plough. There was only one plough in the manor and ploughing had to be done during short periods of time, with the consequence that all of the tenants would want to plough on the same day. It fell to the Reeve to decide upon a rota. This was a problem almost too difficult to contemplate, the plough could only plough one acre a day and in Culm Davy there were about 70 acres of arable land – it is not hard to imagine the abuse to which he must have become accustomed.

Woodwards had an arguably less stressful job, taking care of the manor's woodland, of the timber being used for house construction and of house repairs. The tenants could purchase firewood and there would have been a large area of woodland within Culm Davy, as there still is today. In 1611, however, the woods would have contained hardwood trees. Woodwards came to the court and, on oath, declared the value of timber that they had sold during the year. The record for 1611 is as follows:

Clement Cheriton	3d.	James Holwaye	6d.
William Tooker	6d.	William Trigge	4d.
Robert Bowerman	2s.4d.	Charles Bowerman	20d.
Thomas Aishe	14d.	John Harrys	20d.
Joan Goodale (widow)	20d.		

Almost half of the income from the court came from sales of timber.

This is the account of just one Court baron within Hemyock. Sadly only one parchment has survived. There would have been many more Culm Davy documents and even more concerning the other Hemyock manors.

In Chapter Two we discussed the origins of the place name Culm Davy and how the Domesday

'Comba' (meaning a narrow valley), evolved to become Culm Davy. One of the families who possessed the manor in those early days was Widworthy (or Widworth) and it was a David Widworthy whose christian name was added to the place name.

During the middle ages the manor passed through the hands of the Wogan and Corbet families until it finally came into the possession of the Bowermans in Tudor times, who were represented in Culm Davy until the end of the 19th century.

Some Culm Davy properties date back to the 15th and 16th centuries. Culm Davy Farm, for example, has been described by experts as a classical Devon longhouse dating to around the mid-15th century. Whitehall Farmhouse dates back to a similar time. Long after the Bowermans this property was owned by the Kerslake and Lutley families and is now in the possession of the Courtenay family.

One of the most delightful of the early buildings in Culm Davy is the chapel. It is said to date back to Elizabethan times but may have even earlier origins. There are legends that there may have been a small nunnery on the site dating back many centuries. Future research may well reveal more of the history of this building situated high on a hillside overlooking the valley and hills beyond. It is not possible to date the present building precisely but as with other old buildings in Culm Davy one can say with confidence that they existed at least as long ago as the early 1500s.

In an 18th-century ecclesiastical survey the incumbent of Hemyock and Culm Davy, Edward Rayner, suggested that the chapel might be dedicated to St George. Rayner apparently based this suggestion on the fact that the people of Culm Davy held a revel on the Sunday after St George's Day. In Hemyock itself a revel was held on the Sunday after Holy Rood Day. Changes were made to the chapel in the late-Victorian period possibly around 1860 but certainly before the turn of the century. The present entrance to the chapel faces south whereas before the Victorian 'restoration' the door was on the west side of the building. The interior of the chapel is simple and very peaceful. There are two memorials on the walls. That on the right dates from the 1700s and reads: 'In Memory of Anne ye Wife of Willm GARVIS of Ashculm who died ye 25th. Oct 1705 and was inter'd in ye west end of this chapel.' It is interesting that the lady was from Ashculm, a small community some way from Culm Davy on the other side of Hemyock. The second wall memorial honours Captain Anthony Elmes MC who served in the Royal Artillery with the 8th Army in North Africa. He was mentioned in

George Lowman above Knoll Cottage, 1963.

Dispatches while fighting at Tobruk between April and July 1941, was awarded the Military Cross in 1942 and was killed in action, in Libya, on 31 May 1942, aged 23.

The small graveyard outside the chapel is the last resting place for many well-known local families and some less known. Some of the oldest stones record members of the Mortimer family, including John Mortimer who died in 1831 aged 100 and his wife Jane who died in the same year aged 93. The Culm Davy air must have encouraged their longevity. The Bowermans were still represented in the hamlet as late as 1894.

Other families whose last resting place is at Culm Davy Chapel include Lowman, Southey, Hookway, Follett and Lutley. The earliest extant memorial to the Lutleys relates to Mary Lutley who was buried in 1798 at the age of 66 and her husband Edward Lutley, buried in 1800 aged 73. The Lutley connections with Culm Davy and Hemyock go back much further. The distant origins of the Lutleys appear to be in Staffordshire where the de Luttleys held lands. Early in the 15th century the de Luttley estates passed to Isabel, Countess of Devon. Is it possible that about this time, one of the de Luttleys came to Devonshire and became the ancestor of the Culm Davy and Hemyock Luttleys? Further research in the future might well provide the answer. Chris Dracott's ancestors also came from Staffordshire and his direct ancestor also left that county in the 15th century. So perhaps it was that the descendants of two old Staffordshire families ended up in the same Devon parish!

The Tedders are another family represented in the graveyard at Culm Davy Chapel where Sir Arthur Tedder CB is buried. His memorial reads: 'Late Commissioner of H.H. Customs and Excise 1851–1931.' Sir Arthur's wife and daughter are also interred on the site. A native of Kensington in London, Sir Arthur spent some years with his family living in Surrey. He later purchased 'Windlehurst', a large house built high above Hemyock with views across to Culm Davy Chapel. Apparently Sir Arthur so enjoyed the view that he expressed a wish to be buried there when he died.

Sir Arthur's son, Arthur William Tedder (later Lord Tedder) became internationally famous during the Second World War. Having served in the infantry and Flying Corps as a pilot in the First World War, he became an Air Officer commanding in the Middle East in the second conflict. By 1943 he was in command of all Allied Air Forces in the Mediterranean but his most significant contribution was as Deputy

Supreme Commander under General Eisenhower in the closing stages of the war, in which position he was largely responsible for the initial success of the Normandy landings in June 1944. He became Marshal of the Royal Air Force in 1945 and received his Peerage in 1946. He died in 1967 and his name is remembered by 'Tedder's Close' in Hemyock.

Opposite Culm Davy Chapel is Chapel Farm built some time in the early 1800s by Hugh and Anne Mortimer. The farm was eventually purchased by the Edwards family and James Edwards still farms there, also serving as churchwarden since taking over from Pamela Dowson (née Elmes).

A family that played a significant role in the story of Culm Davy during the late 1800s into the 1920s, were the Folletts. In 1884 Colonel Robert Follett purchased Coombeshead Farm. He was the son of Sir William Webb Follett, the distinguished lawyer who was MP for Exeter and became England's Attorney-General. Sir William himself had already acquired another local farm, Coombe Pyne (now Culm Pyne) in 1843, and his nephew, Sir Charles (Mayor of Exeter 1872–74), used Culm Davy House as his country residence during the lifetime of his first wife before moving to Luggs Cottage when he remarried. It was members of the Follett family who established the short-lived Culm Davy Brick Co. In 1921 Sir Charles Follett died and was buried at Culm Davy Chapel as was his wife.

On 23 September 1921 at the Rougemont Hotel, Exeter, the Culm Davy estate, consisting of 886 acres, was auctioned in 19 lots by Whitton Lang. Park Linhay and Brick Field Cottage, with about 48 acres, was sold privately to one of Sir William's nephews, John Skirrow Follett. The sale realised over £15 000. The tenants for some of the properties at the time of the sale included Mr P.C. Hine and J.R. Wyatt at Chapel Farm, Mr H. and Miss E. Thomas and Mr W. Dyer at Culm Davy Farm, Mr C. Pine at Goodalls Farm, and Messrs J. Flay and P.C. Hine at Coombes Head Farm. Just one of those property names takes us back to the Manor court of 1611, Goodalls, which may well have been the property of Joan Goodale back in Tudor times.

Culm Davy House had passed into the ownership of Captain F.R. Elmes and stayed with his family for a number of years. His daughter, Pamela, still lives in Culm Davy although the family home is now in other hands. The original Culm Davy House was burnt down in 1891 and then rebuilt. It is likely that the original Culm Davy House dated back to a much earlier period. Luggs has for some years been in the possession of the famous wildlife artist Peter Barrett, and his wife Susan.

The old Manor House at Whitehall, where the Court baron was held in 1611, has, for some years, been the home of retired Royal Marines Lieutenant-Colonel, Tim Courtenay, and his wife Jane. By coincidence a 17th-century 'Visitation' of the County

of Devon made reference to 'Henry Bowerman of Whitehall in Hemyock, Lieutenant to Captain Courtenay'. So in the 21st century a Courtenay is living in a house occupied some 350 years earlier by a Bowerman who 'served' under a 17th-century member of the Courtenay family. It should be explained that from 1529–30 the College of Arms made 'visitations' to different parts of the country to establish that coats of arms were being used correctly and to 'vet' new applications. The last such visitation was in 1686.

Like Hemyock, Whitehall had a mill, owned for many years by the Lutley family and until comparatively recent times a smithy, last operated by one of the Culm Davy Lowmans, James. It will be remembered that Whitehall had its own 'halt' in the days of the Culm Valley Light Railway and there are still traces of the halt platform.

Although part of the parish of Hemyock, Culm Davy has a distinct history and character of its own. It has a feeling of space and to a large extent is 'unspoilt', to use a much-abused word. If one of those individuals who appeared before the Court baron in 1611 were to return to their old community they would see that much of the countryside had not changed a great deal in nearly 400 years.

Top: *Jim Lowman at his Whitehall forge (now a dwelling).*

Above: *Captain F.R. Elmes (2nd row, 3rd from the left) with the first local group of British Legion members, c.1922.*

*Hemyock School in the 1930s. The front wall has been removed and has been replaced with iron railings.
The County Library sign is attached to them. The school taught children aged from 5–14 at this time.
Note that the older boys are still wearing short trousers.*

*The School in centenary year, 1977.
Headmaster Clive Richardson is on the right-hand side by the door.*

CHAPTER TEN

Hemyock School

Until the Second World War almost every village had its own school and until the 1950s children were taught from the ages of 5 to 14 or 15 when they left school. The passing in 1870 of the Education Act allowed villages to elect a 'school board' which could borrow money to build a village school. In turn these institutions were subject to a degree of control at national level. Hemyock elected a School Board in 1875 and had built a new school by 1877.

This was not, however, the dawn of education in the parish. In 1708, in the reign of Queen Anne, John Somerhayes sold:

... all but one plot of ground being at the east end of the Church Yard of the said parish of Hemyock which was purchased by the said John Somerhayes of and from Susanna Macey, widow deceased.... And on this plot the Parishioners of the said parish have lately erected or built a new dwelling house and have made it into one with what was formerly the Church or Parish House.

This plot of land was situated on the corner of the churchyard where the war memorial now stands. A schoolmaster was to be 'elected' to keep an 'English and writing school in the said great room for the instruction of boys'. Whether connected with this building or not, we know that in 1745 a school was endowed for five poor children. It would appear that the school did not have a continuous history. A footnote in the burials section of our Parish Registers reads:

In the year 1785 a House of Industry for the education of the children of the Parish poor was established by the Rector, John Land, but dissolved in the year 1792 for reasons painful to relate and therefore perhaps better omitted.

Why does history not give us all the facts? By the 1820s a school was running again because we know

that a Mary Macey taught the following pupils in 1819–20: Mary Walker, Ann Clist, William Stone, Deborrah Wood, John Moon. The following year she had on the roll: Mary Clist, Robert Stone, Deborrah Wood, John Ash and Susanna Wood.

From 1830 onwards, until the Board School was built, the school was running on the same site. Towards the end the teacher was a Miss Ash. She must have done her job well because the Board wanted to appoint her as the head in the new school but were prevented from doing so because she was uncertificated and the new regulations insisted that only a trained teacher could be appointed.

The history of the school is intimately entwined with the history of the village. Almost all of the older residents have attended and received an excellent education there. Every head was supposed to keep a daily school log-book and we are very fortunate that Hemyock's log is very detailed and records both school and village events at great length. Stories of success, of mental strain, of frustration, are all in evidence, usually commented upon openly. We have decided that the history of our school will be led by the contents of the log with numerous extracts from its pages. The Hemyock School Board was elected on 16 March 1875 and had as its members: Mr Edward Lutley junr (134 votes), Mr Benjamin Wood (60), Mr William Hine (53), Revd E.W. Popham (39), Mr John Farrant (38), Mr William Farrant (35), Mr James Hine (13) and Mr George Barton (7).

The first six of these gentlemen were elected and the expenses came to £19.16s.8d. (£19.83p.) Mr William Bennett was appointed Clerk to the Board which immediately set out to buy land to build a new school. Two landowners offered plots – Mr George Barton of the Castle and Mr John Manley of Millhayes. It was decided to build a school in a field called Town Mead, belonging to Mr Manley, at a cost of £160 an acre. It seems likely that the existing school, under Miss Ash, was allowed to continue until the new school was in operation.

The London firm of architects, Messrs Hay and Oliver, who had designed Culmstock and Wellington

Schools, was asked to draw up plans, to be paid five per cent commission (to include travelling from London). Two people submitted tenders to build the school, including one master's house – Mr Diamond of Wellington, for £1384, and Mr Langdon of Minehead, for £960. The original design was for a school built of flint, but Mr Langdon was asked to build it in brick for £950. One wonders why brick was selected, because the saving in cost was only £10 – perhaps it was to create work for the Culm Davy Brickworks? The school was pegged out on 15 January 1876.

It is interesting to note that in the first year the Board met 34 times! In November we read that 'out of diverse applications received, two were entertained' for the post of head. These were from a Mr Sargent of Chawleigh and Mr Hunt of Middlezoy. The first headmaster was to be Mr Hunt, at a salary of £90 a year, plus half the Government grant. From this salary he had to supply his aunt as sewing mistress and his sister as monitor. This method of payment lasted until the 1902 Education Act. It was a means of obtaining good results because the Government grant depended on the regularity of pupils' attendance, their ability to pass an annual examination and the grading which the school received after an annual inspection. It was decided to open the school on 5 February 1877 and although the building was at this stage incomplete, 51 scholars attended on the first day and within a week 70 were on the register. They were reputedly backwards in arithmetic. Mr Hunt bought a blackboard for £1.5s.0d. (£1.25p) and an easel for 8s.6d. (42½p).

The school was identified as a meeting place almost immediately; in the evenings by parishioners and for entertainment by the Hemyock Glee Club. A fee of one guinea was charged. It would be fascinating to know who made up the Glee Club and what type of entertainment they provided!

One week after the opening, the members of the School Board 'viewed the assembled scholars' and 'framed a list of fees to be charged'. There were three other schools that drew some children from Hemyock. These were Mr Brealey's 'British' school at Clayhidon (with about 21 scholars), Mr Wright's at Symonsburrow (with about 25 scholars) and Dunkeswell Abbey (with 11 scholars). Unfortunately, the design of the school was not perfect and within two years the architects had to be contacted because of the weak state of the roof and measures taken to obviate its complete demolition. The roof repairs were carried out by a Mr George Babb for £33.10s.0d. (£33.50p). In 1882 a new Clerk to the Board was appointed. He was Mr Edwin Wide and he remained in this position for many years. Mr Hunt left the school after seven years and his resignation was regretfully accepted. He lived for many more years until his death which is mentioned in the log in 1913. The seven years during which the school was in the care of Mr Hunt were vital ones. It was he who set the high standards that other headmasters maintained thereafter. The initial problems were mainly physical ones. We read of the lack of cupboards in which to store books and materials. The grates were not sufficient to heat the rooms properly and snow came into the classroom through roof joints. Of particular interest – and also upon times a source of amusement – are reasons listed for poor attendance. Some absences were, to say the least, unusual. On one ocasion there were 'Many children away because of a wild beast show at Uffculme' [a circus]; on another there were 'Children absent because of a military review of Volunteers at Uffculme and the militia at Leigh.' Various bucolic activities kept children from their desks and we read of whortleberry picking, acorn picking and apple picking, as well as haymaking and harvesting being causes for absenteeism. Annual 'club' days closed the school, as did the various Sunday School 'treats' and an annual picnic at the Wellington 'Memorial'.

The weather has always played an important part in the life of Hemyock. On 18 January 1881 there was a terrible snowstorm which 'set in during the night and... continued without ceasing the whole day'. On this day the school was closed. The following day the storm continued 'with the same fury' and the school premises were 'blocked up'. On 20 January the storm abated but services had not returned to normal – 'the train has not returned from Tiverton Junction since Tuesday, being snowed in – postal communications cut off.' At the same time it was recorded that the school had again passed 'a good examination, writing especially well done' although worries were also expressed that 'the older children talk too much over their work and ought to know better'. Such songs as 'Pilgrim Fathers' and 'Strive to Learn' were sung on inspection day.

Illness features prominently in the log-books at this time, some of it recognisable to the modern reader, and some ailments appearing rather obscure. We read that Henry Thomas had a 'humour' and was advised to stay away from school for a week. The usual accidents occurred. Henry Hill broke his arm, and rather sadly we read an entry from 2 May 1881 which tells us that Charles Manley:

... who up to last Wednesday afternoon had not missed school once since its opening, died this morning after a short sickness caused by a fall. He is the first child admitted to this school who has died.

Bad feet and broken chilblains, whooping cough, measles, influenza, ringworm, inflammation of the lungs, water pox and scarletina were also mentioned. The latter was the cause of complete closure of the the school for eight weeks starting in October 1883.

Mr Hunt introduced two features to the life of the school that were to remain for a long time, both typically Victorian in thinking. The first was a savings

A very early photo of Hemyock School, with children behind the wall. The schoolhouse is on the right and the structure that holds the school bell is on the roof of the building.

scheme for the children. On 28 January 1881 it is recorded that:

... the system of saving money by postage stamps has been adopted in this school. Capital result – to the 20 depositors who had previously begun, 30 new ones have been added.

Could this have been the forerunner of the famous 'Boot Club' which, linked with the National Savings movement, meant that the saving of even one penny a week ensured that at the end of the year sufficient funds had been put aside to purchase a pair of boots. Today, many of us still refer to the National Savings movement in school as the Boot Club. By November 1881 £70 was in the bank. This had grown to £120 by September 1882, which, considering the value of money and the fact that the country was just emerging from a period of low agricultural prices, was a remarkable achievement. The other innovation was the 'Band of Hope'. Mr Hunt was a staunch teetotaller and was constantly encouraging his pupils to sign 'the pledge' – promising to abstain from alcoholic liquor. In February 1882 he wrote:

I am pleased to see the children are wearing a piece of blue ribbon to show that they belong to the Temperance Party. Both pupil teachers are teetotal, and the master and mistress are.

Later, he added: 'Five girls and four boys signed the pledge after school this evening – they voluntarily came and asked whether I would allow them to do so.'

Teaching had its moments of frustration. Then, as now, the headmaster wrote from the heart when the matter of overwork was concerned.

I wonder what person would be able to stand preaching 5 days a week from 9 to 12 o'clock, such is what we have to do nearly under this code, as the oral lessons have been so multiplied. Sometimes I almost faint away with the overwork, yet I am a young man, in the prime of life, fond of hard work.

Playtime was introduced in 1883 – just 15 minutes in the morning. To counteract this, homework was introduced one week later. Important national events are recorded such as the rather obscure fact that 'sad intelligence of the death of the Duke of Albany was received in this village on Saturday last.' A final mention from Mr Hunt's period in the school should be recorded. It deals with a punishment that was given out. The log-book speaks for itself:

I told Frank Babb twice this morning to go on with his work as he was idling, but he did not do so. In a moment or so I fetched the cane, which was in the window and gave him 2 raps across the knuckles and one on his shoulder for insolence, as he muttered out something which I could not hear. On Friday he broke up his examination tickets. I have had to caution him for writing bad words on the wall and have threatened him for being insolent to the pupil teacher. He gives a lot of trouble when I go into the infant room. In the case of this punishment, in some way unaccountable to myself, the lad got a scratch on his nose. I can't say whether the cane in descent touched his nose, whether the lad did it himself, or whether it might have been done afterwards. But the mother has been in a fearful rage about it. Some 12 months ago she told us to knock him down if he was insolent. I very seldom punish big boys, but in this case I thought it necessary.

Hemyock School, Class 1, c.1910/12.
Left to right, back: Headmaster Mr A.T. Baxter, John Stradling, Sam Cross, Walter Salter, Fred (or Sidney) Hart,
Cecil Pike, Stanley Wide, George Hold, Percy Wide;
3rd row: Ernest Lowman, William Marklew, May Florence (?) Hill, Hilda Parsons, Ida Wide,
Emily Pring, William Baker;
2nd row: Sarah Lowman, Ellen Pike, Alice Cross, Katie Hart, Florence Hart, May Clapp, Ivy Ayres, May Salter;
front: Wilfred George Clist, Charlie Manley, Walter Webber, James Graves, Harold Quick, Walter Ridgeway,
Harold Lawrence, William Granger.

We must now move on to what may be called the middle period of the school's first 100 years. For almost 70 years, with the exception of one term, when a supply headmaster was in place, the school was run by just two heads. Both made sure that the excellent start made by Mr Hunt was continued. In many ways the appointment of a head may be likened to the appointment of an Anglican incumbent. Once appointed, their tenure is such that without their consent, it is difficult to remove them. In both senses Hemyock has invariably been fortunate. Mr Baxter's teaching career is well documented in the log-books. In 28 July 1884 he took charge of the school, after having been selected from 34 applicants for the job and coming to Hemyock from Hay, at a salary of £60 plus half grant (which was £37.19s.5d.). It is obvious that he was the right choice, because after six months, the School Board, which was not noted for its generosity, raised his salary to £92 plus half grant.

What was the school like at this time? The school day bore few resemblances to that of today. We can be sure that at this time almost the whole day was spent engaged in learning the three Rs.

An illuminating entry is made by Mr Baxter after two weeks in the school: 'I find that the reason why Standard IV cannot get on with their sums is because they are not perfect in their tables.' A week or so later he writes: 'Standard II very forgetful in their tables – what they learned apparently well yesterday they have forgotten today.' The annual report, however, speaks of improved behaviour, with the inspector remarking:

I should note that the behaviour of the children, though somewhat free and easy, has decidedly improved. Gradually the timetable is broadened in its scope – a geographical model was made in cement, and the children seem to like it immensely and have improved greatly in geography since its introduction.

The routine of daily and weekly written tests continued as the annual inspection drew nearer. To impress the inspector the school was decorated: 'After school was over, the girls helped the teachers to decorate the schoolroom with flowers.' This seems to have had the desired effect, as the 1886 report read:

Hemyock School, Class 1, 1919.
Left to right, back: Olive Hill, Mary Salter, Mary Morgan, Olive Pring, Stella Clist, Ethel Doble.
upper middle row: Mr Baxter, Mildred White, Queenie Pring, Laura Lowman, Kathleen Peardon, ? Wyatt,
Olive Ayres, ? Salter, Les Hart, Bob Wyatt, Albert Causley;
lower middle row: ?, Victor Stradling, ? Phillips, Ivy Phillips, ?, ?, ?, Edie Slater, Phyllis Manley, ?;
front: ?, Bill Pike, ?, ?, Walter Hart, Edward Lutley or Chris Doble, Denis Pring, ?.

The Excellent Merit Grant has again been awarded. The School has passed an admirable examination. Geography and English are also taught with marked intelligence. The attendance is not as regular as it should be.

In arithmetic we have a glimpse into the technicalities of dealing with money in the days before decimalisation: 'Standard IV are having some difficulty with reduction of money – reducing half crowns to half guineas and florins to guineas etc., it puzzles them!' Time was found for singing. In 1890 a new school song, 'The British Grenadiers', was learnt. Poetry was, naturally, to be learnt by heart. In 1903 the timetable for Class I included 150 lines of 'The Lady of the Lake', for Class II 'Lord Ullin's Daughter' and 'The Destruction of Sennacherib' and for Class III 'Somebody's Mother'.

The teachers had great difficulties over new admissions to the school. The modern practice of compulsory education at five years had yet to be introduced. An example of the problem may be seen in this extract from the log-book of 1890:

Emily Frampton gets on fairly well. She is only lately come to school, and although over eight years did not know her alphabet or figures. People in the outlying districts often will not send their children to school until they are nearly seven and they are too old for the infant department.

Another innovation was the introduction of drawing to the school syllabus in 1890. This was examined by a separate examiner and, if deemed successful, meant that the school would receive an additional grant.

Very occasionally the somewhat dull routine of the school was varied. In 1897, for example, Revd Forbes came into school and gave a talk on a recent journey that he had made to Russia, Germany, Sweden, Norway and Denmark. In 1906 he gave another talk on 'a visit to the scene of the late destruction caused by the eruption of Vesuvius.' He showed his audience specimens of lava and volcanic dust. Sometimes the school was taken outside. One such day was in 1901 when a visit was made to Mr Edwin Wide's house for a practical lesson on bees.

Much of the work was done on slates, although there were moves away from this medium early on in the 20th century. In 1902, for example, Mr Baxter noted that he intended Standard III 'to work on paper with lead pencils instead of using slates.' A mention of the use of teaching apparatus in school was made at this time when it was said that it would be a good idea to have some sets of cardboard coins for teaching money sums to children. A result of the 1902 Education Act was the introduction of one hour's physical exercise each week. The children must have been delighted when practical lessons were introduced. In 1909 they went into the playground to measure out a square pole and into the meadow, which was later to become the Recreation Ground, to measure a square chain. Ten years later, just before his death, Mr Baxter did some work on the height of the sun and the zenith distance by means of shadows cast at noon.

The impact of the First World War was brought home to the scholars in 1915 when the whole of the upper school had a lesson on the British Navy.

Certain extracurricular activities were encouraged, for example by the formation of a 'Branch of the Children's National Guild of Courtesy' in 1906 and a reading circle in connection with the 'National Home Reading Union' in 1910. The first book read was called *The Gorilla Hunters*. Reference is made for the first time in 1892 to children being nominated for the County Council Scholarship. Some classes were organised for adults in the evening (not to be confused with the official evening classes covered later). In 1893 a series was given on 'Fruit Culture'. This had a more practical outcome, when subsequently a model orchard was planted out at Mountshayne by the Agricultural Department. In later years 'Ambulance Classes' were popular, as were those on 'Manures and Feeding Stuffs'. From 1906 onwards, there was a regular appearance of the County Council 'Dairy School' in the village. This is proof of the importance of butter making in Hemyock, where the first mechanically operated butter factory in the West of England had been started, once again at Mountshayne, 20 years previously.

Absenteeism was still just as much a problem at the beginning of the 20th century as it had been when the school first opened. The following are just some of the many reasons given in the log-books for absences. As had been the case in Mr Hunt's time, many were related to agriculture – acorn picking, blackberry picking, apple picking, potato digging, haymaking and corn harvesting, rabbiting, the annual ploughing match and sheep shearing – and these activities were described by Mr Baxter as 'frivolous'!

On 21 December each year the school was largely depleted whilst the children celebrated 'Begging Day'. They went about the village singing this song: 'Christmas is coming and I ain't very fat, Please put a penny in my old box hat.'

In 1893 another interesting aside on rural problems appears in the log when 'W. Cload came in after 11 o'clock, having been looking for a lost cow'. Four years later 'Sarah Sparks was bitten by a dog on her way to school'. Many children were, from time to time, kept home for petty reasons such as having to go on errands and help with washing day. Sometimes one child in a family was kept at home to mind the baby, while another child was at school and the next day, the former was sent and the latter absent. There was a case of a boy who was kept away from school 'actually employed by his father in removing sand from the playground in front of the school!' Even in 1900 pupils and teachers could go off to a choral festival at Exeter. In many ways it was easier to travel from Hemyock in those days. Trains left Hemyock five times a day and travelled to Plymouth, Exeter and Taunton. Even Bristol was easy if you had the inclination and the money. In the same year we read of a child returning to school after an absence of 3½ years for no apparent reason! The list of illnesses is legion. They include whooping cough, colds, diphtheria, scarletina, eruptive spots, bad eyes, bad feet, influenza and inflammation of the lungs, pneumonia, mumps, tonsillitis and infectious rash, quinsey, impetigo, neuralgia, bronchitis, galloping consumption, blood poisoning, a case of appendicitis, ulcerated throat, chicken pox (which in those days meant one month's absence from school), abscesses, ringworm and the more unusual case of Derbyshire neck (goitre?). Elizabeth Hall went blind, Sidney James broke his leg and a death occurred from croup. Listed also was exclusion from school (or even worse isolation whilst remaining at school) because of having a 'dirty head'. Unfortunately, more serious accidents happened then, as now. In 1904:

A terrible accident befell Orpah Moore, one of the VI Standard girls. She was riding in a hay wagon when the horse bolted and in trying to get out of the vehicle, poor Orpah was dashed to the ground and killed on the spot. The sad event has cast a deep gloom over the whole place. I tried to impress this morning upon the children the uncertainty of life.

The same year saw Albert Trickey cut his hand in a chaff cutter (a machine for chopping straw). The continuing appearance of epidemics of measles, diphtheria and whooping cough caused the villagers much concern. This was justifiable because a bad outbreak could actually close the school for up to three months. A Minute from a Board Meeting illustrates this point:

It was resolved that a representation be made to the County Council pointing out that as a parish we were constantly suffering from epidemic diseases and drawing their attention to the unsatisfactory supply of water, both for washing and flushing purposes and asking their immediate attention to the matter.

This protest is understandable because at the time all matter from the school toilets passed along an open ditch just outside the school wall. We read too that all sewage from the top of the village led also into this ditch. Part of the ditch remained open until Castle Park was built in the 1960s. After a particularly bad epidemic of diphtheria in 1911 the school was thoroughly fumigated with sulphur dioxide. The worst epidemic to hit the school was in 1890. In February the school was closed for a week because of a bad outbreak of flu. By early April we read that measles was beginning to appear in the village. On 21 February the log reads:

Measles all over the place. There is hardly a house but some of the inmates have the disease. It is attended, in many cases, with complications, notably bronchitis and pleurisy.

By 9 May seven of the children had died – two from one family in one week – Sidney and Frank Clist.

From time to time the school had some unusual scholars. In 1909 it was recorded that two gypsy children were admitted to school, Defiance and Joseph Orchard. They were 11 and 13 years old respectively, but could neither read nor write. A month later two more gypsy children came, Ellen and Patience Essex, neither of whom had ever been to school before. At the start of the First World War three families of Belgian refugees came to the village. They were guests of the parish and lived at Pencross and Fourways House. Their names must have sounded unusual to the Devonian scholars of the time – Jeanne, Albertos, Marie and Rosalie Diericks (who only spoke Flemish); Johanoes, Carolus, Leon and Albertos Hermans (one of whom spoke French); and Marceline, Amanda and Emil Buys (who remained until 1916). No doubt the mere presence of these foreign scholars would have had a marked effect on Hemyock's inhabitants, for it was an inward-looking parish at this time.

How isolated it was is borne out by an entry made on 18 May 1916:

An aeroplane passed over the place during the dinner hour. This was probably the first time an air machine has been seen in Hemyock. Children greatly interested.

At this stage the war did not have much influence on the village, or the school. In July 1915, however, we read:

Holiday this day on account of the schoolroom being required for entertaining the soldiers of the 3rd Battalion Devonshire Regiment, who are visiting the village on a route march.

The war did leave its mark in a more insidious way. As it progressed the U-boat campaigns sank more merchant ships bringing food to the country. Food became more and more scarce and expensive – even, incredibly, in rural areas. In February 1917 the Chairman of the Managers:

... raised the question of the food problem and suggested if anything could be done in connection with children attending school by giving them some meal as a substitute for bread during dinner hour.

This was solved by dinners being cooked in the Church Sunday School room – five lunches a week were provided for 7d. The effect of a poor unbalanced diet was to show almost a year after the war had ended. The log continues in July 1919:

School visited by Dr. Lightbody, he examined 60–70 children. 13 children required treatment and 5 are suffering from anaemia. It is a noticeable fact that since food has been so dear, especially milk, many of the children have lost their former ruddy appearance and have more the look of town children.

Mr Baxter had problems with his staff too and this comes as no surprise on learning just how much bargaining took place on the appointment of a teacher. 'What is the lowest salary that you will accept?' was the question that was invariably asked when a teacher was interviewed for an appointment. In 1907, for example, the log records: 'The County Council say it is highly improbable that Miss Rowsell be appointed because she requires maximum salary.' (Subsequently she was appointed but the arrangement was not satisfactory and she left after two months.)

Headmasters and their staff have not always agreed on teaching policy either! Occasionally these arguments have developed into questions of principle. The following extract speaks for itself (we are sure that sufficient time has elapsed to quote in full!):

I am very sorry to have to record that Miss Toms' conduct in school has been most unsatisfactory. On Monday (12 June) I explained to her the method I wished her to adopt in teaching Analysis of Sentences to the 2nd Class. On Tuesday I taught the class myself, in her presence, to show what I wanted done. This afternoon she deliberately ignored my wishes and again taught the class in her own way. On my speaking to her about it after school she tried to justify herself by alleging that her method was the better. I pointed out that if she refused to carry out my wishes in the matter, I must report her conduct to the proper quarter. To this she replied that she would defend herself. In fact her whole bearing and tone were most arrogant.
June 20th. *This afternoon I regret to say Miss Toms again ignored my wishes by persisting in having her*

own way in the method of teaching Analysis. I had, therefore, to stop the lesson and change it to arithmetic. I again remonstrated with her afterwards but she was quite insolent, telling me that she was appointed by the Managers to teach the class. I, therefore, told her that as she refused to teach as I wanted, I should place the class under the charge of Miss Reed and that henceforth she must take Standard I and II instead. During my 20 years of service in this school I have never had such conduct shown by an Assistant Teacher, my relations with subordinates having been most harmonious.

On the following day the atmosphere in school continued to be difficult:

In the afternoon Miss Toms added to her previous obstinate conduct by a most flagrant act of insubordination and public affront to myself. She came to me and asked if I wished her to take the singing lesson. On my replying in the affirmative, she said in a loud voice before all the children "Then I refuse to do it. If Miss Reed is good enough to take my class she can take the singing – I am not going to do her work!" On this I dismissed the children at 3.40. A meeting of the Managers is to be called to deal with her conduct.

This meeting took place on 5 July. The Managers told Miss Toms that they were perfectly unanimous in condemning her conduct and that they entirely agreed in supporting the authority of the headmaster. They asked her to make an apology and promise to work harmoniously in future. This she did! In March 1905 Miss Toms informed Mr Baxter that she intended to resign as she had obtained employment in an office in Devonport Dockyard. An appropriate remark concludes this story – 'The Managers, I think, will recommend that she be allowed to leave!'

A rather facetious report from the needlework inspector dating from 1910 also deserves mention:

The directress of needlework gives a favourable report on the needlework specimens submitted to her, but points out that the linen patch should be applied to the WRONG side and not the RIGHT side of the garment.

In Victorian days children were not without bad habits. There appears to have been an especially troublesome habit prevalent at one time – stone throwing. Of course, at this time, the roads and playgrounds were not tarred, so stones were readily available. In 1886 we read 'After dark this evening a stone was thrown by Frank Rabjohns, a farm boy, I am told, which fractured the stained glass window of the school library.' The problem was so bad that the County Education Committee sent a circular letter to the Board about stone throwing by the children. The letter was handed to the headmaster and the Board

must have been reassured by his reply, 'I frequently caution the children.'

A few brief extracts from the log will conclude the life of the school under Mr Baxter. In 1898 the clerk was prosecuted for letting the schoolroom inadvertently for a 'stage play' in the evening. The next year, when choosing a Board Chairman, both Revd Forbes and Mr Lutley received an equal number of votes. The matter was resolved by casting lots – surprisingly the Revd Forbes won! At the turn of the century three mammoth brass Rochester lamps at £1.3s.0d. each and an extra chimney were ordered. In this day of motor transport, we have forgotten the damage that could be caused by horses, as for example was the case when Mr Mortimore was 'asked to repair a pier damaged when his horse and trap backed against it.'

In 1902 the Board was able to assist the Parish Council when it received this request from them: 'The Parish Council made application for the LOAN of one of our baize curtains in school, not now used, for the purpose of covering the hand bier.' Also in this year the school was handed over to the County Council and became Hemyock County School.

In 1904 a rather amusing incident took place. It would appear that the cleaner, whom we will not name, had not performed her duties correctly. In the Manager's Minutes we read 'Mrs Clist to meet *****, and give her instructions on how to clean the school.'

The village was not quiet even in the days before our Leisure Centre. Mr J. Hart booked the room in 1908 for use by the Debating Society, whilst Mr Edward Hill required it for dancing classes. Both were granted – the dancing class, though, had to agree to some conditions. They had to finish by 9.30p.m. and no alcoholic drink or smoking was to be allowed. One is somewhat curious to know what is meant by an application for an 'all-night dance'. Even now parishioners would hesitate before booking the Parish Hall for such an event! The revelry was permitted to take place but had to terminate at midnight. There is an interesting contrast within a year when the subjects for the evening classes were being discussed. It was recommended that 'boys and girls classes be on different nights and that they be not mixed', so it seems that the village could dance together but they could not be taught together!

The state of the school building and its equipment as well as that of the children was often commented upon in the log, as when it was noted that: 'Whilst ringing the school bell this afternoon, the chain broke. On examination it proved to have completely rusted through.' For many generations this bell called pupils to school, until both it and the bell turret were removed in the 1950s. There are many incidents not strictly related to school which are mentioned at one time or another in the log-books. On the following page are just a few of them.

1888 The constable obviously led a very insecure life for on 1 June we read: *'The Horswells have left the village, their father (the constable) having had to shift to Cruwys Morchard at 2 days' notice.'*

1891 The very bad snowstorm of 1891 lasted from 9–17 March. The extract for 10 March reads: *'A terrific storm of snow still rages. Snow piled up many feet deep in places. Roads completely blocked up and no traffic possible. Not a single child at school.'*

1893 National events are not forgotten. On 6 July: *'Today being the wedding day of the Duke of York, later to become King George V, and Princess Mary of Teck, there was a whole holiday. In the afternoon the children were entertained to a splendid tea by the generosity of the members of the School Board. Both before and after tea the scholars marched with flags in procession round the village. 144 children present... sports in the evening.'*

1896 Political feeling could upset the school day. On 27 August: *'The Primrose League (a Conservative Party organisation) held a fête in the meadow behind the school... 84 children absent from school. Tomorrow there is to be a circus in the village.'*

1897 On 21 June: *'No school until 24th on account of the Diamond Jubilee Celebrations of Queen Victoria. The Schoolroom will be wanted for the feasting on the 22nd.'*

1898 On 11 February: *'The new Church Sunday-School is to be opened this afternoon – both teachers and children will witness the ceremony.'*

1898 On 14 July we have what must be one of the first references to a school photograph (taken by a lady photographer!): *'This morning the children were photographed by Miss Stewart of Exeter.'*

1900 On 1 March we have a patriotic reference to the Boer War: *'News has just arrived that it is officially confirmed that Ladysmith has been relieved – children therefore granted a half holiday.'*

1901 On 7 January: *'I am sorry to record that during the holidays little Willie Rugg was drowned in the millstream whilst playing with other children.'*

1901 On 24 September: *'A half holiday on account of the consecration of part of the new cemetery by the Bishop of Crediton.'* The other half was left unconsecrated for the use of Nonconformists.

1902 On 2 June: *'The welcome news of PEACE (in South Africa) being declared. There was a half-holiday...'*

1902 On 20 June: *'There will be 1 week's holiday on account of the Coronation of His Majesty King Edward VII.'* Unfortunately, the King became ill with appendicitis. On 24 June: *'Sad news arrived this day of the serious illness of the King – the celebrations will consequently be postponed.'*

1905 On 12 October: *'A new chapel opened at Dunkeswell Abbey (Baptist) in the afternoon – 14 children absent in consequence.'*

1906 On 4 May: *'A disastrous fire took place in the Square yesterday. 3 cottages being destroyed, one of these was occupied by Miss Manley (a teacher) and her mother.'*

1908 On 21 February: *'Holiday this day in honour of the visit of the Bishop of Exeter, on the occasion of the thanksgiving service for the re-hanging of the church bells.'*

1910 On 20 May: *'No school, on account of this being the day of the funeral of his late revered Majesty King Edward VII. At 1 o'clock a united service was held in the Parish Church. The school children, school managers, parish councillors etc. went in procession to the church.'*

1911 On 17 March we read: *'Have given lessons on the coming census and showed the older children how the census papers should be filled in.'*

1915 On 11 June there was a fatal car accident: *'Mary Burrows, a child in Standard II met with a fatal ACCIDENT while going home from school this afternoon. The poor little girl suddenly rushed across the road just as a motor car was approaching and she was knocked down. She received such injuries that she died in less than an hour after being taken to Dr. Huth's surgery at Culmstock. The accident has cast quite a gloom over the place.'*

1917 On 21 June an interesting meteorological phenomenon is recorded – could this be a fireball? *'Severe thunderstorm in the afternoon. During its course a terrific peal appeared to crash above the school. At the same time I observed a burst of bluish light in the middle of a class. This was accompanied by a crackling sound as if a whole box full of matches had been ignited at once. I have learned since that a tree and outbuildings just outside the village was struck by lightning and considerable damage was done. It is a matter for great thankfulness that the school escaped injury.'*

1919 *'A request from the Managers was sent to the Automobile Association for some "Danger" signs to be erected near the school. They agreed to provide three of them.'* For many years these yellow signs were a prominent feature in the village.

1919 On 26 November: *'Mr Baxter died. An exciting period of 35 years of the life of the school had ended. He was buried amid every sign of respect from parents and other parishioners.'*

Above left: *School girl gardeners, c.1938/40. Left to right, back: Rose Pike, Pat Guppy, Aylwin Alway; middle: Yvonne Summers, Joan Hassan, Peggy Howe; front: Pam Stokes, ?.*

Above right: *School boy gardeners, c.1938/40. Left to right, back: ?, ?, ?; middle: ?, ?, Michael Northam; front: Mervyn Shepperd, Michael Pike.*

Below: *Hoeing on the school allotment during a dry spell, 1938.*

We must not allow this period of the school's development to end without mentioning briefly the very successful evening classes that were held each winter from 1894–1911. These were extremely well run and attended by up to 50 pupils. A great range of subjects was studied, both theoretical and practical in nature. The classes for 1894 covered arithmetic, reading and writing, chemistry and drawing. A fee of 1d. a night was charged which was refunded if an attendance of 75 per cent was reached. In subsequent years shorthand, needlework and wood carving were added. On looking at the chemistry syllabus one is surprised that the school building still survived! Quite complicated experiments were carried out using the most elementary equipment. One would like to know what products resulted from the distillation experiment! The season of lectures ended with a special supper. There are details of the supper in 1907:

After supper various games were indulged in with great spirits until 11p.m., when Mr S. Farrant Chairman of the Board, distributed the prizes. Both the Chairman and the Rector gave short addresses – the meeting terminated with a hearty vote of thanks to Mr and Mrs Baxter.

Hemyock School was left without a headmaster because of the sudden death of Mr Baxter. For four months there was a temporary head, Mr A.J. Coles. Hemyock was lucky to have had such a well-known author in charge of the school (it being Mr Coles who wrote the very popular books in Devonshire dialect under the pseudonym Jan Stewar). Unfortunately he did not write as much in the school-log as he did in the books that he published!

On 12 April 1920 Mr P.H. Prowse took over as head. The school not only gained an excellent headmaster, but in the person of Mrs Prowse, an excellent assistant teacher as well. So started a husband and wife team that was to be the backbone of the school for 32 years. Many people in Hemyock today have good reason to thank Mr and Mrs Prowse for the grounding in basic education that they received from them – although pupils did not always see it in this light at the time. Mr Prowse obviously got down to work quickly – for on 29 April he wrote:

Up to the present I have not been able to carry out instruction in accordance with the time table. In the first place the stock of writing paper and exercise books is exhausted, and I have such an overwhelming amount of re-organising to do that it is not possible for me to cope with it in the evening.

Almost immediately he set about arranging the school garden that was to remain such an important part of school life for 30 years. Within one month he was making a request to the Managers that he be allowed a small portion of the sports field for a school garden. In November the Horticultural Superintendent came to school to give advice on the project and in June the following year we read: 'The school gardening class has commenced.' As is so often the case, some unforeseen problems were encountered. In July of the following year Mr Prowse noted:

... the school garden has been seriously damaged by trespass of sheep and much growing crops spoilt. With the consent of the managers I have purchased wire netting and spent the whole afternoon with the boys of Class 1 in fixing the netting in place.

Trespass by sheep was to occur again in 1927 when a two-year experimental plot was obliterated. An idea as to how successful the school garden was may be gauged from this report on the garden in 1927:

This is an excellent school garden. While the boys receive a thorough training in simple practical horticulture, including cultivation of vegetables, flowers and bush fruits, the girls are also interested in the management of the flower borders. The most valuable results are due to the Headmaster's enlightened conception of the garden as a means of giving reality and interest to the ordinary lessons in English, arithmetic, natural science and drawing.

Mr Prowse had some problems with the state that the school was left in after the room had been let for an evening meeting. On 4 November 1922 for example:

On examination of the school this morning I found the right pedal of the piano broken. 15 of the children's drawings on the floor, spoilt by being trampled upon, a large drawing made by the infant mistress to hide the untidy back of the harmonium, detached and lying on the floor, cigarette ends on the ledges and woodwork burnt. The room had been let for a dance on the 27th.

This was a problem that was to persist at the school until the Parish Hall was built in 1927. Until then, the school was the only suitable place for social gatherings to be held.

An almost unbelievable scenario was recorded in the 1930s. The infant teacher, Miss Hurley, married another teacher at Hemyock School, a Mr Conduit, in 1934. Although the Managers did everything that they could to try to keep her as a teacher, the Devon County Council would not allow it. Their policy was that married women could not remain as schoolteachers!

Overcrowding in school has it seems always been a problem. In 1927 the money was not available for building new classrooms and an ingenious compromise was worked out. The Wesleyan Sunday School, later the Methodist Sunday School, was rented for

£25 a year. This arrangement, which initially was on a temporary basis, was to last for more than 25 years, until the new secondary school was built at Uffculme. Mr Elliott moved there with Standards III and IV.

As generation succeeded generation in school life we all took our turn in walking in crocodile to the new schoolroom. That particular classroom was especially unpleasant on wet days when the children were not allowed to return to the main school to play. In April 1931 another small school was closed, that at Dunkeswell Abbey. The children who attended that school were dispersed to neighbouring schools. Four came to Hemyock, together with two cupboards, one table, one chair and some surplus stock.

The school continued to receive good reports during the HM Inspections which were held from time to time. The one that took place in 1932 was typical and is well worth quoting:

This is a good school. The annual concert, the school flower show, the encouragement of thrift by means of National Savings, a clothing club and the operation of a House and Prefect system are examples of social activities of schools which have been well developed.

In fact, this report was so good that a letter of appreciation was received from the Devon Education Committee. Whenever one cares to examine the reports of inspections of the school, whether they are from the early days, the middle period (as with this one) or more recent times, they are always good.

What must have been a tremendous boon to the school was the installation of electricity in 1933 when the village was supplied with electricity by the old Culm Valley Electric Company.

Further evidence of shortage of space was noted in 1939. The old L-shaped shed in the corner of the boys' playground was demolished. In its place a wooden craft-room was erected and was brought into use just after the outbreak of war in September, 1939. In November of the same year the new playground in the Recreation Field was brought into use (now the car park for the Parish Hall). In 1947 the other prefabricated hut was built in the boys' playground, in response to the 1944 Education Act which made education compulsory until the age of 15. During its construction the log notes: 'The mechanical concrete mixer makes worthwhile work impossible.' Older pupils of the school will remember the wood partition between the two classrooms in the main building – complete with convenient spy holes to view events in the other room (depending on which classroom you were in!). This was removed and replaced with a brick wall in 1949.

In the same year, in January, four children were admitted from Clayhidon. From this date all children from that school were sent to Hemyock

School when they reached the age of 11 years. This, of course, meant that Clayhidon School would only accommodate the younger children. Looking back this seems to have been the 'beginning of the end' for a separate school in that village. At this time, Mr Prowse spent quite a lot of time on his research for a Government report on 'Rewards and Punishments'.

In July 1949 school sports were revived after having been discontinued for the duration of the war and several years afterwards. At the same time house competitions were held and that year Culm won the cup. In July 1951 the first school trip took place when the senior school was taken to Plymouth to visit the Festival of Britain's ship, *Campania*. They also saw the Aquarium and went sightseeing in the estuary of the River Tamar.

On 6 September 1951 there was 'a considerable influx of infants... admitted to school.' The post-war baby bulge was beginning to impact on the local education resources.

In February 1952 the school received a visit from Mr Philip, the Chief Education Officer for Devon. He discussed the reorganisation of secondary education in the Culm Valley, which in turn led to the building of the new school at Uffculme two years later. An example of the way in which Mr Prowse thought constantly of the welfare of the children was the expenditure, 25 years earlier, of £2 to provide a cupboard to hold shoes and stockings in the event of the children arriving at school with wet feet. Many other interesting items crowd into the log-books and Managers' minute-books completed during Mr Prowse's headship.

Records of illness were far less numerous than had been the case in the late-19th century. The usual epidemics of whooping cough, measles, chicken pox, etc. took place, but they took their course without upsetting the life of the school to any great extent. Dr Lightbody visited the school in 1920 and he found 'that defective eyesight and septic teeth' were the most numerous complaints. More emphasis was placed on preventative medicine. For instance, in May 1941, Dr Griffin (senr) came into school and inoculated 60 children against diphtheria. Again in 1948 80 per cent of the parents agreed to let their children be tested in a survey on tuberculosis. A slightly different type of medical inspection was introduced in the 1920s. In 1924, a Dr Truman, a 'mental specialist', came to examine 2 children. Quickly the term 'county psychologist' appeared. One is tempted to speculate as to whether or not they cured or caused some cases that they came to visit! The school dentist seemed to strike terror into the children when he appeared at the school. Dental treatment was not compulsory. We have evidence of this, when on a visit in 1920, out of 112 children in the school, the dentist actually treated 51 children, whilst 61 brought written objections from their parents.

The school was visited by educationalists from overseas, including, in 1931, an Indian. Mr San Yat was enquiring into rural education with a view to seeing whether any principles to be found here could be applied to education in rural India. In 1936 another gentleman from the East came to see the school and spent two days here. He was Mr Maung Tint Swe from Burma. He, too, was looking at rural education to see if any of our methods could be used in organising village social life in his own country.

Many people will remember the Inter-House Shield which used to be awarded to the best school house each year. Miss Agar presented this trophy to the school in 1934 and the children were, apparently, delighted. The Good Fellowship Prizes were another popular introduction the following year. This record from the log on 30 July explains the system:

The election took place this morning for the first award of the "Good Fellowship" prizes promised each year by Mr and Mrs F. Melhuish (of Fircroft). These prizes are awarded annually in July to the boy and girl who, in the opinion of their classmates, is the best "fellow". The choice was made by ballot, following strictly parliamentary procedure and the presiding officer was the Rev. Ketchley, Chairman of the Managers. The two children elected were Cyril Tancock and Eileen Casely.

This annual event created tremendous interest and the results that came from the ballot box were eagerly awaited each year. The winners had their names placed on a special Honours Board.

A pleasing addition came in the war years, when an extra £2 was made available so that the two separate 'Good Fellows' could be chosen by the evacuees from their number. This is another example of the way in which the village has always been prepared to integrate new arrivals quickly.

It is surprising how easily we come to accept a new system and forget how we managed to carry on before. A case in point was the provision of school transport. The first mention of mechanical transport to school was in 1929 when discussion took place about the provision of a car to convey some children from Culm Davy. This must have seemed something of a luxury in those days when some children (not many!) walked over three miles to school. In 1933 a bus for children from the Madford area was provided. What a far cry this is from today when buses radiate in all directions from Hemyock to bring children to the school.

It is not known whether the telephone was installed as a result of the delivery of a demonstration set in 1935, but it created a lot of interest.

Intense preparation was apparent in school in 1935 for King George V's Silver Jubilee. A Miss Hacker came to teach the children some maypole dances. These required a lot of practice but the pupils were ready for Jubilee Day. This was a great occasion and all of the scholars went up class by class to receive special mugs. Soon afterwards the old King died and the first mention of a radio in the school is recorded, on 22 January 1936:

I assembled children of Standards I–VII in the main room to hear a Broadcast of the ceremony of the proclamation of King Edward VIII. This took place from 9.55 to 10.45a.m.

The water mains finally arrived in Hemyock in 1939 and the gangs of men who laid the pipes shattered the quiet daily routine. Mr Prowse wrote:

Considerable difficulty is being experienced this week in carrying on the work in school owing to the excavating which is being done in the roads outside. A large gang of men and two pneumatic drills have been busy all the week laying a water main.

Managers had made the request for a piped water supply to the village almost 30 years before! The various local councils had acted in a lethargic way over the installation of this water supply. Subsequently they acted with remarkable speed and condemned most of the wells in the village, thus forcing the householders to connect up with the new water pipes. It was at this time that our famous Pump in the centre of the village ceased to provide water to anyone who was thirsty! As if this upset was not enough to contend with, two months later, the roads were dug up again to lay telephone cables and cause further disruption to school routine!

The school canteen opened in September 1943. The meals came from Culmstock where they were cooked in a central canteen situated in their Parish Hall. On the first day 116 children and 7 staff enjoyed the meal. Bad weather, however, put a stop to the food during the snowstorm of 1947. It lasted from January to early March. A single entry covers the period from 5–14 February:

Frost continues, the heavy fall of snow on the 8th made matters worse. The bus and cars cannot run – on average only 25 children present. No dinners on the 10th and the 14th, due to curtailment of electricity because of the coal crisis.

In fact the full service from the central kitchen was not resumed until 25 February.

The Second World War, naturally, had a great impact on Hemyock School. In 1937 a number of remarks made by Mr Baldwin were discussed by the seniors and a lesson given on 'Peace and the League of Nations'. In September 1938 the storm clouds were clearly piling up. Mr Prowse observed:

Owing to the extreme tension occasioned by the international situation and the excitement caused by A.R.P.

(Air Raid Precaution) meetings and gas mask demonstrations, work has been very difficult to carry on throughout the week. I have also had considerable interruption owing to callers in connection with my duties as Air Raid Warden.

School re-started after the outbreak of war, a few days late. Nine unofficial evacuees were already in the village and came to the school. The next week every available piece of the school garden was planted in order to increase the food supply. In February 1940:

Mr Lowry, the local billeting officer, called and warned me to expect evacuees the next day. 18 children from the Guardian Angel Roman Catholic London County Council School, Stepney, arrived at about 6p.m. They were given tea and billeted by the local committee.

They varied in age from 4–13 years upwards and not having been to school for a long time, it was found that their education had been sadly affected. They were soon happily installed with us in the school. The first batch of evacuees really did settle down well, although on reflection the move from Stepney to Devon must have been a shattering experience. Soon one of their teachers, a Miss de Lacey, came to the school as well, as did 8 tables, 16 chairs and 16 'tidy boxes' from the LCC store in Taunton. By May the situation in France was critical. This was the period immediately before the Dunkirk evacuation. Schools were ordered by wireless to cancel the Whitsun holiday and reassemble. In mid-June the large contingent of evacuees came; 121 and 4 teachers arrived from Hazelbury Senior Girls School in Edmonton. These children were scattered all over the village. Mr Prowse wrote: 'It was decided to merge the 2 schools. The local children attended in the morning and the evacuated ones in the afternoon.' The teachers from Edmonton, the Misses Turner, Cox, Mortimore and Douthwaite, were to teach classes of town and country children. The school population had reached over 300. The Parish Hall was used with a curtain across the centre to make two classes and the church Sunday School was also taken over. This was almost a little school on its own. The babies and top infants were taught there and, with the consent of Mr Knowlman, the cattle market was used as a playground. How the staff managed to cope with this situation is hard to imagine.

The author recalls that it was when it came to singing that trouble set in, as the Hemyock children had never been taught such songs as 'Shenandoah', 'Bobby Shafto' or 'Rio Grande' but the London teachers thought that they were exhibiting their inherent stubbornness when they failed to join in – London punishments were not the same as Hemyock ones either.

The school was kept open throughout the summer holidays and the pupils were involved in a campaign to rid the village of cabbage-white butterflies, and even received payment from the school for catching them. In September more unofficial evacuees from London arrived because the bombing had intensified.

Even during wartime Christmas was still a time of celebration and the staff were pleased when the senior children devised and produced an impromptu concert one afternoon. Time and food were found for three parties. February 1941 brought a War Weapons Week when the children were all encouraged to invest heavily in National Savings Funds and the same month saw the bombing campaign switch from London to provincial cities. The school had 31 more children, this time from Bristol, under their teacher, Mr J. Howard, who stayed until he went off to join the RAF. Although he did not stay here for long, he is still remembered fondly by quite a number of Hemyockians. He formed a unit of the Army Cadet Force, which operated for some years, and he had a liking for 'buzzers' – used for sending Morse-code messages. All of the boys made their own buzzers, and for a short while, the village sounded like a swarm of bees! Fairly frequent Ministry of Information films varied the routine. These showed pupils how the war was progressing and their propaganda was an effective morale booster at a time when things were not in fact going at all well for the Allies.

By the end of 1941 some of the evacuees had returned and the number on the roll fell to 250. The gas masks were checked in December 1941 and additions were made to them. In 1944 there was a 'Book Drive' in the school for the Armed Forces. As a result 2500 books were sent off. Gradually the endless strain that the staff had been exposed to began to tell. By June 1944 three teachers remained on the staff to teach 154 children. On 30 June the school was closed 'to provide a break for remaining staff, 2 members showing signs of over-strain.' In July a further 26 evacuees arrived – no doubt as a result of the 'V-bomb' attacks on London. Illness set in amongst the teachers and on Monday 9 October Mr Prowse was forced to close the school as there were no teachers available. The following day, however, two teachers arrived and school continued.

The Christmas of 1944 was an exceptional one. By this time the aerodrome at Dunkeswell had been given up by the RAF and taken over by the US Navy. On 20 December representatives of the latter attended the school Christmas party. They brought a generous supply of sweets for all present and even returned the hospitality. The next day we read: 'The staff accompanied 70 of the youngest children to a Christmas party at Dunkeswell aerodrome given by members of the U.S. Navy to children of the locality.'

VE Day (Victory in Europe) finally arrived on 8 May 1945 and this school, along with all others, enjoyed a two-day holiday. Mr and Mrs Prowse retired in July 1952 to a bungalow built on the outskirts of the village, not far from the school that had been their lives for 32 years. Unfortunately Mr Prowse did not live long enough to enjoy the retirement that he deserved. Some years later the Parish Council was unanimous in naming a new estate in the village 'Prowses' in the couple's memory.

In 1952 the school's first post-war headmaster was appointed. He was Mr J. Reed, an ex-RAF pilot. His arrival heralded a new generation of heads, who did not necessarily aim to stay in the same school for their entire career. Mr Reed was able to introduce fresh ideas, ones that we now take for granted and in 1952 the classes were arranged as follows:

Teacher	Children aged		No.
Mr J. Reed	14+		11
Mr F. Warren	11+	to 13+	34
Miss M.O. Baker	8+	to 10+	37
(later Mr Clist)			
Miss G. Fowler	7+		27
Mrs E.M. Culverwell	5+	and 6+	46
(and Mrs Warren as nursery helper)		**Total**	**152**

In June 1953 there was a week's holiday to celebrate the Coronation of Queen Elizabeth II. A feature of this event was the installation of a temporary TV set in the craft-room, so that the children and adults could actually watch the crowning.

The school garden was still in operation but 1953 was not the most trouble-free of years, for on Boxing Day Mr Reed wrote:

5 heifers belonging to Mr Hill were found in the school garden and by lack of anything green (except wallflowers) had been there some hours. What has not been eaten has been trampled into damp ground.

Basket work created in the school craft-room whilst Mr J. Reed was the headmaster.

The reorganisation of secondary education was uppermost in the minds of those at the school at this time. A Mr Lee, Research Fellow of the Institute of Education (UCSW), came to the school and the educational set-up in the Culm Valley was discussed. This change took place in September 1954, when Mr Warren and all senior children left the school to go to the new secondary school at Uffculme. The school numbers were cut by almost 30 per cent at once. This was the most fundamental change that the school had seen since its start.

At the same time the Methodist Sunday School was no longer required as a 'temporary' classroom. The HMI report of February 1955, six months after the change, shows how quickly the new regime had settled down. It also gives an insight into the teaching methods of the day and it is worth quoting:

The most promising feature of this Primary School is that its doors are open to let the children out into the attractive countryside to learn at first hand something of the wonder and delight which comes from the study of nature and of the interesting human activities which are going on in the vicinity. The hedgerow, the stream, the farm, the egg packing station, the bungalow rising from its foundations and the like, all serve to give opportunities for exploration and discovery. With such a programme it is obvious that every moment of the school day is fully and happily occupied. The children reflect in their behaviour, whether at lessons, play or at their mid-day meal, the good training that they receive here.

It must have been pleasing for the staff to receive such an encouraging report. Indeed, the new 'feeling' was apparent when, on 30 June, the first Open Day was held. Parents were encouraged to come into the school to see how things were run.

The year 1960 was crucial during Mr Powell's period as headmaster. On 8 September the Clayhidon children came to Hemyock School, their own primary school having been closed in July – yet another loss of a small village school and with it an important local focal point, not only for education, but also for parochial needs. The children made the transition very easily, the more so, because one of their teachers, Mrs Berry, came with them. Their former headmistress, Mrs Bowden, acted as a supply teacher in Hemyock several times. The same year also saw the foundation of the School Reference Library – a grant of £30 was sufficient to start this venture. Our first television set arrived in 1962.

A few months later saw the 'big freeze' of 1962–63. From 28 December until early March school life and village life were disrupted. Numbers at school seemed to level out at 24 for several weeks. Mr Richardson arrived in the school in 1967, as our first deputy headmaster. Almost immediately a change in emphasis took place in the attitude adopted towards

Left: *Senior School PE, March 1954. Left to right, back: John Churchill, John Barrow, Christine Howe, Brenda Warren, Yvonne Gibbs, Margaret Hallett, Michael Bradford, Tom Bright; middle: Phillip Martin, Michael Ashton, Harold South, Elsie Doble, Janet Lowman, Margaret Manley, Annette Maltby, Gordon Lowman, Michael Bishop, Winston Scoble; front: Nigel Pring, John Doble, Pauline King, Sylvia Bright, Mr Frank Warren (senior master), Anne Cox, Diane Mitchell, Brian Spiller and Derek Hadley.*

Right: *In May 1953 the first of the annual educational outings took place. Mr Reed and Miss Baker took a party of 40 children and 22 adults on a visit to London Airport, followed by a river trip to Maidenhead, to return home via Ascot and Windsor.*

Left: *Hemyock School pupils in historical costume, Christmas 1956, with teacher Mavis Clist at the back. Left to right, back: Marilyn Jones, Raymond Drew, Tom Fouracre, Rosalind Bourden, Maureen Granger, Michael Knott, Christine Henson, Carolyn Dew, Janet Granger, Rosemary Hurd, Janice Fuller, Roy Perrott; front: Brian Doble, Trevor Coles, Malcolm Edwards, Gwen Kallaway, John Lawrence, Keith Gammon, Christine Middleton.*

Right: *School Open Day, June 1955. Those at each table beginning in the bottom left going clockwise around the room and around each table.*
Table 1: *Raymond Granger (bottom left), Doreen Howe, Derek Granger, Ronald Kallaway, Heather Cox, Janet South;* ***Table 2:*** *Brian Jenkins, David Kallaway, Raymond Vian, Monica Bright;* ***Table 3:*** *Heather Grabham, Shelagh Bourdon, John Northam, Alan Ridler, Jean Burston, Shirley Troake, Bill Guppy, Raymond Salter;* ***Table 4:*** *Andrew Clements, Mary Sanders, ? Edwards;* ***Table 5:*** *Michael Sweetland,*

Jennifer Smith, Patricia Maltby. **Parents and teachers,** *left to right: Mrs Drew, Mrs Mutter, Mrs Evans, Mrs Coles, Mrs Burston, Mrs Perrott, Mrs Edwards, Mrs Grabham with Coralie, Mr Jack Reed (headmaster) Miss Mavis Baker (mistress), Beryl Sanders, Mrs Sanders.*

music. The first musical production was *The Turtle Drum*. The £18 raised by the collection was to be used to purchase musical instruments. Early the next year the music inspector, Mr Hollingsworth, came and discussed two operettas. He also offered the school additional musical instruments. The operettas were performed in July 1968 and the following year a more ambitious entertainment was produced, HMS *Pinafore*, to an audience of more than 300 people on two nights.

In 1968 some doubt was expressed in the village (and recorded in the log) as to whether parents understood the methods of teaching maths, science and English:

Some 30 parents came back to school in the evenings, working in pairs they spent some time doing school assignments in these subjects. It was the general impression that an enjoyable time was spent finding out how the modern school works.

*School football team 1979.
Left to right, back: Teacher J. Ellis, D. Sparks, L. Sloman, ?, R. Bowden;
front: B. Denning, C. Jones, ?, ?, G. Payne.*

Just before he retired, Mr Powell called a meeting to discuss the formation of a playgroup:

This afternoon a meeting was held in the T.V. Room of mothers with pre-school age children to start a Play Group in the Hall. Negotiations regarding this have been proceeding for some months and it has the County's sanction, but since it was divorced from the school (officially) it was not necessary to have the Managers' permission.

The playgroup was quickly set up and operating. It has flourished ever since and still has an extremely active membership of budding scholars for Hemyock School!

On 18 July 1969 Mr Powell retired and on 9 September Mr Richardson took over the school as headmaster. It was at this time that the head felt that the children should be given the opportunity to travel outside this country. The first school trip abroad was to Belgium and for a time journeys to the Continent were a biennial event. Parties averaging 45 children and parents travelled to Switzerland and Germany.

The second teachers' strike took place in 1969 when three teachers stopped teaching for half a day.

This was over a pay dispute. In 1975 the heating system was changed. References to smoking chimneys and fumes in the classrooms cease in the log at this time because electric night-storage heaters were installed. The effect of heavy unemployment amongst teachers was felt even in a country school. In 1976 when a teaching post was advertised, there were 215 applicants to fill the one position!

As long ago as the 1930s people began to say that Hemyock needed a new school. One of the earliest plans from the post-war period actually identified an area of land on what is now a part of the Hollingarth Estate as a site for the new school, with the Recreation Ground and Parish Hall still being kept available for use by the children. Until recently the Parish Council had little control over the planning decisions. In our case either Councils in Tiverton or Exeter had the real power as to where developments could take place. When the Hollingarth Estate was built the site earmarked for the school was filled with houses. We thought that our new school would never materialise, but in 1980 Devon County Council announced that they had enough money to build one school – either to be in Plymouth or in Hemyock. At this time Parklands Estate was under construction and a site for the school was found there and Hemyock chosen. The position was not ideal but if no site had been found Hemyock would not have been selected. A very modern school with room for 180 pupils was built and it opened in 1982. The move from the old school to the new building went remarkably smoothly, with little apparent upheaval under a very capable headmaster, Mr Roy McQueen.

At the time of writing we still have a very successful school under the headship of Mrs Gill Peters and in 2002 the school will have been in existence for 125 years. The children are taught in a new school, the curriculum and the methods of teaching are very different from earlier days, but it is gratifying to know that our young residents are still benefiting from a good education provided by a team of dedicated teachers.

As the result of an idea of a local doctor, Dr Jonathan Meads, the old school was converted into flats to house elderly people and so is still serving the community well.

A selection of the shorthorn calves after distribution in Hemyock Market which was behind what is now the Catherine Wheel.

The animals are paraded at Millhayes looking towards what is now Lower Millhayes.

CHAPTER ELEVEN

Young Farmers

The history of the Young Farmers Movement began in Hemyock over 80 years ago. The First World War had a great influence on the life of the nation and a whole generation of young men had left their homes to fight for their country, many of them never to return. And the war had a great impact at village level too. As a result of intense U-Boat attacks many merchant ships bringing food had been sunk and there was a genuine shortage of food, even in Hemyock. Some eight months after the war had ended, the following was noted in the school log: '... school visited by Dr. Lightbody, he examined 60 to 70 children, 13 require treatment and of those 5 are suffering from anaemia.' Comment was also passed on how the complexions of the children had altered to make them appear more like town children than girls and boys from the country (see Chapter Ten). And this in a village that not only had many dairy farms, but its own milk factory too!

The milk factory had been locally owned until half way through the First World War when it was sold to a much larger dairy group, Wilts United Dairies, which operated at a national level. The milk shortage was a nationwide problem. Somehow our farmers had to be persuaded to increase their milk production but this was difficult to achieve at that time – producing more milk would have required more stock and extra cows were hard to come by during the war. When a solution was found it was a very ingenious one. Perhaps the proponents of this scheme were unaware of how successful it would become, or indeed how far reaching its influence would be. A movement for young country people had been in operation in Canada for several years under the banner of the '4H Clubs'. These clubs had both an educational and social purpose and had become very successful. It so happened that in 1920 a Canadian dairy specialist had been sent to the milk factory in Hemyock as a Manager and quite quickly saw that an organisation formed along similar lines

would be of benefit to the children of the village.

In October 1920 a 'meeting of agriculturalists' was arranged to discuss the idea. The meeting took place on 14 October and a week later the club held its first annual meeting when seven girls and a dozen boys became members. The club was called United Dairies Ltd. Calf Club No.1, with the phrase 'Unity, Industry, Prosperity' as its motto. Each child was provided with a heifer calf which they had to rear themselves, attending fortnightly meetings along the way for instruction. At the end of a year their calf (which by then had become a yearling) would be judged and sold. The process then continued with a second distribution of calves. The first year's calves were described as 'roans' and were basically of the dairy shorthorn breed. The one condition was that their dam (mother) had to have produced 600 gallons of milk a year, some 50 per cent more than our local cattle yielded at the time.

The third year saw an unusual development in that Ayrshire calves from Scotland, including a bull calf to maintain the breeding line, were purchased. These came from cows that were producing over 800 gallons of milk annually. The system operated as follows. United Dairies bought the calves and charged the children £5 each for them, but the sum was not collected until the animals were sold a year later. It was anticipated that the heifers would be bought back by the parents of the members and incorporated into their milking herds, which is exactly what transpired. Within a few years United Dairies was obtaining the additional milk that it needed and at the same time had founded a Calf Club that was quickly copied all over the country and eventually became the Young Farmers Movement.

The first consignment of calves arrived in Hemyock at the end of January 1921 and they were distributed to the Calf Club members on 31st of that month at a special event held in Hemyock Market (behind what is now the Catherine Wheel). The factory Manager's three-year-old daughter drew the numbers and these were matched to club members'

Left: *The method of calf allocation at the first distribution, 31 January 1921. Rosemary Sandford takes a club member's name from a hat which is matched with a calf's name from the other hat.*

Below: *Each member received a Christmas card from little Rosemary Sandford.*

Dixcroft.
Hemyock.
Xmas, 1921.

Dear Member,

Your Club Mascot sends you Greetings for the Festive Season and trusts Daddy Xmas will put something nice in your Stocking for the kind way you have looked after your Calf.

Will you give it something nice for dinner Xmas day.

From
ROSEMARY

Above: *Wilfred Ackland and William Tucker with their calves.*

Left: *This letter was sent out to local farmers to invite them to a meeting to discuss the formation of the Calf Club. Less than two weeks later the club had been formed.*

Below: *The calves running with their new owners through Hemyock Square.*

Above: *The first three pages of the Calf Club minute-book. This was the first Young Farmers Club to be formed in the country. The minute-book gives details of this important event.*

Below: *By 1922 the calves have become yearlings, which are seen here behind the milk factory at Millhayes. Two old cars and an early Albion lorry can be seen in the background.*

Above: *Young ladies going to Canada (at London Railway Station).*

Right: *The logo of the newly-formed Calf Club bearing the four-leafed clover and the motto.*

In 1923, Ayrshire calves were chosen and a bull calf, seen on the left, was even bought to make sure that the breed would remain pure in the Culm Valley.

names which were drawn from another hat. This method ensured that the system of distribution was completely fair. The young people were provided with a printed book, with sufficient space for them to record weight gain, the type of food fed and any problems that were encountered.

Some of these diaries make interesting reading: '... calf 14 had a lump, calves 1, 9 and 11 had scours, calf 10 had a swollen jaw and calf 5 had lice'. Some of the remedies to treat the conditions were equally unusual; for instance one would not have thought that a tablespoonful of starch and another of ground coffee would be used today to clear up scours! One of the members, Doris Fry, wrote in her diary:

My calf, Star 2nd, weighed 107lbs on Jan. 31st 1921, at the end of 12 months she weighed 736lbs and on April 23rd 1923 she presented me with a nice, rich, red heifer calf.

The prices of the feeding stuffs used to rear the calves were as follows:

Linseed cake	£18.10s. a ton
Calf meal	£22.0s. a ton
Flour	2d. a lb
Hay	£7 a ton
Mangolds	£7 a ton
Milk	10d. a gallon (2p a litre)
Skimmed milk	3d. a gallon.

The rearing costs for each animal ranged from £9.30s.0d. to £17.30s.0d.

The social side of the club was not neglected. Visits were made to Welwyn Garden City, The Dairy Research Institution at Reading, The Ideal Home Exhibition and both Empire Exhibitions in London in 1923 and 1924. The Calf Club found an early and generous sponsor in the *Daily Mail* newspaper which arranged and financed some of these visits. The young members were driven around London in a double-decker bus, which was suitably emblazoned with the Calf Club logo. Two of the original members, Mildred White and Gordon Salter, were sent to Canada for three months, to visit and work on farms.

The vision that led to the formation of this club was an inspired one. In 1925 a conference was held at the Ministry of Agriculture to 'consider points of policy and procedure in regard to the Young Farmers' Clubs Movement.' Clubs represented at this meeting were Hemyock, Barns Green, Buckland, Loughborough, Hornsey, Heston, Kirdford in Sussex, Heathfield, Northaw, Buckingham, Clifton and Kingsclere (which was the second Calf Club to be formed). From this meeting we learn that the Ministry of Agriculture had taken over the general supervision of the clubs in 1924 and that it was felt that the time had come to link the movement with agricultural education in general. Our original club in Hemyock had developed into a national system of clubs within three years and over succeeding years into the thousands of branches that exist today.

In 1981, to celebrate the 60th anniversary of the Calf Club's formation the County Rally was held in Hemyock in a field at Regency House. For a couple of days the field was a sea of tents which contained the exhibits required for a successful rally. Our club is still flourishing in the name of the Culm Valley Young Farmers Club.

CHAPTER TWELVE

The Defence of Hemyock

This chapter is principally concerned with the subject of home defence from Tudor times to the Second World War. We do not refer here to the men and women of Hemyock who served their country in the Crimean and Boer Wars or the many other conflicts including the two world wars and subsequent campaigns. The village war memorial names those who made the ultimate sacrifice in the First and Second World Wars and Malaya.

For many centuries in England there has always been some sort of system for raising men to take arms in the defence of their country. The origins of a formal method in gathering fighting men date back to the Fyrd and the Anglo-Saxon days of King Alfred and his successors Then there was a force of thegns, the Anglo-Saxon military elite, who were obliged to bear arms for their ruler. Under Alfred one half of the Fyrd was on duty whilst the others were resting – these were the men largely responsible for defeating the Norwegian King Harald Hardrada at the Battle of Stamford Bridge before marching hundreds of miles south to face the invading force of William of Normandy and defeat at the Battle of Hastings.

Following the Norman Conquest the obligation to bear arms for the king was known as Knight's Service where the king's tenants in chief were obliged to provide a number of knights to serve for a particular period (usually, in peacetime, about 40 days). In 1181 Henry II issued an Assize of Arms which determined the weapons and equipment required of each knight, freeman and burgess. Not only were men liable for military service but they had to provide certain items of equipment at their own expense. The unfree peasantry were also liable for military service from the 13th century and the situation remained much the same until 1558.

In that year Commissions of Array were appointed by the Crown. The Commissions were to compile Muster Rolls which listed all those available for military service on a county by county basis. It was the responsibility of the parish constable to raise the necessary levies under the direction of the Lord Lieutenant of the County or his deputy. Apart from being of general historical interest the lists are of local interest as they deal with each parish individually.

The Devon Muster Roll of 1569 lists over 70 men of Hemyock, aged between 16 and 60, together with the weapon or equipment which they were required by law to keep. Some of the names of the Hemyock men have a familiar ring to them, among them Lawrence Bowreman (later Bowerman) who had a corselet, one pike, one harquebus (an old hand pistol) and a murrion (helmet). Another Bowreman, Andrew, was not so well armed and simply had a longbow. A Robert Manley was also among the harquebusiers and Peter Holway was a pikeman. This Muster Roll is the earliest document detailing men of the parish who were required to be ready for conflict.

Hemyock was fortunate not to see any fighting until the advent of the English Civil War, which broke out in 1642. At that time the Popham family were the principal landowners in the village, among whose properties was Hemyock Castle. The Pophams were Parliamentarian supporters and Hemyock Castle was garrisoned by Parliament and used to house Royalist prisoners. Along with many of the cloth-producing villages of the Culm Valley, Hemyock was almost completely united against the King. When Charles I summoned East Devon to appear on a posse 53 inhabitants of Culmstock, 34 from Clayhidon and 29 from Hemyock refused to attend. In March 1644 a large insurrection against the King broke out here which led to the siege of the castle (see Chapter Five).

Only a few years after the Civil War and the Restoration came the Monmouth Rebellion (or Western Rebellion as it was sometimes called). James Duke of Monmouth was an illegitimate son of Charles II and when Charles died in 1685 his

115

Roman-Catholic brother James came to the throne. He was not a popular choice. The Protestant Duke of Monmouth, who was living in exile in Holland, decided to challenge for the throne. Monmouth felt that he had more than enough support to succeed in his challenge and was hopeful that the country would rise against James II. How wrong Monmouth was. A combination of bad advice, a dearth of funds and a lack of a clear and cohesive purpose would be his undoing.

At first the Duke's prospects looked good. He landed at Lyme Regis with a few supporters and within days the men of the western counties, mainly Dorset, Somerset and Devon, had flocked to his cause. Monmouth began his march across country to the north, passing through the east of the Blackdown Hills en route to Taunton and Bridgwater. More flocked to his side at Taunton, Wellington and other local towns. Monmouth found himself with an army of some 6000 'volunteers'.

The whole enterprise was to founder disastrously on the Somerset Levels near Weston Zoyland on 5 July 1685 where Monmouth's army was totally defeated by King James' forces. Monmouth's men were either slaughtered or taken prisoner, or made good their escape into the countryside. Monmouth himself took flight but was captured in Hampshire, taken to London and executed on 15 July.

The aftermath for those involved in the rebellion, most of whom were not even professional soldiers, was grim. Those who had been taken prisoner at Sedgemoor or captured later were to find themselves in front of the infamous Lord Chief Justice, Sir George (Judge) Jeffreys at the Bloody Assize. The Assize was held at Winchester, Salisbury, Exeter, Taunton and Wells. Over 300 men were executed, nearly 1000 transported to Barbados and many others whipped. Little mercy was shown. Public executions were the norm and they were pretty gruesome affairs. Prisoners were hanged but kept alive whilst their entrails were removed and burnt before their eyes, then the corpses were quartered, boiled in salt and dipped in pitch to preserve them. The parts were then placed in public places as a lesson to the population at large. Judge Jeffreys died in 1688 having tried to flee the country disguised as a sailor. He was arrested at a Wapping pub and died in the Tower of London.

What has all this to do with Hemyock? Were any of the villagers involved in Monmouth's Rebellion? The names of some 4000 people involved in or suspected of being so are listed in a 'Roll Call' of rebels prepared from a number of historical documentary sources. The list includes men and women from towns and villages all around Hemyock and the Blackdown Hills, Wellington, Taunton, Honiton, Cullompton, Uffculme, Luppitt (34 men from this small village were listed), and even one lone gentleman from Culmstock – but not one name from Hemyock appears. This does seem rather unlikely, but perhaps the village resisted the fervour that swept across the West Country. Was everybody in the village totally loyal to King James II or is it that the authorities were unable to establish a connection between any villager and the Duke of Monmouth's cause?

After Sedgemoor the difficult task of collecting the names of suspected Monmouth supporters began. The constables from each hundred were ordered to submit lists of men in all of the villages within their jurisdiction who had been 'absent from their homes during the rebellion of James Scott late Duke of Monmouth'. Perhaps the constable responsible for Hemyock was less thorough than he should have been in this task? Of course, the hangings that had taken place in Hemyock after the siege of Hemyock Castle during the Civil War may have discouraged villagers from getting involved in any form of insurrection, political or otherwise.

Nonetheless, there are many names in the Roll Call of rebels that were familiar in Hemyock at that time and in later years, among them Blackmore, Bowden, Lutley, Pring, Clode, Scadding, Lowman and others, but these particular individuals were apparently from other parishes. There is every chance, however, that some Hemyock families of today had an ancestor or kinsman who fought for Monmouth. One man on the list who certainly was not from Hemyock, was Henry Dracott of London, accused of being 'concerned in the rebellion in the west'. He managed to obtain a pardon! It has not been established whether he was a distant kinsman of one of the authors of this volume.

The closing years of the 18th century were to see the biggest threat of invasion prior to the Second World War. During the Napoleonic Wars the fear of invasion was heightened when a number of French troops landed at Fishguard, Pembrokeshire, in February 1797. It was a fairly feeble attempt by the French who were quickly overwhelmed by local forces, but it did serve to concentrate the minds of the Government and military in England. Plans had to be made and these plans were wide-reaching, involving the regular military, the militia, volunteer forces and the civilian population.

Not surprisingly the South West was considered to be particularly at risk and Hemyock was one of the parishes that had to prepare itself for war and evacuation. The parish is extremely fortunate in that certain documents relating to its proposed arming and evacuation have survived the passage of time and are still available for study. Virtually none of these official records have survived elsewhere in Devon or in other counties throughout the South West so they are extremely rare. Before discussing these valuable documents it may be useful to give the reader some idea of the general build up for home defence at this point in time.

The Militia Act of 1757 stipulated that militia would be provided on a county basis, a quota being apportioned among parishes. Men between the ages of 18–45 were to be selected by ballot although they could 'buy' themselves out by paying £10 for a substitute. Militia men initially served for three years and later five years and could serve anywhere in the country. They were subject to military discipline. In 1758 parishes were able to offer 'volunteers' which would count towards their local quotas in place of militia. Volunteers were exempt from the militia ballot so volunteering was quite popular. There were various changes made to the status of both the militia and the volunteers in succeeding years and in 1793 volunteers became separate from the militia with their own officers. Volunteers were either infantry or cavalry (yeomanry). In addition to the militia and the volunteers there were also men known as 'fencibles'. These were regulars raised for the purposes of home defence only. Apart from defence the volunteers could also be used to suppress local disorders, riots and other disturbances. Events in France had made the authorities very wary of the possibility of revolutionary tendencies erupting in England as they had done over the Channel.

Hemyock raised its own Corps of Volunteers and the Devon Lieutenancy Papers show that on 22 August 1800 General John Graves Simcoe, Commander in the West of England (see Chapter Eighteen) recommended raising 'a Corps of Infantry in Hemiock under the command of Charles Baker Esq. Consisting of 78 rank and file.' It was ordered that the recommendation be accepted and forwarded to the Lord Lieutenant for his approval. Volunteers were required to complete a certain amount of training and exercises, for which they were paid a small sum of money. The Volunteer Pay Lists and Returns in the Home Office Records at Kew give details of the Hemyock Corps from 1800–02. The Corps comprised:

Captain	Chas. Baker
Lieutenant	Jewell Collier
Ensign	John Southey
Sergeant	Charles Bray (permanent pay)
Sgts.	Geo. Southey
	John Southey
	Wm. Standerwick
Corporals	Wm. Channon
	John Gillard
	A(?) Gillard
Drummers	Wm. Berry
	Saml. Southey

There were also 63 privates, among them Edward Manley, George Fry and John Fry. In 1803 Hemyock combined with Culmstock as part of the East Devon Legion with Jewell Collier as Captain. The Devon Lieutenancy Minutes also indicate there was a Volunteer Cavalry Corps in Hemyock.

The plans for the civilian population are covered by what are described as Defence Lists, the Posse Comitatus lists of 1798 made under the Defence of the Realm Act, and the Levee en Masse Lists of 1803–04 made under the 1st and 2nd Defence Acts – all prepared by order of the county's Lord Lieutenant. Printed circulars were sent to the petty parish constables instructing that certain returns should be completed and sent to the Lord Lieutenant. It is the parish copies of some of these papers that survive in Hemyock. Official form filling has never been anyone's favourite pastime so imagine the reaction of Hemyock's constable on receipt of the following:

To the Petty Constable of the Parish of Hemyock…
By virtue of Instructions hereinafter stated, given by the Right Honourable Hugh Earl Fortescue, Lord Lieutenant of the said County, at a General Meting of his Majesty's Justices of the Peace for the said County, holden in the Castle of Exon on 20th day of January in the 38th year of the Reign of King George 3rd to the Justices then and there convened and assembled you are hereby required to give notice to the Ministers, Churchwardens and Overseers of the different Parishes within your constablewick. That in vestry assembled for the Purpose, they make forthwith a faithful and accurate Return of the Males resident in their respective Parish, according to the Form of the Return marked 'A', hereunto annexed for the purpose of raising and establishing the Civil Power, for the general defence of the County; to suppress any Riot or Insurrection or to repel Invaders; And also to recommend in Case the Number to be levied in any Parish within the Age prescribed in the annexed Return should exceed One Hundred Men, the names of two or more proper and fit Persons from which may be chosen a Chief Commander of the Men to be hired as aforesaid and also proper persons to be Petty Commanders of and over every 20 men to be hired as aforesaid; and so in Proportion for every Hundred men two or more names fit be selected for a Chief Commander and for every 20 men, fit persons to be selected as Petty Commanders, according to the Form of the Returns hereunto annexed, and also the Names of such Persons fit to be selected for Directors of Stock and for Drivers in each Parish respectively agreeable to the Return to be made marked 'B' hereunto annexed and also the number of Waggons, Carts and cart Horses in each parish respectively which may be used for the removal of Dead Stock or conveying Soldiers or Baggage etc.

And the said Minister, Churchwardens and Overseers of the Parishes respectively are to make their Returns to the Justices acting within the Hundred of Hemyock at a special Sessions to be holden at Tiverton in the said County on Monday the Nineteenth Day of February Instant in Writing under their Hands containing the respective Articles according to the Form of the returns hereunto annexed.

Herein fail not. Given under my Hand this 7th. Day of February 1798. **Robert Fry. High Constable**

described as servants, the balance being labourers or apprentices. A number of men in the Hemyock Return are listed under 'Armed Force'. This is taken to mean men prepared to take up arms of any sort and fight, as distinct from formal members of the 'Volunteer Corps' as outlined earlier.

Return 'B', Live and Dead Stock, is only a working copy but is taken to be fairly accurate. The detailed livestock included 47 oxen, 237 cows, 270 young stock (which may have included both young cattle and colts as did a subsequent return in 1803), 1296 sheep and 202 pigs. The dead stock (harvested crops in store) comprised 144 quarters of wheat, 60 of oats, 35 of barley, 73 loads of hay, 15 of straw and 201 sacks of potatoes.

The plans for defence were taken a step further in April 1798 when further preparations were to be made for the removal of the aged and the women and children from the path of the invading French. A 'Standing Committee of Civilian and Service Representatives' was established in Exeter to keep the plans under review. Part of the Act of Parliament that set all these plans in motion, sums up the Government's thinking:

Proposals for rendering the Body of the People instrumental in the General defence saving their Property and distressing the enemy, by removing the Means of Subsistence from Threatened Parts of the Country, as also for insuring the necessary supplies to his Majesty's Forces, and facilitating their Movements in the case of invasion, without making any expensive preparations.

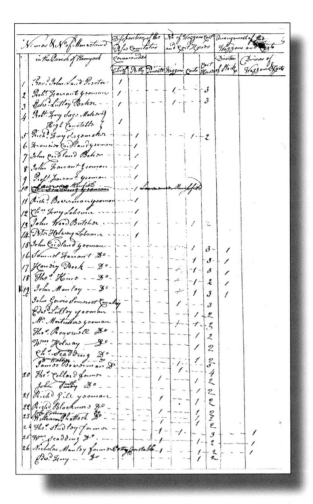

This document (just one page of several) lists 26 men. The first three columns show their rank in the proposed defence force (separate from the militia and volunteers), Chief, Petty and Privates. The other columns list their wagons, carts, cart horses and 'Directors of Stock'.

It was to be scorched-earth policy. If a French force arrived in Hemyock, or any other village or town, they would find no people, no crops, no live or dead stock, absolutely nothing for the army to live on. This aspect of the plan in Hemyock was covered by a 'Removal Paper'. In this document the 'Directors of Stock' were named as Henry Pook, Thomas Hine, Nicholas Manley, Robert Fry and Peter Holway. In all 58 'Proprietors of Stock' were named and 21 men appointed as drivers of stock and assistants. The following were appointed as 'Guardians': the Revd John Land, John Cridland senr, John Mortimer, Samuel Farrant, Jas. Bowerman, Mark Quick and Richard Gill. Edward Lutley senr and Edward Fry were originally listed as 'Guardians' but their names were crossed out and entered under the heading 'Superintendent of Women and Children and Infirm Persons'. The wagons, carts and horses were to muster under the control of Directors John Manley and Richard Fry.

Destinations had been established for every parish in Devon, that the whole village was to set out for in the event of invasion; one was in Somerton in Somerset, the other on Dartmoor. The route to be taken by the population of Hemyock to Somerton was set out as follows:

Form 'A' included column headings and sub-headings as follows: 'Parish', 'No. of Men returned to the Magistrate', 'Disposition and arrangements of the Posse Comitatus: Chief, Petty', 'Privates', 'No. of Waggons, Carts and Cart Horses returned to the Lieutenancy', 'Disposition and Arrangements of the Waggons and Horses', 'Directors of Stock' and 'Drivers of Waggons'.

The individuals involved in completing this form were John Cridland (churchwarden) and Richard Bowerman and John Manley (overseers). The names and occupations of 240 men were listed in Hemyock including the Reverend John Land who was to be a Chief Commander. The other three Chief Commanders were Robert Farrant, a yeoman, Edward Lutley, a baker, and Robert Fry, a serge maker who was also High Constable. Ten Petty Commanders were appointed including Charles Fry and Peter Holway. The transport fleet numbered 6 wagons and 20 carts. Some 64 draught horses were available and 26 drivers were nominated, 11 being

The Directors of Stock for the Parish of Hemyock do fix on the Town of Hemyock for the place of our Rendezvous and to assemble the livestock of the said Parish on Blackdown near Simonsborough about 2 miles from Hemyock and from thence to seven Mile House on the said Down about 4 miles (crossing the Turnpike Road leading from Taunton to Honiton) and from thence to Ashel Forest about 5 miles, and so on the Direct Road to Somerton if so ordered.

The Hemyock documents, which are unfortunately incomplete, contain further removal orders for 1803 which give the evacuation routes to Somerton and Dartmoor:

If the Route should be towards Somerton the place of Rendezvous is to Simonsburrow and thence to Staple and Hatch Inn, to Curry Rivel to Langport and Somerton. Or if the Route be towards Dartmoor, the place of rendezvous is to be Castle Hill from thence to Kentisbeare to Bradninch, to Thorverton, to Creedy Bridge, to Barnstaple Cross, to Bow, to North Tawton, to South Tawton to West Zeal to Dartmoor.

What a journey. It is presumed that the choice of Somerton or Dartmoor was to be decided according to where the French landed.

Of course the French did not invade in 1798 and in March 1802 England ended hostilities with them at the Treaty of Amiens. By 1803, however, we were at war once again, and once again defence plans were drawn up under the Levee en Masse. This time the returns were far more comprehensive and were to include the following groups: (1) all men aged 17–55 giving names, occupations and infirmities, arranged in four categories according to age group, marital status and numbers of children aged under 10; (2) all householders giving names, sometimes occupations and ages and whether Quakers or Aliens with numbers of males and females in each household; (3) non-combatants who would need to be evacuated, women, children, the old and infirm being incapable of removing themselves, giving names, sometimes occupations and ages; and (4) some of the men aged 17–55 formed into posses of pioneers and special constables. Miscellaneous categories included lists of millers, bakers, wagon and barge owners, guides, stockmen, wagoners and those holding weapons. Also schedules of farm animals and amounts of corn and fodder to be removed were listed.

Once again all possible effort was put into completion of such forms but it was all to no avail because the French never did invade.

The completed 1798 return listing (in groups) all of the Hemyock men who would form the 'Active Service' force.

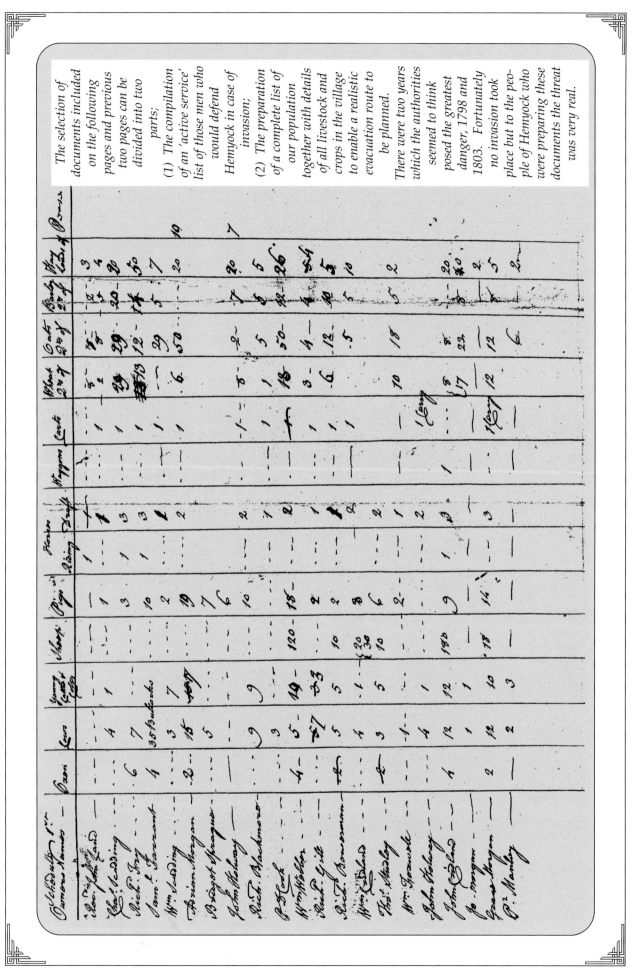

The selection of documents included on the following pages and previous two pages can be divided into two parts;

(1) The compilation of an 'active service' list of those men who would defend Hemyock in case of invasion;

(2) The preparation of a complete list of our population together with details of all livestock and crops in the village to enable a realistic evacuation route to be planned.

There were two years which the authorities seemed to think posed the greatest danger, 1798 and 1803. Fortunately no invasion took place but to the people of Hemyock who were preparing these documents the threat was very real.

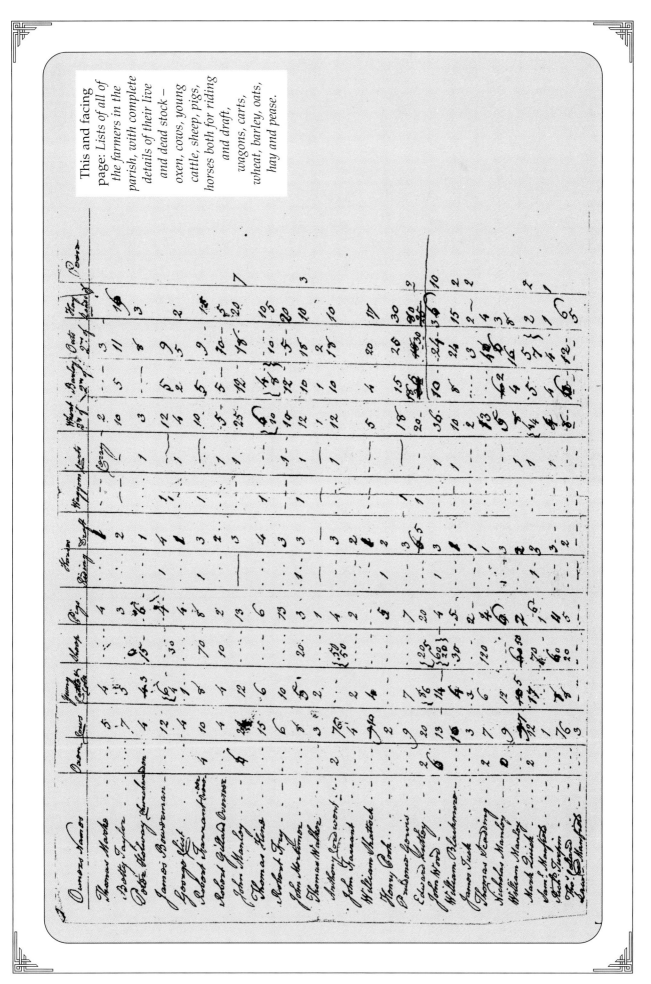

This and facing page: Lists of all of the farmers in the parish, with complete details of their live and dead stock – oxen, cows, young cattle, sheep, pigs, horses both for riding and draft, wagons, carts, wheat, barley, oats, hay and pease.

Oxen	Cows	Y Stock	Sheep	Pigs	Wheat	Oats	Barley	Hay	Straw	Potatoes Sacks	
1	10	4	30	2	3¾	2	—	4	1	—	J. B
2	12	6	10	2	10	2	3	5	2	4	J. W
1	4	4	—	2	2	—	—	1	—	—	J. S
2	7½	4	60	2	2	—	—	—	—	—	R. F
2	8½	2	27	17	4	2	—	—	1	7	N. J
	8½	6	12	3	3	—	2	2	1	2	T. K
	8	4	1	7	2	3	—	2	1	—	R. G
2	10	3	5	2	4	4	2	2	1	3	N. J
	4	2	10	2	—	—	—	—	—	—	W. H
	3	2	7	4	—	—	—	2	—	7	R. W
	8	5	33	2	5	—	—	1	—	—	E. L J. W
	9	7	—	2	2	—	—	1	—	—	J. B
	5	—	1	3	—	—	—	—	1	4	J. E
	2	—	—	—	—	—	—	—	—	—	
2	8	10	24	2	4	4	2	1½	—	6	N. M
2	16½	20	40	9	4	2	3	1½	2	20	
	8	1	—	—	—	—	—	—	—	—	
2	12	7	12	5	4	—	—	—	—	—	
4	16	14	90	11	7	3	2	6	2	—	
		—	52	—	—	—	—	4	—	—	G. V
	4	—	—	2	—	—	—	—	—	30	L. M
	1	3	20	10	—	—	½	—	—	—	
3	1	1	—	2	—	—	¼	—	—	—	
	2	—	—	—	—	—	—	—	—	30	
3	4	1	—	2	—	—	½	—	—	—	
	10	—	40	1	3	—	—	2	1	—	
	9	8	50	1	3	—	—	1	—	—	
2	7	8	60	10	6	6	3	1	—	15	
	1	1					1	10	1		
21	106	130	583	110	71	28	22	43	14	129	
26	131	140	713	92	73	32	13	30	1	72	
47	237	270	1296	202	144	60	35	73	15	201	

	208										
	131										
	339										
47			79	846	130						
	233	151	425	50							
	98	220	1271	180							
	331										

> This is a summary of the animals and crops in the village, prepared from the documents on pages 120–121.

Mr Rich. Fry — Wheat 250 Bushels / Barley 160 Do / Oats — 250 Do / Hay — 20 Load

Mr Robt Fry — Wheat — 80 Bushels / Barley 100 Do / Oats — 40 Do / Hay — 20 Load

Wm Scadding — Barly — 40 Bushels / Oats — 250 Do / Hay — 7 Load / Cart 1 Horse

P. L. Cook — Wheat — 10 Bushels / Barley — 40 Do / Oats — 40 Do / Hay — 5 Load

Adran Morgan — Cows 15 — Hefers 5 — Oxen 2 — Calfs 11 — Colts 1 — Pigs 19
Wheat ——— 50 Bushels
Oats ——— 400 Do
Pease —— 80 Do
Hay ——— 20 Load

Henry Manleys Wife & 2 Children		+
E. Gillard	2 Do	+
Robt Wood	2 Do	✓
James Sandors	3 Do	+
Aaron Scadding	1 Do	✓
Thos Lee	1 Do	✓
Henry Perry	2 Do	+
Henry Moons Wife &	2 Do	+
Cathn Wood	2 Do	✓
Wm Sprague	1 Do	✓
Thos Wood	4 & Do	✓
Jno Manley	4 & Do	✓
Robt Hitchcock	2 Do	✓
Hanna Salter	3 Do	✓
Joan Hartnole	1 Do	✓
Francis Hart	1 Do	✓
Peter Broomfield	2 Do	✓

Honor Sandors	1	Children
John Harts Wife &	2 Do	✓
James Clist	2 Do	✓
Peter Sarle	2 Do	✓
Robt Burrow	4 Do	✓
Wm Fry	1 Do	
John Wilde	1 Do	
Robt Spark	2 Do	
Saml Hine	4 Do	✓
John Hine	1 Do	✓
John Chard Wife &	3 Do	+

The top section of this document summarises the crop totals in the various tythings with the parish. The lower section lists labourers and their children.

Mr Robt Fry's Cart wife & 2 Children
Jas Harwood

6   *Saml Hine — 4 Childn*
John Hine

Mr Saml Farrants Waggon

Robt Woods — 2 Children

Hanna Salter + 3 do   *Robt Wood*

Joan Hurniold & Child 2

Francis Hart — 1 Child

Pr Bromfield — 2 do

Honor Sanders — 1 do

John Harts wife & 2 do

7   *Jas Clist — 2 do*

Peter Sorle — 2 do

Robt Burrow — 4 do

Anna Salter —
Ann Morgan
Mary Morgan
Ann Carter
Sarah Moon
Isaac Jones & wife
Ann Ridgway
Robt Manley

Jas Masey's wife & 1 Child

Thos Mark's Cart   Robert Manley

James Cofes 2 Children

7   *Judith Hart & Child*
John Clode — 2 Child

Mr Robt Farrant Waggon Robt Masey
Your Family 3

Wm Manley's wife & 2 Children

8   *Jas Benniford wife & 4 do*
John Scadding & wife
Provision & horsepower for the Poor

Mr Gervis Waggon
her Family 4

9   *Robt Clode wife & 3 Child*
Geo Moor's — 2 do
Pr Holway —
Mary Holway

Thomas Hine's Waggon

Cathr Loworthy — 2 Childn

Wm Sprague — 1 Child

Thos Wood — 4 Childn

5   *John Manley — 4 do*

Robt Hitchcock — 2 do

Betty Hitchcock Son 2   Driver

Sarah Hart — Son 2   John Hine

Susanna Manley —

Wm Fry — 1 Child

John Hide — 1 do

Robt Spark — 2 do

Mr Bowerman's Waggon   Jas Browning
Driver

Hanna Salter — 3 Childn

Joan Hurniold & Child —

6   *Francis Hart — 2 do*

Pr Bromfield — 3 do

Honor Sanders — 1

John Harts Wife — 2 do

Jas Clist — 2

Peter Sorle — 3

Robt Burrow — 4

Jas Masey wife & Child 2

Mr Clist a Cart
his wife

8   *John Manley's wife & 4 Children*

John Manley a Cart   Robt Burrow drive

Wm Manley wife & 2 Children

9   *John Scadding & wife*
Robt Sanders & 2 Children

Removal

Ashculme Tything Mr Cridlands
Waggon to take ——————

+   John Greenslades   3 Children
     Wm Burrow's ——   2 do
     John Pring's ——   1 do
     Wm Luxton's ——   2 do
     John Marshall's — 3 do
     James Thomas's —   1 do
     Richd Blackmore's — 2 do
     Wm Wright's — 2 do
     Wm Holway's ——   1 do
Thos Wm Holway's ——   1 do
     Judith Hart ————   1 do

+   Mr Cridlands Cart to take ——————
     Sarah Toler ——   Driver
     Dorothy Hitchcock ——   Roger Knight
     Eliz Greenslade ——   Wm Wright
     Thos Bromfield & wife ——

Culmdavy Mr Lutley's Waggon Driver John Clarke
     Geo. Salter's — 2 Children
     John Buncombe's — 2 do
     Edwd Chard's ——   4 do
     Cathn Hitchcock & Child
     Hannah Hitchcock & 2 Child
     Hannah Greedy's — 2 do
     Henry Toogood son
     Pr Holway
     & Mary Holway

John Mortimer's Waggon —
     Robt Chard's 3 Child
     Geo Moore's 2 do
     Robt Browning's Boy
     Wm Bennett's wife 3 Child
     John Chard's ——   2 do
     John Willey ——
     Thomzin Blackmore's 2 Child
     Hannah Ackland
     Ann Raphel
     Mary Holway —
     Rachel Hitchcock

Thomas Studley's Waggon to take ——
     his wife & 3 Child
     Daniel Jennings 3 Children
     Richd Manfield's — 1 do
     John Colling's ——   3 do
     John Woodrow's — 1 do   Driver
                                   Thos Moor
4   Robt Hutchings Child 1 do
     Roger Masey —   1 do
     John Elige   2 do
     Sarah Perry & — 1 do
     Thos Moon ——   1 do
     James Coles   2 do
                         Eliz Lane

Madford Mr Quick's Cart to take Geo. Morgan
            Jas. Tucks Family — 3
1   Henry Browning ——   1
     Thos Browning wife 2
                              Robt Grant
Nichs Manley's Cart to take do
            his 2 Child
2   John Perry's Family 3
     Bott Hitchcock & Child 2
            Eliz Sanders ——

     Saml Dorham
Thos & Wm Scadding's Cart Waggon
            his wife & 3 Child
     Wm Chard & wife
     Moses Scadding & Wife
4   Eleanor Scadding
     Mary Moon Mary & Mary Perry

Wm Manley's Cart —
     Mary Moon, Mary Carey
     Henry Moon's wife & 2 Child
3   Henry Perry's — 2 Child
     Aaron Scadding — 1 Child
     Thos Moo ——   1 do
     Jas Sanders   3 do

Mr Richd Fry's Cart
     Henry Manley's wife & 2 Child
5   Edwd Gillard's — 2 do
     John Chard wife & 3 do

Mr Scadding's Cart
     Mary Morgan, Ann Carter
     Sarah Moon, Isaac Jones & wife
     Ann Ridgway —

An Acco.t of Waggons and Carts — Oxen & Horses — Drivers

+ Mr John Redland one Waggon — — } 4 Oxen & 3 Horses { Roger Knight +
+   D.o — one Cart —   W.m Wright

  Mr Robert Farrant one Waggon — — } 4 Oxen & 3 Horses — { Robert Masey +
  D.o — one Cart

+ Mr Edw.d Lutley — two Waggons — 2 Oxen & 5 Horses { John Clarke +
    Geo. Salter

  Mr Jas Bowerman one D.o — — 4 Horses — James Browning +
+ John Mortimer — one D.o — — 3 D.o — Hugh Morgan +
+ Thomas Studley — one D.o — 2 D.o — Tho.s Moon +
  Mr John Holway — a Carry — 2 D.o — Tho.s Chard
  William Shattock — 2 D.o

  John Wood — a Carry & Cart — 3 D.o & 4 Oxen { John Doman +
    Rt.d Browning
  Mrs Gorwis — a Waggon — 0 D.o
  Grace Morgan — a Carry — 2 D.o 2 Oxen — Sam.l Loaman +
+ Thomas Hine — a Waggon — 3 D.o — John Hine +
  Rich.d Gill — a Cart — 1 D.o — E. Manning +
  Rob.t Gillard — a Cart — 2 D.o — E. Gillard
  Geo. Clist — a Cart — 1 D.o
+ William Manley — a Cart — 2 D.o — Jas. Manley +
  John Manley — a Cart — 2 D.o — Rob.t Burrow +
  Adrian Morgan — a Cart — 2 D.o — W.m Scadding
  William Webber — a Cart — 2 D.o
  Rich.d Blackmore — a Cart — 2 D.o — John Blackmore
+ Rich.d Fry — a Cart — 2 D.o — Henry Willey +
+ Charles Scadding — a Cart — 2 D.o — Jas Moon +
+ Mr Mark Quick — a Cart — 2 D.o — Geo. Morgan +
  Peter Holway — a Cart — 2 D.o
  Richard Bowerman a Cart — 1 D.o
  Richard Turpin — a Cart — 3 D.o — Rob.t Turpin +
  Thomas Collard — a Cart — 2 D.o — Francis Willey
  Thomas Marke — a Carry — 2 D.o — Robert Manley
  Betty Taylor — a Cart — 2 D.o
+ Nich.s Manley — a Cart — 2 D.o — Robert Grant
+ Mr Rob.t Fry — a Carry — 2 D.o — Henry Flay —
1.st + William Scadding — a Cart — 1 D.o — Tho.s Wo
+ Mr Samuel Farrant a Waggon — 2 D.o & 4 Oxen Rob.t Wood / W.m Hitchcock +
  Tho.s Scadding — a Waggon — 1 D.o & 1 Oxen Thomas / John Dorham
  Mrs Gorwis — D.o 3 D.o — John Serle

The final list of the farmers, their wagons and carts, the oxen and horses to pull them, and the drivers.

CIVIL UNREST

Both volunteers and militia had not had to face the reality of invasion but as the 19th century dawned, they were called upon to deal with civil unrest – in this case in the form of food riots which broke out at the end of 1800 and early 1801. The prices of grain, bread and butter, and indeed food in general, rose, putting many items beyond the means of most ordinary folk. Mobs began to intimidate farmers and merchants trying to force them to lower their prices, and there was a certain amount of arson (although with minimal personal injury). The riots were widespread – being seen in Exeter, Taunton and Wellington, Honiton and Exmouth – in fact virtually everywhere. Unfortunately in many places the volunteers were actually involved, sometimes being the ringleaders. The 'Establishment' tended to sympathise with the population, General Simcoe, for example, describing them as 'being driven by want'. He even made a handsome donation to a fund in Honiton to help alleviate the problems of the needy; in many places the gentry and better off did their best to improve the situation.

Hemyock was not involved in these riots. As with the Monmouth Rebellion so many years before the parishioners decided to keep a low profile and gave the authorities no cause for alarm. In fact, on 7 April 1801, the Revd John Land, Rector of Hemyock, wrote a lengthy letter to General Simcoe about the situation locally, especially in nearby Wellington. Land wrote that although the poor of Hemyock were suffering they refused to take part in the 'tumultuous & Disgraceful Proceedings of that Town'. Those 'tumultuous Proceedings' in Somerset did lead to some hangings at the Stonegallows in Taunton, but fortunately the disturbances were not long lived and peace was soon restored to the countryside.

SECOND WORLD WAR

We now move to the next threat of invasion, which came with the Second World War, when once more a home-defence force had to be created, the Home Guard. This time the threat of invasion came from the Germans not the French. Soon after the outbreak of war the LDVs (Local Defence Volunteers) were formed, later to become the Home Guard. The Hemyock Home Guard was commanded at first by Captain Cubitt with Lieutenant Lowry. The NCOs were Sergeant Pooley and Corporal Hutchings. Gradually, with extensive training the local Home Guard became a very useful defence force.

A number of Hemyock evacuee boys dressed as 'Junior' Home Guard members.

The headquarters for Hemyock's Home Guard was at the milk factory, an ideal place because many of the men worked there. As with everywhere else in the country, uniforms and equipment, and particularly guns, were scarce. The Home Guard often had to drill with broomsticks until rifles became available. Once they arrived, the men were taken for shooting practice at the ranges on a 'Redwoods' bus. The Home Guard patrolled the parish boundaries and the hills, and they also helped guard the White Ball railway tunnel. Fortunately, like the volunteers of the 18th century, they were never called upon to do battle with the enemy in Hemyock or elsewhere in the country.

A platoon of the Army Cadets was also formed in Hemyock, with Lieutenant Howard (an evacuated schoolmaster from Bristol) as the Commanding Officer and Cecil Lowman the Sergeant. 'Skip' Lowman subsequently came to fame with the Scout Group he formed and led in the village. A copy of an order issued to an army cadet (then aged 13) reproduced on page 128 shows what a responsible position the young cadets had in time of war.

What impact did the Second World War have on the village of Hemyock and its people? Among the earliest signs that trouble was brewing were leaflets about precautions against possible air raids and the use of poison gas which came through parishioners' letterboxes, but the large cities were at a great distance from us and the villagers remained confident that war was an urban not a rural threat. Even when in 1939 residents were called to the local school to be issued with individual gas masks, they didn't really think that they would ever be needed. Soon afterwards the village learnt that it had to prepare for a possible war.

Air Raid Wardens were appointed and trained. Their purpose was to ensure that the windows of every house were blacked out, so that no light from any house could be seen from outside. The wardens had to be on the streets should an air raid occur. Billeting Officers had to be in place to receive and find homes for evacuees.

An Auxiliary Fire Service was established manned by volunteers from the village and they had at their disposal a new trailer water pump, purchased by parishioners from an obscure fund that was collected some years before to provide a swimming pool for the village (a plan which had foundered because of a dispute over whether there should have been mixed-sex bathing and whether the pool should be open on Sundays). This pump was kept in an implement shed in the Castle and remained there for some time after the end of the

Hemyock Home Guard, early 1940s.
Left to right, back: Geoff James, Leslie Hart, Stanley Salter, Stanley Lowman, Chris Doble, Frank Lowman,
George Salter, Percy Pike, Albert Salter, Stanley Doble, Harry Richards, Leonard Stuart, Jack Wood,
Roy Granger, Harold Durman;
middle: Arthur Shire, Bill Pike, Jack Trenchard, Frank Simmonds, Dennis Pring, Cedric Jenkins, Eric Cubitt,
? Chichester, Jim Hart, Dr Muir, George Gammon, Dick Granger, Walter Lee, Jack Lilley;
front: Fred Clark, Fred Lawrence, Jim Lowman, Bill Alway, Bill Trickey, Dick Pooley, Harold Cubitt, H. Lowry,
R. Thorne, George Franks, Bill Hutchings, Jim Woodgate, Harry Bale, Bill Bradford, Harry Trickey.

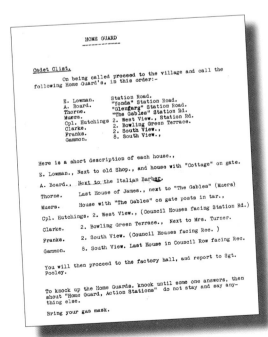

war. Its eventual whereabouts remain a mystery to this day.

The pump was never used to extinguish any fires caused by enemy action. However, during the war, on one occasion, it was used for a whole week in an attempt to put out a fire that had set alight a hedge made of peat. The glow was visible to any aircraft flying overhead – an event which is perhaps best forgotten.

War was declared on 3 September 1939 and the impact of this declaration was almost immediate in the village. Four days later nine unofficial evacuees arrived. On 28 February 1940, 20 more arrived from Stepney, on 18 June 121 children and their teachers arrived from Edmonton and in February 1941, 31 came from Bristol. Finally, in July 1944, the last

Left: *Orders issued to an Army cadet in the event of an invasion taking place.*

contingent of children arrived – this time there were 38 of them and they were sent from London, 'as a result', so it is recorded in the records, 'of pilotless raids on London'. These were of course raids by the V1 rockets which became known as 'Doodlebugs'. Chris Dracott remembers these weapons well, having lived in London through the Blitz, and V1 and V2 attacks when a regular experience was listening to the droning of the V1 engines, the eerie silence after the engines cut out, the suspense as the weapons glided down to their targets and the tremendous explosion seconds later, sometimes some distance away, sometimes uncomfortably close.

Naturally the evacuees did not all remain in Hemyock for the duration of the war, they came and they went back intermittently. It was the job of the Billeting Officer and his helpers to find homes for evacuees who arrived in the village, usually with less than 24 hours' notice. Great tact was required in their placement because the children who were better dressed and more attractive were the easiest to find homes for. It is interesting to note that some evacuees later married local people and are still living with us today.

The advent of the blackout meant that at night it was extremely dark; there were no street lights, the few cars that there were in the village could not use their headlights (a shade had to be fixed over the lens with just three narrow slits in it), bicycles had to have lights with a curious semi-spherical hood covering the light source, and all the house windows were blacked out. Fortunately in the days when everyone walked almost everywhere all the potential hazards in the village were known, so groping about in the dark was not too difficult.

The church bells were silent; they could only be rung to announce an invasion. All evening church services were cancelled for the first few years of the war. All the signposts indicating the direction of nearby villages and towns were removed, causing additional problems. As time wore on more and more parishioners, both men and women, were conscripted, and those who remained were either too old to do military service, were in reserved occupations, or had a medical problem that prevented active service. In consequence the remaining workforce dwindled and it was normal practice for farmers, who before the war had a full-time farm worker, to have to share their employee with another farmer. Petrol was very scarce and was rationed and cars could only be used for essential journeys. A zone of some ten miles from the coast was sealed off almost completely.

Food was strictly rationed but fortunately, being a rural parish, there was always just enough. Every effort was made to produce food, and gardeners concentrated on vegetables. The farmers were directed to grow certain crops by the much disliked 'War Agricultural Executive Committee' whose local knowledge of the land (or lack of it) led to some bizarre decisions. To assist with the shortage of labour Land Girls arrived, and obviously became very popular. Hemyock had two whose unpleasant job it was to kill rats to help prevent too much valuable food from being wasted.

There were pursuits for children to engage in during the war, but they were far from normal. In the summer of 1940 there was a plague of cabbage white butterflies in the area and during the school holidays there was a campaign to catch them; children went throughout the district netting them, after which they would take them to the school to receive payment.

To provide additional food parishioners were encouraged to fatten a pig to be used for home consumption. Sheds to house these animals appeared everywhere and the village even had an official pig club! Educational classes were arranged to teach people how to preserve the pork by salting. In wartime food for these pigs was scarce, and to supplement their rations children were encouraged to collect acorns (known locally as mace), which were sold for 7d. a peck (3p for 3 kilos).

To ensure that babies had a healthy start in life theywere issued with rosehip syrup free of charge. Once again, the rosehips had to be collected by hand and this took place in the autumn. We must not forget jam making! This was organised on a communal basis by the Women's Institute, a special allowance of sugar being made available for the purpose and great quantities of jam being bottled and sent off to a central collecting point.

With no less than three airfields on the surrounding hills the village had a large influx of service personnel. The airfield at Dunkeswell, built for the RAF, was quickly taken over by the US Navy. It was from Dunkeswell that the late President Kennedy's brother flew on his last fateful mission. The airfield at Upottery was constructed as a base for the invasion of Europe and it housed American soldiers with their Dakota aircraft and accompanying gliders. At Trickey Warren (later renamed Churchstanton) a fighter aircraft station was established, manned at first by Czech and Polish airmen. Hemyock seemed to be full of military vehicles, especially jeeps, invariably driven at high speed on the wrong side of the road. Because of this presence the parish was bombed on several occasions; and not all of the bombs exploded.

Ministry of Information films were shown in the village and residents were encouraged to be watchful of the surrounding area. Everyday life was taken over by rumour. Was the research chemist with a German-sounding-name and seconded to the milk factory to do research, actually a spy? The elderly Italian who opened a barber's shop in Station Road was similarly suspected. Hemyock was indeed an interesting place to live in during the war.

The unexploded bomb at Mackham Farm during the Second World War with members of the Forbear family (and the dog) posing for the photo. Presumably the soldier had defused the bomb? At least one other unexploded bomb still remains buried in the area.

A number of the evacuees who stayed and still live in Hemyock, May 2000.
Left to right: Betty Arnold, her brother John Dimmock and Ted Tartaglia.

CHAPTER THIRTEEN

Entertainment

 In 1931 a few people in the village decided to form an amateur theatrical group. Calling themselves the 'Hemyock Players', they staged their first production, with the delightful title of *Lady Gorringe's Necklace*, in the same year. The producer was Dr John Griffin (senr). The players in that production were the Revd Ketchley, Mr Anderson, Bill Griffiths, Dot Fox, Ted Hassan, Kathleen Curtis, Mrs Farrant, Mr Cundict, Mrs Agar and 'Queenie' Pring.

Another of these early productions was *Lord Richard in the Pantry* in which Dr Griffin acted this time instead of directing, with other members of the cast including Mr Prowse, Mr Cundict, William Griffiths, Miss Agar, Revd Ketchley, Mr E. Hassan, Mrs Cundict, Miss Ella Hookway, Miss Queenie Pring, Miss Phyllis James, Mrs E. Farrant and Miss Laura Cload.

The people of Hemyock also had the benefit of going to the pictures in the late 1930s and early 1940s. There was no cinema in the village but two enterprising gentlemen, namely Bill Griffiths and Richard Pooley, set up G.P. Pictures (Hemyock) and screened popular films of the day in the Parish Hall, these films being hired from the Gaumont Cinema in Taunton. Comedy was a favourite and the films that were most popular included *Boys will be Boys*, starring one of the most famous actors of the silver screen, Will Hay, and Stanley Holloway in *Road House*. Admission to these performances was 6d. and 1s.0d. (including tax). Children were, of course, half price. These film shows continued during and after the war for some years. During the war and in the immediate post-war years some village entertainment was provided by the 1st Hemyock Guides, Scouts and Wolf clubs. More details about these activities will be given in Chapter Seventeen.

The milk factory also produced a number of shows over the years, especially pantomimes. One such production was staged to raise money for the Hemyock Welcome Home and Victory Fund. The

pantomime, *Sinbad the Sailor* (written by Margaret Carter) was presented by the Wilts United Dairies (Hemyock) Social and Welfare Club. The producers and stage managers were Ronald Edmondson and William Griffiths, with the lead role of Sinbad being played by Elsie Board.

Over the years various groups within the village have produced concerts and shows too numerous to list but they included the *Good Old Days* and the *1940s Show*, both staged in the 1980s.

There is little question, however, that the world of 'entertainment' in Hemyock has been dominated by the 'Hemyock Singers' for the past 25 years or so. The Singers evolved from what was known as the Hemyock Leisure Centre or Hemyock Leisure Group. Established in 1971, the aim of the Leisure Group was to encourage villagers to participate in a variety of leisure activities on a 'pay as you go' basis with voluntary leaders. It was an attempt to tap the various skills, talents and interests within Hemyock for the benefit of individuals and the community as a whole. The principal meeting place was the old Hemyock Primary School, then under the headmastership of Clive Richardson. The first committee, as shown in the minute-book, consisted of Mr J. Bustard, Mrs E. Culverwell, Mr M. Dear, Mrs M. Gregory, Mr R.J. Lipscombe, Mrs J.D. Meads, plus the school's headmaster. The Chairman was John Eden. The project was quite a success in the early days, and the activities and studies included woodwork, play reading, embroidery, local history, languages, painting, photography and music. The music group began as a musical appreciation gathering, where members would listen to a wide variety of gramophone records and simply enjoy the music. With the passage of time this developed into giving concert performances of Gilbert and Sullivan and other works. Eventually, under the leadership of Clive Richardson, the group progressed to give full stage performances.

The Leisure Centre was wound up in 1983. Some of its activities had been successful, others less so. The local history group, for example, produced a

EARLY ENTERTAINMENT

Left: *The Wilts United Dairies Pantomime, c.1947/8. Left to right: P. Lowman, S. Northam, P. Northam, Shirley Northam, B. Northam, J. Leckie, R. Trickey, V. Weeks, J. Summers, A. Board, S. McKee, E. Alway.*

Right: Lord Richard in The Pantry, *c.early 1930s. Left to right, standing: Dr John Griffin senr, Mr Prowse, Mr Cundict, Bill Griffiths, Miss Agar, Revd L. Ketchley, Ted Hassan; seated: Mrs Cundict, Miss Ella Hookway, Miss Queenie Pring, Miss Phyllis James, Mrs E. Farrant, Miss Laura Cload.*

Bottom left: *A poster for Hemyock Film Show.*

Left: *The Wilts United Dairies pantomime chorus, c.1947/8. Left to right: Y. Summers, A. Alway, K. Trickey, W. Ashton, W. Northam, ? Alway, R. Lowman, J. Hassan, J. Hawkins; front: B. Trickey, J. Miller, R. Pike, P. Wilson, B. Bird, B. Perrott.*

Below: Lady Gorringe's Necklace, *c.early 1930s. Left to right, back: Revd Leslie Ketchley, Mr Anderson, Dot Tose (?), Bill Griffiths, Ted Hassan; in front: Kathleen Curtis, Mrs E. Farrant, Mr Condict, Miss Agar, 'Queenie' Pring.*

HEMYOCK
Parish Hall.
WEDNESDAY, 19th OCT.
Doors Open 6.30 p.m. Commencing 7 p.m.

G. P. PICTURES (Hemyock)
PRESENTS
STANLEY
HOLLOWAY
IN
ROAD-
HOUSE
Certificate A   ALSO
BIRD SANCTUARY
also SUPPORTING PROGRAMME
The Management reserve the right to alter the
Programme if necessary.

Admission 6d. & 1/- (including Tax)
LIMITED NUMBER AT 9d.
CHILDREN HALF-PRICE.

valuable historical booklet entitled *Hemyock v France* in 1974, but the real success story is that of the Hemyock Singers.

In 1973 the music group (as it then was) gave a concert performance of Gilbert and Sullivan's *Iolanthe*, followed in 1974 by a concert performance of *The Gondoliers*. Next came three performances of Stainer's *Cricifixion* and in 1975 the Singers staged their first full stage performance, HMS *Pinafore*. *Merrie England* was their show for 1976, *The Mikado* in '77, followed by a return to their early shows – *Iolanthe* in 1978 and *The Gondoliers* in 1979. The 1980s began for the group with *The Pirates of Penzance* in 1981, *The Sorcerer* the following season and *Patience* in 1984. Gilbert and Sullivan music was always a favourite with performers and audiences alike.

By 1984 the dedicated band was no longer part of the Leisure Group but had become the 'Hemyock Singers' under the chairmanship of Jack Jones whose magnificent bass voice will never be forgotten by those who heard it. The musical director/producer for the concert and stage performances was Clive Richardson until his retirement in 1980, when he was followed by Ron White.

In *The Pirates of Penzance*, Revd Tony Grosse played the role of Major-General Stanley, and the Pirate King was played by Ron White with Clive Richardson as Samuel, Ron Coe as Frederic and Mike Aston as the Sergeant of Police. The principal ladies' roles were performed by Barbara Churchill, Barbara Bowden and Patsy Ruffell-Hazell as the General's daughters Mabel, Edith and Kate. One of the 'greats' of the Hemyock Singers, Polly Eden, was cast as Ruth. The chorus was joined by the audience who were supplied with song sheets for each performance.

Every year, apart from producing a stage show or concert performances, the Singers have also sung choral works in the church at Easter and have performed at other venues outside the village. The choral performances have been a long-standing tradition continued to this day and works have included Vivaldi's *Gloria*, Handel's *Messiah*, Faure's *Requiem* and many others.

In 1985 came a marked change of direction for the Singers; a move from the traditional to the popular large scale musical shows. The first of these was *My Fair Lady*. The group had a new director, the multi-talented Nick Lawrence, a man who was always able to get the very best out of his cast. Performed for three nights this show was a tremendous success. The way had been paved for the Singers to produce many great musicals, and to become members of the National Operatic and Dramatic Society (NODA), winning a number of top awards for their productions. Such was the significance of *My Fair Lady* that the names of those involved should not go unrecorded. The role of Professor Higgins was played by Tony Grosse, Eliza Doolittle, the cockney flower girl who became a lady, by Patsy Ruffell-Hazell, Alfred Doolittle by Ron Coe, Colonel Pickering by Chris Dracott and Mrs Pearce by Polly Eden. Graham Whitlock played Freddie Eynsford-Hill. Other roles were played by Pat Ewins, Elsie Board, Alan Bell, David Bawler, Faye Patten, Magda Gilroy, Lily Quantick and David Palmer. In the chorus were Gwen Barnes, Janice Bawler, Sylvia Child, Joan Coe, Shirley Dracott, Janet Elworthy, Ros Ford, Pearl Gentle, Eve Gilroy, Joan Lutley, Ann Rochell, Jean Wayland, Rene Wright, George Barnes, Francis Bustard, Dick Drew and Ted Wassink. Piano accompaniment was provided by Joan Lawrence and Frances Hart. A future Chairman of the Singers, Muriel Bater, was the prompt. Graham Whitlock later became a professional actor and Janet Elworthy, after years as a performing member of the group, became a producer in her own right.

In 1986 came *Fiddler on the Roof*, produced and directed by Nick Lawrence. Tony Grosse took the lead role of Tevye with Polly Eden as his wife Golde. New members had joined the group and took important roles in this production, among them David Stepney, Chris Poole, Martin Root, John Mallinson and Andrew Sandilands. One scene, done in the best possible taste of course, involved Tevye and Golde sharing a bed on the stage. During one performance this led to a gentleman with a very loud voice and broad Devon accent, declaring, 'Here, Vicar be in bed with Mrs Eden' – the audience loved it. Sadly this was to be Jack Jones' last performance.

The show in 1987 was *Finian's Rainbow* with Chris Dracott playing the alcohol-loving Irishman, Patsy Ruffell-Hazell his daughter and Magda Gilroy the all-important leprechaun, Og. Once again Nick Lawrence directed.

The following year the Singers found themselves in the Wild West of America with the very popular *Annie Get Your Gun*. The lead part of the sharp-shooting Annie Oakley was played by Sue Batten, Nick Lawrence, as well as directing, played the 'romantic' lead Frank Butler, Tony Grosse was Charlie Davenport, Chris Dracott was Buffalo Bill Cody (with home-grown whiskers for the part) and Dave Stepney a superbly attired Sioux chief, Sitting Bull. As often happens in amateur productions, many of the best moments are completely unintentional. In one scene Annie Oakley had to display her skills as a crack shot. This entailed her aiming her stage rifle high into the air, and following the sound of a shot a stage hand would throw a stuffed pigeon on to the stage and the cast would applaud. Unfortunately in one performance the timing went a bit awry. Annie pointed her rifle, the pigeon was duly lobbed on to the stage, then as an afterthought, the shot was heard – another classic.

The following year saw the Singers in ancient Greece with Offenbach's *La Belle Helene* with Tony Grosse as Calchas the High Priest of Jupiter (an

133

❧ The Hemyock ❧ Singers

Below: Iolanthe, *1978. Left to right: Gwen Barnes, Alan Bell, Bryony Aston, John Ellis, Barbara Bowden, Tony Grosse, Polly Eden, Jack Jones, Penny Trickey, Ron Coe, June Sparks.*

Above: Merrie England, *1976. Principals – standing on the left, Alan Bell as Sir Walter Raleigh and Barbara Bowden as Bessie Throckmorton, standing front right Polly Eden as Queen Elizabeth and Jack Jones as the Earl of Essex, kneeling are John Ellis, Penny Trickey, John Ives, Sally Jackson, Tony Grosse and Judith Lord with the full chorus.*

Left: HMS Pinafore, *1975.*

Below: *A scene from* My Fair Lady, *1985. Left to right: Tony Grosse as Professor Higggins, Patsy Ruffell-Hazell as Eliza Doolittle and Chris Dracott as Colonel Pickering.*

Below left: *Award-winning programme for the show* Oliver, *1995.*

Above: Scrooge, *1990.*

Right: No Time For Fig Leaves, *1999. Left to right, back: Caroline Pinder, Julie Bailey, Alison Robson, Bob Hawkes; middle: Sally Cartledge, Sarah Summers, Christine Stepney, Stuart Summers, Anne Monk; front: Nicola Bailey, Catherine Wall.*

Above: Fiddler on the Roof, *1986. Left to right: Tony Grosse, Paulette Daniels, Janet Elworthy, Polly Eden as Golde, Faye Patten, Rebekah Bawler, Anne Rochell and David Stepney.*

Right: *Tony Grosse as Fagin in his den with his gang of young thieves from* Oliver, *1995.*

Above: Calamity Jane, 1997. *In the Golden Garter Saloon, left to right: Tony Baker as Wild Bill Hickock, Sally Cartledge, a saloon girl, David Bawler, in front of him Annie Metcalfe as Calamity Jane with Monica Smith, Christine Stepney, David Sprague, Jack Hull and Nicola Keith. Seated are Alan Coles and Stuart Summers.*

Above: The Wizard of Oz, 1993. *Left to right: Lucy Eveleigh as Dorothy, David Stepney as the Lion, Tony Grosse as the Tinman and Steve Warden as the Scarecrow.*

Right: Wind in The Willows, 1991, *showing the award-winning scenery with the gypsy caravan. Left to right: Tony Grosse as Mole, Patsy Ruffell-Hazell as Ratty, Chris Dracott as Toad and of course the horse hiding Thomas Palmer and James Palmer (unrelated).*

inspired piece of casting), Janet Elworthy as the beautiful Helen, Queen of Sparta, David Stepney as Paris, a prince of Troy, Chris Poole and Ron Coe as Kings Ajax 1 and 2 and Chris Dracott as Agamemnon. Once again Nick Lawrence directed and Lynn Caygill conducted the small orchestra.

In 1990 the singers tackled the Dickensian world of *Scrooge*. The miserly Ebeneezer Scrooge was played by Chris Dracott with Chris Poole as Scrooge's unfortunate clerk Bob Crachit, Martin Stepney as Tiny Tim – who brought a tear to many an eye – Geoff Sworder was duly frightening as the ghost of Jacob Marley and the ghost of Christmas yet to come. Eve Grosse was the ghost of Christmas past and Janet Elworthy the ghost of Christmas present. Other members of the still growing company played the many cameo roles offered by this musical and the chorus. A particular feature of this production was the increased number of youngsters taking part, from the very young to teenagers. Many of these young people were to appear in future productions and hopefully will continue to do so. One youngster, Martin Stepney, subsequently appeared in productions on television and at the Brewhouse Theatre in Taunton having acquired the taste for acting and singing with shows such as *Scrooge*. The award-winning programme for the show was designed and drawn by Eve Grosse. It outlined the whole story as a series of pictures in the style of a Victorian comic and was a work of art in itself.

Obviously a large support team was required for ambitious productions such as this. Apart from Nick Lawrence, the musical director, and Andrew Sandilands, the producer, the all-important stage manager was Muriel Bater (by now Chairman of the group), Claude Capel was responsible for the lighting, Jo Wilson-Hunt took care of the costumes and appeared on stage, Barbara Churchill acted as prompt, and David Bawler, as always, was the stage builder/carpenter. Added to that there were numerous people dealing with props, the stage hands, the front of house 'volunteers', and the two musicians, Joan Lawrence on the piano and Norman Leighton playing the violin. All in all 41 individuals appeared on stage and another 18 worked off stage, so it was quite a sizeable company.

The year 1991 saw a musical that was a complete contrast to *Scrooge, The Wind in the Willows*. A new director had come on the scene in the shape of Graham Balchin and Veronica Barnes was musical director. One of the most important features of this production was the magnificent, award-winning scenery, designed by Eve Grosse and constructed by David Bawler and others. The costumes and make up were also of the highest quality.

The riverside quartet of Kenneth Grahame's immortal tale were played by Chris Dracott, Patsy Ruffell-Hazell, Tony Grosse and Janet Elworthy as Toad, Ratty, Mole and Badger respectively. Eve

Grosse was a suitably evil Weasel and Pat Keith a far nicer Mrs Otter. Once again, this show brought in many more children.

Wally Cotgrave was the new producer for the 1992 offering, *Annie*. Because of laws governing the appearances of children on stage the lead role of the orphan Annie was jointly played by Cheryl Loker and Johanna Elworthy, the young ladies performing on alternate nights.

Another American-style musical followed in 1993, *The Wizard of Oz*, in which the lead role of Dorothy (played in the film version by Judy Garland) was played delightfully by Lucy Eveleigh. Her travelling companions Scarecrow, Tinman and the Lion were played by Steve Warden, Tony Grosse and David Stepney. This trio were almost unrecognisable in their make up and costumes. One scene that brought the house down at every performance was when the Wicked Witch of the West (Patsy Ruffell-Hazell) was thrown into her cauldron and re-emerged very much reduced in size (the miniature witch being played by Sarah Summers).

In 1994, *Hello Dolly* was produced by Shaun Patchett with Hilary Wickham as musical director. Tracey Hayes was a big hit as Dolly with a supporting cast that included Caroline Pinder, Matt and Steve Warden, Tony Grosse, Georgie Mudditt, David Stepney, Ian Oliver, Anne Rochell, Janet Elworthy, Pat Keith, Ron Coe, Kevin Bessell, David Bawler and many more. This production was dedicated to the man who had played such an important part in launching what became the Hemyock Singers, Clive Richardson. Clive and his wife had gone to live in Australia after his retirement where he sadly died a month before the show was performed.

In 1995 came the award-winning *Oliver*, produced by Janet Elworthy with Hilary Wickham as musical director. For the first time the company ran a show for five nights. With a nightly audience of 150 it was watched by 750 people in one week – not bad for a village group. Two young Hemyock lads, Oliver Cartledge and Daniel Blackmore, shared the lead role. The scheming Fagin was played by Tony Grosse. A terrifying Bill Sykes was played by David Stepney with Joanne Wilson-Hunt as the doomed Nancy. This was a highly successful production and the efforts of the large cast and all others involved in the performance resulted in *Oliver* receiving the National Operatic and Dramatic Association's Regional Award for Excellence, plus NODA's area programme award (designed by Debbie Keith).

By way of a change the following year the Singers presented a concert which comprised a selection of songs and poetry reflecting the four seasons of the year directed by Shaun Patchett with musical direction by Norman Leighton.

In 1997, it was back to the Wild West with *Calamity Jane*, produced by Janet Elworthy. In common with many singing and dramatic groups,

The Hemyock Singers were finding it difficult to fill leading parts, particularly male roles. Fortunately some new blood was forthcoming for this show and Calamity Jane was played with gusto by Annie Metcalfe, her friend Wild Bill Hickock by Tony Baker, Lieutenant Gilmartin by Bob Hawkes and Katie Brown by Joanne Wilson-Hunt. Chris Dracott played the saloon keeper Henry Miller and Venetia Nowell was his niece Susan. Chris Poole was Francis Fryer. This show also won an area programme award from NODA for a programme designed by Debbie Keith.

There was another change of producer in 1998 when Mary Willis produced *Anything Goes*, once again an American musical comedy. Lead roles were played by Jo Wilson-Hunt, Tony Baker, Annie Metcalfe, Venetia Nowell, Bob Hawkes, Alan Coles, Caroline Pinder and others.

In 1999 lack of numbers and difficulty in finding a producer meant that a musical was out of the question and instead a small group of the singers staged a comedy, *No Time for Fig Leaves*, set in a post-nuclear-war England. The cast produced and directed the play themselves with considerable success. The 'players' were Sally Cartledge, Anne Monk, Christine Stepney, Caroline Pinder, Bob Hawkes, Julie Bailey, Stuart and Sarah Summers and Alison Robson with Nicola Bailey and Catherine Wall. The performances were dedicated to David Stepney, a stalwart of the Hemyock Singers for some years, who sadly died in October 1998.

Yet another change of direction came in 2000 when the Singers performed the pantomime *Cinderella*, with Alison Robson as 'Cinders', Caroline Pinder and Anne Monk as the ugly sisters and Gillian Hawkes as the wicked stepmother. Stuart Summers scored a hit as Buttons. Gary Butland was Prince Charming and Matt Warden was Dandini. Bob Hawkes, Sally Cartledge and other familiar and not so familiar faces filled the variety of parts called for in this panto. Pantomime is always a popular choice with audiences young and old and a tradition of performing panto had begun in the village at the milk factory decades earlier. The decision to revive the custom went down well and although there may not be one every year it seems likely that pantomime will figure largely in the Singers' plans now and then over the next few years.

The future of the Hemyock Singers should be a bright one. Many of the 'old stagers' have gone but there seems to be a good supply of new blood. The choral aspect of the singing has continued to be very well supported year by year under the guiding hand of Norman Leighton ably supported by Joan Lawrence. Many old friends have died, including the much loved Muriel Bater, but no matter what the future might hold for the Hemyock Singers, the show will always go on.

There is one very important aspect of staging these sort of productions that merits a mention. The performances staged by the Hemyock Singers are always put on in the Hemyock Parish Hall which is inevitably heavily booked by groups and organisations throughout the year. In recent years the Singers' productions have been staged during the autumn half term. One of the principal reasons for this is that when a production is being put on a complete stage and set have to be built over the weekend preceeding the show, lighting rehearsals have to be held plus a dress rehearsal, the seats have to be put out and a multitude of other tasks undertaken. All of this can only run smoothly thanks to the willingness of other groups to give up their hall bookings for the whole period of stage building, the show and the dismantling process. It is very much a Hemyock affair and illustrates extremely well the spirit of co-operation that exists in the village.

A final postscript. Hemyock does not always rely on its own resources for entertainment. Over the years the village has been fortunate enough to be visited by many well-known choirs, singers and orchestras, including the Devon and Cornwall Police Band, the Caerphilly Male Voice Choir, the internationally renowned harpist Annie Mawson, a Norwegian Youth Orchestra and many more. Drama has been catered for by the Cygnet Theatre performing Shakespeare, and after building a stage the Common Players gave open-air performances on the village Recreation Ground. All of these performers have found appreciative audiences in Hemyock and many of them have vowed to return again.

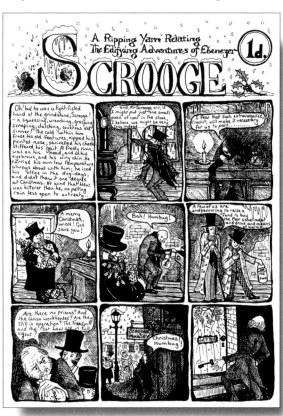

Eve Grosse's wonderful programme for Scrooge, *1990.*

CHAPTER FOURTEEN

Sporting Life

Hemyock today is fortunate in having a number of thriving sports clubs. There is a splendid bowling green, a tennis court and the Recreation Ground where the seasonal sports of soccer and cricket are played. For those more inclined towards indoor sports there are snooker and badminton clubs and of course skittles teams.

BOWLING

Pride of place as the oldest club in the village goes to the Hemyock Bowling Club although soccer and cricket were probably played in the village at the beginning of the 20th century if not earlier. The Hemyock Bowling Club was founded in July 1905, so its centenary is not that far away. The founders were a group of local businessmen, farmers and the headmaster of Hemyock Primary School Mr A.T. Baxter. The first President of the club was Revd John de Burgh Forbes. In the first bowling season, 1906, there were 32 registered members, a total that included 11 'lads'. The lads paid a membership fee of 1s.6d. a year, full members 3s.0d. a year. Fortunately Mr Baxter, who was Secretary for some years, kept excellent minutes which make fascinating reading.

In the early days Mr W. Tait was Treasurer and he had to handle sums of money and outgoing expenses which his more recent successors would no doubt be quite envious of. The first set of figures in the minutes, for example, records members' subscriptions totalling £3.19s.6d. – this income being boosted by generous donations of £32.2s.6d. The club expenditure included one year's rent to Mrs Tapscott of £1.5s.0d., 1s.0d. for rolling the ground and another 1s.0d. for grass cutting.

The first Bowling Club Committee consisted of Revd de Burgh Forbes, W. Tait, J. Clist, H.B. Whyte, C.J. Carrick, A. Wide, R. Tait and A.T. Baxter. The committee was later joined by G. Clist and M.

Lowman. Obviously one of the primary needs of the club was a clubhouse (described in the minutes as a bowls house) and in March 1906 the idea was put forward to obtain an old tramcar from the Metropolis. Presumably plenty were available in those days. The matter was investigated and at a committee meeting in May the Treasurer stated that a disused tramcar could be obtained from London for between £3 and £6. Added to that Pickfords would require £2.10s.0d. for putting the car on the rail at Paddington and the cost of transporting it to Tiverton would be a further £6. This was all considered far too costly a project and the problem was eventually overcome by approaching one of the club's Vice-Presidents, Sir Charles Follett (who owned a property at Culm Davy) for some larch trees with which to erect the clubhouse.

One expense the club was happy to meet was in December 1905 when 16 tons of beach sand were purchased from Bude at 7s.3d. a ton, which included the cost of transporting it from Bude to Hemyock Station. When it was decided to replace the green in 1907 there were various of ideas about where to obtain the turf from, one being to dig it up from around the Wellington Monument. Eventually an 'expert' from Taunton, aided by members, relaid the green.

Fortunately in the formative years the bowling club received generous financial help from local individuals such as John Clist, Samuel Farrant, C.J. Carrick, D. Strawbridge, R. Barton and members of the Wide and Hyde families and in due course the club was able to purchase the green and some extra land from Mrs Tapscott.

The very first match played by Hemyock Bowling Club was an away match against Wellington Park on 1 June 1906. Hemyock won by 52 shots to 24 although Wellington won the return match at Hemyock 94 to 64. So began a long and flourishing club history.

For many years bowls was very much the province of the village menfolk but what of the ladies? As early as 1911 it was proposed by a

First members of Hemyock Bowling Club, c.1906.

Hemyock Bowling Club, 1910.
Left to right, back: John Hart (?), Mark Lowman, Robert Graves, ?, Robert Tait, John Clist, ?;
seated: Dick Strawbridge, James 'Sonny' Farmer, William Tait,
Revd de Burgh Forbes, ?, Charlie J. Carrick.

Postcard of Hemyock Bowling Club, 1920.
Left to right, back: Mr Shepherd, John Clist, ?, Sam Farrant, C.J. Carrick, Dick Strawbridge, Mark Lowman;
middle: Vernon Paul, Harry Summers, Tom Sandford, Mr Phillips, Jack Sandford, Bill Griffiths,
Reg Barton, Jack Exton, Mr White, Antony Richards;
front: Revd de Burgh Forbes, Mr William Tait, Robert Tait, Mr Wheeler, Bob Hill,
PC Moulder (policeman), George Paul.

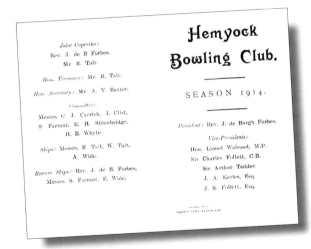

Above and right: *Bowling Club Fixture card with results, 1914. From the card it is clear that the Bowling Club travelled around a great deal – visiting such towns and villages as Uffculme, Crewkerne, Cullompton, Wellesley and Exonian in a single season.*

Hemyock Bowling Club.

SEASON 1914.

Joint Captains:
Rev. J. de B. Forbes.
Mr R. Tait.

Hon. Treasurer: Mr R. Tait.

Hon. Secretary: Mr A. T. Baxter.

Committee:
Messrs. C. J. Carrick, J. Clist,
S. Farrant, R. H. Strawbridge,
H. B. Whyte.

Skips: Messrs. R. Tait, W. Tait,
A. Wide.

Reserve Skips: Rev. J. de B. Forbes,
Messrs. S. Farrant, E. Wide.

President: Rev. J. de Burgh Forbes.

Vice-Presidents:
Hon. Lionel Walrond, M.P.
Sir Charles Follett, C.B.
Sir Arthur Tedder.
J. A. Eccles, Esq.
J. S. Follett, Esq.

MATCHES.

Date	Team	Place	Result	For	Agnst.
May 23—Sat.	Exonian	Away	L	58	94
„ 28—Thur.	Uffculme	Away	W	58	50
June 1—Mon.	Cullompton	Home	W	81	42
„ 6—Sat.	Wellesley	Away	L	46	72
„ 11—Thur.	Uffculme	Home			
„ 13—Sat.	Athletic	Home	L	49	63
„ 18—Thur.	Crewkerne	Home	W	55	54
July 18—Sat.	Cullompton	Away	L	47	73
„ 23—Thur.	Cullompton	Home			
„ 24—Fri.	Wellesley	Home	W	70	54
„ 31 Fri	Crewkerne	Away	W	73	65
Aug. 3—Mon.	Exonian	Home	W		
„	Uffculme	Away	L	55	
„ 22—Sat.	Uffculme	Home	W	93	39
Sept. 5—Sat.	Athletic	Away			

member that ladies might be allowed to use a couple of rinks once or twice a week but to play croquet not bowls. The proposer of this idea thought 'that it would enable the ladies to enjoy a pastime and would augment the revenue of the club'. The proposal was not even seconded and died an immediate death. At the Annual General Meeeting of the club in 1921 it was unanimously agreed that ladies be allowed to be members of Hemyock Bowling Club at the same subscription as the men. It was, however, to be many years before a lady joined the club to bowl despite a proposal in 1932 that ladies be admitted as playing members and be allowed a separate rink by the committee. Further similar proposals followed in 1933 and 1936. Finally at a meeting of the club in Hemyock Parish Hall on 30 November 1956 a proposal, made by Mr C.J. Hannaford and seconded by Mr N. Lowman, was accepted that a ladies section of the club be formed. This got off the ground in 1957 and is still going strong. In 1996 and 1997 the ladies won the prestigious Mid-Devon Ladies' President Trophy. (Interestingly, beyond the South West, female bowlers tend to be referred to as women rather than ladies.)

Nowadays there are a number of trophies played for within the club including one for the 'Under 18s'. One of the trophies, the Melhuish Cup, has an interesting history. Frank Melhuish was a member of the Club Committee and Captain in 1928. He became Club President in 1943. At a General Meeting in March of that year it is recorded that Mr Melhuish promised a two-guinea Silver Challenge Cup for the winner of a single competition run throughout the year. The following year this became the 'Melhuish Cup'. In March 1940, at the AGM, it was noted that the competition for the cup had not been completed and it was decided to give the trophy to the player with the highest score. A new cup was donated by Mr Melhuish in 1941 but the original Melhuish Cup was presented to Hemyock Bowling Club in the year 2000 by a relative of one of the club's early bowlers. This original has two names engraved on it, H.L. Wide for 1937 and M. Lowman for 1938. No name was shown for 1939.

Today's clubhouse was opened on 16 July 1987 by the then three-times and current World Bowls Champion David Bryant. Mr Bryant brought three family members to compete against Hemyock who provided stiff opposition. At that time the Club Chairman was Don McCulloch and Club Secretary Reg Hotten. Other members present at the opening included Martin and Gareth Dear, David Jenkins, Bob Hackwood and Fred Lawrence.

Hemyock Bowling Club has gone from strength to strength over the years and now has a thriving membership of both sexes and all ages, so there is no reason to see why it should not be going strong for another 95 years or more.

Above: *The Ladies after receiving the 'Ladies' President Trophy', 1996. Left to right, back: Jean Andrews, Beryl McCulloch, May Saunders, Helen Lancaster, Anne Gale, Muriel Collins, Sue Piers, Di Groves, Geraldine Gibbins, Maggie Knowlman, Pearl Hurley, Daphne Symes, Gladys Thompson; seated: Mollie Lutley, Nellie Fox-Robinson, Maureen Robertson, Ann Barnden (Captain), Mary Hawkins.*

Inset: *Opening of the new clubhouse by David Bryant, 16 August 1987. Left to right: Reg Hotten, Don McCulloch, David Bryant, David Jenkins, Bob Hackwood, Martin Dear, Fred Lawrence, Gareth Dear.*

FOOTBALL

It is fortunate that the story of the Hemyock Bowling Club is so well recorded. Other village clubs do not have the benefit of such detailed records but have good oral histories coupled with photographic material. Hemyock Amateur Football Club was certainly up and running by the 1927–28 season, when they were in the Tiverton and District League. In that season the club held the Tiverton and District League Shield and the Fox Cup. The President in that season was the Revd L. Ketchley, the Vice-President was Frank Melhuish and Club Secretary was William 'Bill' Griffiths.

The team continued in this league into the 1930s, winning the Walrond Cup in the 1933–34 season. After the war Hemyock AFC was soon back in action and were the Walrond and Hospital Cup Holders for 1948–49. On 1 October a crowd-pulling friendly match was played on the Recreation Field in Hemyock. The local side's opponents were the FA League (Div. 2 side) Brentford. Brentford won the game 4-2. This was followed by a return match at Brentford's home ground, Griffin Park. Brentford won 3-1 but Hemyock acquitted themselves well in both games. Interestingly one of the Hemyock side was an ex-Italian POW shown on the match programme simply as 'Abbey'. This young player's name was, apparently, Alberis, but he was always known as 'Abbey'. During 1949–50 Hemyock played ten English players and one Italian, top clubs today seem often to play one Englishman and ten foreign players, many of them Italians. Was Hemyock's Italian a first? The Hemyock side went on to win the Victory Cup in the 1951–52 season.

For some years Hemyock have played in the Taunton and District League. In April 1984 they reached the final of the Seward Cup which was played at Taunton. Hemyock defeated West Somerset Hospitals 2-1 to take the trophy.

One individual whose name has been associated with the club for very many years is Tom Humphreys. Tom became Club Secretary in 1969 and served in that capacity for no less than 29 years. He was really much more than the Secretary, however, playing his part in team selections, and when it came to touchline decisions about players going on or coming off it was down to Tom. By chance both Tom and one of the writers of this book, Chris Dracott, went to watch matches at Brentford in the early post-war years but neither of them were lucky enough to see the Brentford v Hemyock game.

Youngsters in the village are encouraged to start playing as early as possible with the Hemyock Youth Team and who knows what success may lie ahead for Hemyock football players in the future?

CRICKET

Cricket on the village green has always been a part of English country life and Hemyock has been no exception. There have, however, been gaps over the years where cricket has been less popular. In the 1950s there was a regular side but the game really took off again when the club was reformed in 1985. Apart from playing regular matches with clubs from Devon and Somerset, including old rivals such as Culmstock, the Cricket Club has played a number of friendly matches against opposition from some very exotic locations. One such cricket side hails from Das Island. The two sides contested the 'Hooper's Annual Challenge' match for the 'Naughty Gnome Trophy'.

At present that much-treasured trophy is held in the Cricket Club showcase on Das Island 100 miles off the coast of Abu Dhabi in the Persian Gulf. Perhaps, one day, the Hemyock Cricket Club will travel to the island and fight to retrieve the trophy in surroundings far removed from the lovingly cared for cricket pitch in Hemyock where the backdrop is Pencross instead of a very hot island thousands of miles from home. The current cricket side now plays in the East Devon League.

An evocative photograph of a cricket match in progress on Hemyock Recreation Ground, with Pencross Hill in the background behind the houses of Southview.

Hemyock AFC, 1927–28. This team held the Tiverton and District Shield and Fox Cup.
Left to right, back (Committee): E. Passmore, W. Cload, R. Howe, H. Bickle, F. Cork;
middle: P. Rowse (trainer), F. Melhuish (Vice-President), Revd L. Ketchley, D. Pring, S. Lawrence,
H. Marks, H. Murray, E.B. Anderson (Hon. Treasurer) W.J. Griffiths (Hon. Secretary);
seated: R. Baker, F. Passmore, T. Bright (Captain), L. Hart, V. Bale;
on ground: A Salter, P. Howe.

Hemyock Football Club, 1948. Left to right,back: W. Hutchins, F.J. Bradbury, W. Trickey, F. Trickey,
W.H. Bennett, W. Cload, C. Tancock, W. Guppy; middle: R.E. Edmondson, T. Alberis, R. Casely,
F. Hurst, G.T. Bright, A.G. Bale, L.J. Bright, D.E. Smith; front (sitting): J. Parkinson, L.J. Salter,
L.V. Rowland, R.H. Bright (Captain), F. Slowman; (kneeling): HG. Bright, J.R. Thorne.

The 1949–50 season and the return match against Brentford FC at their ground Griffin Park.
Left to right, back: ?, W. Greenslade, W.J. Andrews, J. Pitman, F. Hurst, S. Mather, R. Casely, ?;
front: G. Bale, T. Alberis (known locally as 'Abbey'), L. Rowland, L. Salter, R.H. Bright.
In the background can be seen part of an advertisement '....ER'S BEE..'. This was for Fullers Beer,
which was brewed at Fullers Brewery, still a thriving family concern, a couple of miles away.

The 1983–84 season and the club after winning the Seward Cup in Taunton.
Left to right, back: R. Alford and A. Fuller (Committee), B. Churchill, T. Slater, M. Bailey, R. Hallaran,
N. Cridge, T. Bull, T. Humphreys (Secretary);
front: D. Jenkins (Committee), S. Knight, F. Greenhalgh, P. Mathews, A. Moon, G. Sparks,
A. Brinsford, G. Salter.

Above: *The club, late 1950s. Left to right, back: M. Hadley, M. Casely, T. Young, R. Culverwell, L. Salter; front: L. Bowden, D. Wide, G. Salter, C. Wide, T. Fouracre, M. Bowden.*

Left: *Julian Clist (Captain) receives the 'Naughty Gnome' from John Hooper.*

Hemyock Cricket Club, 1984–85. Left to right, back: Kevin Salter, Dennis Gubb, Julian Clist, Phillip Hawkins, Nigel Gubb, Simon Clist, Gerald Salter, Jim Hawkins, Nigel Cridge, Derek Hart, Jessie James, Paul Mitchell; front: Andrew Perrott, Terry Mitchell, Julie Nelhams, Neil Hawkins, Pam Gubb, John Bater.

OTHER SPORTS

Hemyock also has a thriving tennis club with two courts next to the Bowling Club. There was once also another court at the milk factory. The exact details of the Tennis Club are not known but it was certainly active in June 1920 when it entertained the club from Kentisbeare.

There is also a Badminton Club and a well established Snooker Club, which began with the Hemyock Recreation Club created in October 1928. The first committee comprised R. Barton, H. Marks, P.H. Prowse, R.H. Strawbridge, J. Norman, E. Hassan, R. Pooley and Chairman Mr E.B. Anderson. A number of rules were set out, which amongst other things, instructed members not to smoke over the table, debarred all freak shots and forbade gambling. The minimum membership fee was 5s.0d., and very soon there were 40 members. By 1942 the group had become the Hemyock Recreation (Billiards) Club, eventually to become the Hemyock Snooker Club. Over the years members have played in various matches and tournaments. In the 1988–89 season, the club won the Tiverton District League Trophy and they repeated this triumph again in 1991–92.

No self-respecting village would be without one or more skittles teams. Apart from men's and women's teams at the village pub, the Catherine Wheel, there had always been teams at the factory. One of the trophies played for each year by the factory's team was the Leonard Maggs Cup (established by one of the factory's earlier Directors).

The future for sporting activities indoor and outdoor looks rosy in Hemyock. The young people of the village have always been encouraged to participate in the wide range of sports available, and will hopefully continue producing generations of players for a long time to come.

Above: *Snooker winners of the Tiverton District League, 1991–92. Left to right, back: Kevin Salter, Mark Eldridge, Les Bowden; front: Andrew Perrott, Nigel Gubb, Bill Howell.*

Top: *Factory Skittles Team with Leonard Maggs Cup, c.1980. Left to right, back: Fred Perrott, Arthur Fuller, Royston Perrott, Arthur Bradbeer; front: Roy Perrott junr, Fred Bradbury, David Jenkins, George Young.*

147

✏ Hemyock Doctors ✏

Left: *Dr John Griffin (junr) in the car and Dr Jonathan Meads outside the surgery, c.1972.*

Below: *Dr John Griffin (senr) opening the new surgery, 7 December 1978. Next to Dr Griffin are his wife, their son Michael and his wife Sheila. Dr John Griffin (junr) is on the far right in a light-coloured raincoat (next to a small girl).*

Presentation of a cardiograph to the surgery, 1977. Left to right: Dr John Griffin (junr), Dr Roger Wells, Terry Doble (Chairman of the Parish Council), Dr Jonathan Meads, Christine Young and Brian Clist (Parish Councillors).

Mr Kenneth Clarke, Minister of Health, opening the newly enlarged surgery, 3 March 1982. Left to right: Dr John Griffin (junr), Mr Clarke MP, Dr Jonathan Meads, Dr John Griffin (senr), Dr Roger Wells.

CHAPTER FIFTEEN

Medical Care in Hemyock

Hemyock is lucky enough to have a modern surgery with five doctors plus nursing and support staff, but in all probability only a few parishioners are aware of the fact that prior to 1925 there was no doctor based in Hemyock at all. If the services of a medical practitioner were required before that date, a doctor had to be consulted from nearby Culmstock or the town of Wellington. In order to paint a full picture of how medical care was made available to the population of Hemyock it is necessary to go back 100 years or so to the village of Culmstock.

It is likely that there was a doctor in Culmstock as far back as the early 1800s; certainly the author R.D. Blackmore, famed for his book *Lorna Doone*, wrote of a doctor being there in the early-19th century in his novel *Perlycross* (of which more later in this book). That Blackmore based most of his characters on real people suggests there was a medical practitioner in Culmstock at quite an early date. Blackmore's own doctor was falsely suspected of 'body snatching', not, fortunately, an allegation levelled against any medical practitioner in our story.

Whatever the situation in 19th-century Culmstock, there was a succession of doctors in that village who served the people of Hemyock. The first was a Dr Nott followed by a Dr Horton and then Dr Date until 1912. In 1913 Dr Sydney Huth (apparently pronounced to rhyme with 'Ruth') arrived from Bath taking up residence in Warden House, Culmstock. He visited Hemyock on a regular basis and conducted a branch surgery at Miss Em Clist's house in the High Street. Dr Huth seems to have been quite a colourful character, described as being a man of teutonic appearance with a bullet-shaped, close-cropped head. (Readers with an interest in the derivation of surnames may think that 'Huth' suggests a name of German origin, which could account for the Teutonic appearance of the gentleman.) In later years Doctor Huth drove a big brown open-topped Austin-12 tourer and was usually accompanied by several dogs. He would give rides to children to whom a trip in a car was a novel treat. Even for his time Dr Huth was thought to be old fashioned, his favourite remedies being castor oil taken internally and methylated spirits applied externally. He smoked big cigars and, it is said, for years after his death one could smell the aroma of cigars in his rooms. It is not surprising, perhaps, that with his love of smoking Dr Huth suffered with asthma. When his breathing was bad he would drive up to Culmstock Beacon to get some good fresh air. Eventually his asthma became so bad that when he visited patients in their own homes they would have to be carried downstairs because he could not get up to the bedroom. Dr Huth and his wife had five sons, two of whom were killed in the Second World War, one being awarded the Military Medal.

During the 1920s some basic surgical procedures were carried out on the kitchen table. The late Mr Leonard Redwood, for example, had his tonsils removed on a kitchen table by Dr Huth and a Dr Laidlaw. If surgical procedures were required that could not be managed on a kitchen table, or if a second opinion was sought, patients were referred to Taunton where there were practitioners with specialist experience. One such group in Church Square consisted of Drs Meade-King, Birkbeck, Iles, Ellis and Marshall.

Over the years patients in the upper parts of the Culm Valley could call on doctors from Wellington. A list of some recorded practitioners (many of them with rather Dickensian-sounding names) includes: Frank Sealy Bridge (1777), Samuel Bridge (1795, Surgeon to the Militia), Prideaux, Lewis, Crannum, Scraff, Brentcamb, Rowe, Merediths (two doctors had this name), Jocelyn, Hillier at 'Luson', Bain, Spettigue (who wore a top hat and visited on horseback), McClements (a Communist and Seventh Day Adventist), Johnson, 'Babs' Johnson (his daughter), Cecilia Fox, Harding, Rhodes and Willis.

In 1925 Hemyock decided that it should have its own doctor. Four prominent villagers decided to advertise the position. They were Alfred Wide, a businessman in the egg, rabbit and garage trades; William and Robert Tait, retired businessmen who had retired to Hemyock; and E.B. Anderson, Manager of the milk factory who was a great gardener, President of the Alpine Society and author of *Seven Gardens* (one of which was 'Dixcroft').

Dr T. Core-Porter was appointed. It was considered professionally unethical, although not illegal, to set up in practice in the same area – an activity known as 'putting up your plate'. Dr Core-Porter only stayed for 11 months and left to take up a position as Medical Officer to a colliery in Wales.

Dr Porter had wanted £120 pounds for the practice but his successor, Dr John Lysaght Griffin, who had no capital, was able to buy in for £100. Dr Griffin's background was very interesting. His father, also a John Griffin, qualified in Trinity College, Dublin, then came to England looking for work. He found a position as Assistant in General Practice at a very low salary in Birmingham and then Worcester before acquiring his own practice in Sussex Place, Bristol. He worked hard and built up a popular list. He unfortunately developed pneumonia and died within two days. Had antibiotics been available he would have been saved. This tragedy in the pre-social-security era left the family in financial difficulties. John Griffin (the 2nd) was, at that time, a medical student at Bristol General Hospital and relatives clubbed together so that he could complete his studies.

After qualifying he became assistant to a Dr Dixon working in the slums of Southville in Bristol but as was so common in those days amongst young doctors and nurses it wasn't long before he caught tuberculosis. The travel magnate and philanthropist Sir Arnold Lunn (which name still exists in the holiday industry) funded a charity that sent young consumptive doctors to benefit from the clean Swiss air where beds on a balcony in the cold mountains provided the only treatment. John Griffin (the 2nd) appeared to benefit from this simple treatment and recovered. He then looked for a very cheap practice in rural fresh air. Hemyock, only established for a year, was ideal.

Dr John Griffin's account books show that in the first three months of 1927 there was an influenza epidemic which brought him receipts of £100 for which he was very grateful. In those days a consultation in the surgery with medicine was 2s.6d. and the fee for a visit was 5s.0d. A repeat bottle of medicine was 2s.0d. (so by subtraction the original consultation must have cost 6d.). Dental care in Hemyock was provided by Mr Edward Farrant of Wellington who ran a weekly surgery in the village. In an emergency Dr Griffin would extract teeth. Mrs Evelyn Pike recalls him removing a wisdom tooth and charging six shillings for the pain.

Dr Griffin's first delivery was an anxious one with the baby weighing in at 12lb. Perinatal mortality was high and maternal mortality not rare. He was not long qualified and often found himself single-handedly facing life-and-death decisions. Most babies were born at home with a few mothers going to the Wellington Maternity Home built by the Fox family. For general cases the Wellington Cottage Hospital had been founded by the Edgerton-Burnetts in 1892, and the Tiverton and District Hospital founded in 1852.

When Dr Griffin moved to Hemyock the village had arranged for him to rent a house next to Mr Reg James' egg-packing station (now Mr Goddards'). With their first child on the way Dr and Mrs Griffin moved up Station Road to a house then called Sandhurst next to the Manse. Consultations took place in the front room with patients waiting on a bench in the hall. At surgery time the family moved into the kitchen.

To start with Dr Griffin travelled on a Douglas motorcycle but he soon acquired an open, bull-nosed Morris car more suitable to his position. Patients requiring a visit would need someone to come in to the village to fetch the doctor. When telephones were first installed the doctor's number was Hemyock 6; when the automatic exchange was built this became 206 and subsequently 680206.

In theory the doctor was on call 24 hours a day for 365 days a year but he did manage to take his family to the seaside or the pictures occasionally. Mary Morgan in the Post Office would keep messages for him and in an emergency even have them flashed up on the cinema screen – a far cry from the age of mobile phones we live in now.

Mr Jack Hart built on to the side of Sandhurst a small consulting room with a tiny dispensary attached. There was a range of about 15 stock medicines and about 10 sorts of pills. Ferris and Co. of Bristol supplied medicine in concentrated form in large Winchester bottles. One fluid ounce of this was poured into an 8oz medicine bottle and, out of sight of the patient, 7oz of tap water added. The dose would have been one dessertspoonful twice a day but miserly patients would eke it out in little sips. Some overconfident patients were observed to drink the whole bottle on the way out. Being in a reserved occupation and with a history of TB, Dr John Griffin was exempt from active service during the Second World War. He was nominally made a Captain in the Home Guard but only once put on the uniform for a group photograph.

He had for many years been giving anaesthetics to dentists in Wellington and developing an interest in that speciality. After an exhausting day's work he would settle down to study the book 'Aids to Anaesthesia' underlining key passages in red ink. He passed the Diploma in Anaesthesia exam, and later was promoted to a Fellowship of the Faculty of

Anaesthesia, in the Royal College of Surgeons. To help him in his practice work he engaged a Scot, Dr Thomas Logan, who arrived on 14 August 1947 aged 25. Dr Logan had experience in only one house job, which was six months in a sanatorium where he had developed quite a talent for treating chest problems. He soon broadened his skills and he was a very popular doctor with an excellent bedside manner.

With the inception of the National Health Service Dr Griffin became a Consultant Anaesthetist to the Somerset Group of Hospitals and moved away from Hemyock to live on the Quantock Hills. Dr and Mrs Logan moved into Sandhurst renaming it 'Heatherlea' to remind them of Scotland. (A later occupant, retired farmer Mr Farrant, renamed the house 'Hatherleigh' after the Devon town.)

Dr Griffin had bought a building plot from Miss Ruby Ackland and on this Dr Logan built a lavish bungalow with a wing containing a sur-

Dr Jonathan Meads on his favourite mode of transport for house calls, c.1972.

gery, waiting room, toilet and dispensary, calling the property 'Bean Close' from the field name. He continued to build up the practice. Dr Logan was friendly with a Dr Probyn at Churchinford and in 1956 they formed a partnership. There were branch surgeries in Culmstock, Dunkeswell, Ashill, Blackborough, Upottery and Yarcombe.

In 1955 because of an increasing workload at the surgery Dr Peter Hayne was employed as an assistant with a view to a partnership. He was very popular, especially in his home village of Culmstock, and integrated well into the social life. The partnership did not develop, however, and Dr Hayne took a single-handed practice in Carlisle, later moving back to a practice at Chilton Polden.

In 1958 Dr John Griffin (3rd) joined as an assistant. The population served then stood at about 4700. There was one part-time unqualified dispenser and some help was given by Mrs Joy Logan. Each weekday there was a morning surgery from 9a.m. until the last patient had been seen. Evening surgery was also without appointments starting at 6p.m. Doctors in those days normally wore a suit and a white shirt with detachable collar. Dr John Griffin, who had become accustomed to wearing a hat in the

Army, continued to do so in order that it could be raised when he saw a lady.

After the long surgeries the doctors went on the rounds. There was a lot of visiting to do. Every patient discharged from hospital, even for a minor complaint, received a follow-up visit when they came home.

In November 1966 Dr Logan suffered a severe stroke which largely deprived him of speech. He was only 44 and never worked again. However, he returned bravely to the village to officially open the Day Centre when it began in the old Methodist Chapel in the High Street. His speech to the gathering though hesitant was warmly applauded. He died on 8 February 1983 aged only 60 and there is an oak tree planted in the churchyard in his memory. In the emergency heralded by Dr Logan's illness the two other partners sent to Musgrove Park Hospital for their best houseman, and Dr Jonathan Meads joined as a third partner to replace Tom Logan in 1967.

The practice had to vacate Bean Close so Mr Jim Hart let them have a plot at the top of Station Road where Dr Griffin's brother built the first simple surgery with two consulting rooms, waiting room, office cum dispensary and three toilets all at a cost of £4300.

Dr Probyn resigned from the practice to go into the hotel business and Dr Terry Franklin bought his house with the attached surgery known as 'Hollybank' in Churchinford. This is now a care home for the elderly.

In 1975 Dr Roger Wells succeeded Dr Franklin and remained until 1990 when he became a full-time Consultant Psychotherapist. On 13 March 1982 Mr Kenneth Clarke QC, MP, who was then just newly appointed Minister of Health, officially opened the imaginative, newly-enlarged surgery built by Mr Dennis Hart at a cost of approximately £122 000. By now the practice had some 5200 patients and the area covered was nine miles north to south and eighteen miles east to west. Branch surgeries were, despite local protests, dropped, with the exception of Dunkeswell, which was moved to a purpose-built suite in the new Highfields housing estate. With help from the Violet Chapman Trust a large extension to the Hemyock Surgery to accommodate the extra services and staff was undertaken in 1992.

The practice was joined by Dr Donald McLintock as a fourth partner, and in 1992 Dr John Griffin (the 3rd) retired and was replaced by Dr Mark Couldrick. Known affectionately as 'Doctor John', John Griffin was a wise, caring and medically astute if very slightly eccentric GP described as being an archetypal Dr Cameron, the partner of Somerset Maugham's fictitous Dr Finlay. Dr Griffin knew the patients and their interrelated families well, and such knowledge was essential in any General Practice but particularly in a rural area. Having been brought up in the Blackdown Hills proved a considerable advantage. He was very much involved, both medically and socially, in all aspects of country life and the lives of his patients. Riding to hounds, acting as medical officer at gymkhanas, motor cycle scrambles and football matches formed just a part of his involvement with the community. He also lectured and examined for St John's Ambulance.

'Doctor John' cared very much about his patients and their rights. When the Somerset Geriatricians wanted to hand over to Exeter the care of the practice's elderly patients living in Devon he was outraged. This would have meant that patients living in Devon would have had to travel the much further distance to Exeter rather than Taunton. The patients could not have wished for a greater champion of their needs. Thanks to innumerable letters, a demonstration and an appearance on television the plan was dropped.

In 1993 Dr John Davies joined the team and helped in the move from the practice's 1975 Devon Lady sectional wooden surgery in the Churchinford Village Hall car park. In 1997, with Nick Hawksley the Practice Manager and the architects Higgison, Brown & Stuckey, Dr Davies was involved in the design and layout of a new state-of-the-art surgery in Fairfield Green Estate, Churchinford.

In 1999 Dr Jonathan Meads retired. He has been, quite rightly, described as an outstanding General Practitioner with dedication and vision. He was largely responsible for the building of the new Surgery; the Day Centre which is now called the Cameo Club; for the conversion of the old Hemyock School building into 11 flatlets for the elderly and the setting up of the Blackdown Support Group and luncheon clubs in Clayhidon and Culmstock. A kind, caring man he had an excellent bedside manner and had a way of making his patients feel very much at ease even in sometimes very difficult circumstances. One patient, no doubt expressing the view of many others, described Dr Meads as a gentleman and a gentle man. In retirement he continues to be very much involved in Hemyock activities and those of other local parishes.

The original partners, as a principle of policy, were committed to personal care of their own list of patients and have always aimed to undertake minor surgery in the village rather than refer patients to hospital. The Blackdown Practice, as it is now called, has been at the forefront of innovations in General Practice; leading to cervical cytology screening, immunisations, health screening, weight control, management of heart disease, blood pressure and diabetes, family planning, infant and child developmental assessment, psychotherapy and parenting classes. 'Care in the Community' has always been the goal. More recently they have shared their premises with practitioners in osteopathy, acupuncture, homeopathy, counselling, hypnotherapy and also complementary therapies such as reflexology, aromatherapy and spinal touch therapy.

The practice now cares for 7000 patients from an area of 200 square miles. The Government's rush to introduce new ideas and yet more changes to the NHS have meant that much of what was good and personal in patient care has been lost. However, changes in medical care that have been of benefit to patients have been readily introduced into the practice.

The practice now has five GPs, Doctors Donald McLintock, Mark Couldrick, John Davies and two job-sharing lady doctors who replaced Dr Jonathan Meads, namely Doctors Susan Brocklesby and Amanda Leach – all supported by a dedicated nursing staff and administrative team. The Practice Manager is Nick Hawksley.

This brief story of medical care cannot be concluded without mention of the Blackdown Support Group. The brainchild of Heather Stallard, Susan Doggett and Dr Jonathan Meads, the group was started in April 1991, and, to quote from its literature: 'It cares for young and old, for those in need of extra help when sick or suffering from accidents, disabilities, or advancing years.' The group helps people who are in danger of falling through the net of support provided by the NHS and Social Services, and folk who have moved to the practice area where they have no immediate family to keep an eye on them when they are ill or recovering from operations – or when they are simply lonely. In addition the group aims to provide transport to hospital perhaps for outpatient treatment where an individual cannot drive or is not fit enough to use public transport.

The Blackdown Support Group is manned entirely by volunteers. At the first public meeting back in 1991 there were about 35 volunteers, and that number has now risen to 70. The Co-ordinator of Volunteers is Brian Simpson. Recently one of the 'founder members', Susan Doggett was awarded the MBE principally in recognition of her work with the group. The honour can perhaps be looked on as recognition not only of Susan's own work but that of the Blackdown Support Group as a whole.

CHAPTER SIXTEEN

Farming

There is evidence to suggest that early man settled around Hemyock about 7000 years ago. At first these settlers would have been mainly hunters but at an early stage they would have been gathering seeds from grasses and early grain-bearing plants. As the years progressed, so did early man. Areas of land were cleared by burning, sufficient to grow small plots of better cereals. Farming as we know it had begun. By the late Iron Age and Roman times a degree of diversification into individual industrial processes had taken place and a large amount of iron was being produced from a great number of small furnaces. These early inhabitants were able to produce enough food by farming the land and to make money from their semi-industrial activities.

The standard of farming improved slowly over the centuries but a dramatic improvement was heralded by the arrival of a group of agricultural monks (the Cistercians) who settled in nearby Dunkeswell Abbey in 1201. These incomers brought with them advanced farming techniques. In medieval times much more grain was grown on local farms and trade developed with other regions. Gradually, following a period of climatic change when rainfall increased dramatically, the weather conditions became more favourable for the growth of grass, and so more livestock appeared in the parish.

For several hundred years, until the early 1800s, the woollen industry, so important to the Culm Valley, made sheep the most profitable animals on our farms. As the woollen trade dropped off, however, cattle came into their own and more and more cows appeared in Hemyock. The breed that became most popular was the Red Devon, a dual-purpose breed that produced both beef and milk. All of the milk, except that needed for domestic use, was made into butter which was eventually despatched to large towns and cities. A by-product of butter manufacture was skimmed milk, which was fed to a rapidly growing population of pigs.

Eventually, at the end of the 1800s, a butter factory was developed, which in turn meant that even greater numbers of cows (and pigs) were kept. This pattern of farming remained virtually unchanged until the end of the Second World War, except that over the years the cattle had been bred to produce more milk and, of course, poorer beef (see also Chapters Six and Eleven).

Every farm had a great many hens, and the cash that came from the sale of the eggs invariably went to the housewife. There were so many hens that Hemyock had two egg-packing stations to pack the eggs and to collect rabbits that had been caught in the fields. With the advent of war, however, this pattern of family farming changed. Food shortages saw the Government encouraging increased food production by giving generous subsidies.

The second half of the 20th century saw many changes. Almost every branch of farming has been intensified and many smaller farms, unable to finance specialisation, have disappeared – as also have the milk factory, the railway and the two egg-packing stations. Hemyock is left with fewer but larger farms and the traditional picture of farming with some hens and pigs and cattle around a working farmyard has gone. Is our village any better or happier as a result of these 'improvements'? The photographs that accompany this chapter will give some idea of what agriculture was all about in the not too distant past.

An advertisement for Alfred Wide's diverse operation at Hemyock.

In the 18th century Burrow Hill Farm was a typical Hemyock farm and would have remained so down the centuries except for two events that occurred in 1779 and 1783. On each occasion there was a forced sale of the farmer's effects because of his inability to pay the rent or mortgage interest. The family of Peter Manley, whose goods were sold in 1779, had arranged a mortgage of £870 in 1736 from Samuel Southwood, and it was assigned to Peter Manley himself in 1750. But in 1779 he must have been unable to settle his debts with his landlord. On 23 February they 'were to be sold by virtue of the distress'. Burrow Hill was subsequently leased to Samuel Fry, but in 1783 he suffered the same fate. The particulars of both sales survive and in the case of Peter Manley they are very detailed. Not only do we have information about his stock and equipment, but we also have an inventory of his furniture and of the rooms of the farmhouse.

In the Kitchen
One clock and case
One long board table (the table stood presumably on trestles)
One dresser
One settle
12 pewter dishes
26 pewter plates
One pewter tea-pot
2 brass pans
2 brass kittles
One bellmetal pot
One copper boiler
One copper tea kittle
One iron pot
2 Brass skilletts
2 brass ladles
One copper saucepan
8 horn plates
2 iron candlesticks
One iron flesh pick
Some earthen ware
3 chimney croaks (pronounced 'crock', a cast-iron cooking pot with legs)

In the Parlour
2 round tables
4 chairs
One cubboard
One tub with some barley
One peck (a measure of volume; grain was sold volumetrically, 4 pecks = 1 bushel)
One half peck
One looking glass
One brass warming pan (for heating the bed)
8 pewter plates
One 'but' (to hold liquid)
One beam and scales
One hacking saddle
One pair of fire dogs
Some lumber (useless or disused items of furniture)
One iron bar

In the Cellar
One hogshead full of cyder (a hogshead was a barrel for storing liquid and contained around 50 imperial gallons)
4 empty hogsheads
One pipe (a barrel for port or sherry)
One half hogshead
3 barrels
One tub
One saw
One hatchet and some timber

In the Passage
One pail
One hook
One bridle
One lade pail (a peculiar pail with one stave longer than the others, thus forming a handle, used for dipping hot water from a copper, or making cider)

In the Wring House
5 tubs
One churn
2 cheese wrings
One barrel
One brass kittle
One range (a sieve for straining liquids, used in cheese and cider making)
2 basketts
One sieve
Some lumber

In the Milk House
11 brass pans
One brass kittle
One pair of tongs
One dripping pan
3 large leads (for pressing butter or cheese)
One pewter plate
Some earthenware

In the First Chamber
2 beds performed (assembled)
One large chest
2 tubs
2 barrels
One side saddle
One pillion and cloth (a seat for a woman behind a man's saddle)

In the Second Chamber
2 feather beds and bolsters
One sheet
2 blankets
One rug
One quilt
2 bedsteads
One clock and case
One hanging press
4 large sheets
3 small boxes
2 chairs
One barrel
A quantity of oats
22 cheeses
One cheese rack

In the Third Chamber
9 empty hogsheads
4 tubs
A quantity of cheese vats
Some lumber

In the Fourth Chamber
One bed and bedstead
One sheet
One blanket
One winnowing sheet (used in separating the grain from the chaff)
One table board
One turm
5 gibbs
One trendle (large oval tub used for scalding pigs)
One tub
4 stools

*T*his extensive list of the contents of an average farmhouse 230 years ago is fascinating. It is obvious that the farmers' wives were not yet house proud (or were not allowed to be!) because even the bedrooms were full of farming equipment – even 22 cheeses! Between listing the goods to be sold and the actual day of the sale the landlord 'gave' the following goods to Peter Manley: 2 brass skimmers, 12 brass ladles, 1 copper saucepan, 4 pewter dishes, 6 pewter plates, 1 brass kettle, 1 bell metal pot, 1 frying pan, 8 stone plates, 2 candlesticks, 1 iron flesh pick, 2 chimney crooks, 1 fire pan and tongs, 1 table board, 3 chairs, 1 looking glass, 1 pair of fire dogs, 2 or 3 barrels, 1 tub, 1 hatchet, 1 pail, 1 hook, 1 range, 2 basketts, 2 beds, 1 chest, 1 clock and case, 22 cheeses, 1 brass warming pan, some wood, 1 tea kettle and some other things. The fact that Peter Manley was allowed to keep some of his own possessions meant that he would at least have had the means to live a simple life. The sale document lists his livestock and dead stock too, so we are able to find out what type of farming was carried on at Burrow Hill.

IN THE HOME BARTON
(In this case, the barton means an area of land set aside for keeping cattle)
6 cows
2 steers
Some timber
One fat pig

IN MANMOOR BARN
A quantity of wool
One fan (for winnowing grain)
2 sieves
One pick and rake

IN LOWER MANMOOR
One bull
2 yearlings

IN THE COURT ON THE HILL
One put and wheels (a tipping cart)
One pair of draggs (for preparing seed beds)
One pair of harrows

IN THE MOW BARTON ON THE HILL
(where corn ricks were placed)
One wheat mow (a rick of wheat
2 oaten mows
2 ricks of oats

IN THE STRAW HOUSE
A quantity of reed (for thatching)

IN GREAT PITLAND (a field)
One bull
3 cows

IN BARN CLOSE (a field)
4 sheep

IN LONG LEA (a field)
A quantity of wood unmade (not sawn)

IN THREE CORNER CLOSE (a field)
Wheat in the ground (growing)
Some wood unmade

IN FOUR ACRES (a field)
Wheat in ground

IN BONDLAND (a field; originally bond land being that held at the will of the lord of the manor)
54 sheep
One rick of hay

IN COFFER CROFT (a field; perhaps coffer shaped)
32 sheep
2 horses
2 steers
One sull (the Devonshire word for plough)
One yoke (for tethering cattle)
2 bows and chains
collars (for horses)

IN THE DOUBLE CRIBHOUSE
(small shed used for rearing cattle)
3 steers
One heifer

IN THE TALLETT (the area on the first floor above a barn, usually open fronted)
A small quantity of hay

IN HIGHER WESTLAND (a field)
Some wood

IN FIELD UNDER LOWER CRIBHOUSE
3 steers
One heifer

IN LOWER WESTLAND ORCHARD
Some wallestt (brushwood, usually tied into faggots)

IN THE STABLES
3 pack saddles
One hacking saddle
Some girts (oatmeal)

IN WRING HOUSE
Some lumber

IN WRINGHOUSE CHAMBER (above the Wring House)
11 empty hogsheads
Some lumber

Village Crier's notice of the forthcoming auction.

Market day in Hemyock, always held on a Monday. A Red Devon bull is in the wagon in the centre of the picture – what other breed would be so docile? Two traps on the left have already had their horses removed.

Hemyock Cattle Market was held behind the Catherine Wheel (as it is now known). The cattle are penned in by mobile wooden hurdles. Later the market had metal-railed pens.

The sale was to commence at 10a.m. on Tuesday 23 February 1779 and was to continue until all the goods were sold. A great number of people from Hemyock and the surrounding villages would have been there, some people wanting to buy Peter Manley's possessions, but the majority perhaps curious onlookers, eager to follow the auctioneer around the fields and barns and even keener to follow him inside the house, to see what Peter had and how he lived.

Farm sales must have provoked the same interest then as they do now. In the late 1700s there were no local newspapers, no telephones and no post as we know it, so how did people who lived outside Hemyock know the time and details of a farm sale? In fact the sale was 'cried' – a man was hired to visit local villages to shout out details of the sale. The 'cry' survives and a copy of it is printed on the previous page. The crier visited Honiton, Broadhembury, Uffculme, Culmstock, Dunkeswell, 'Hemiock',

Clayhidon, 'Lupit', Churchstanton, West Buckland, Wellington, Bradford, Angersleigh, Corfe, Taunton and Trull.

Burrowhill Farm was leased subsequently to a Mr Samuel Fry of Hemyock, but in 1782 he too was unable to pay his rent and his goods were distrained and sold. An inventory of his possessions was taken on 5 June 1782 by two local farmers William Manley and John Manley (probably related to Peter Manley) with the sale itself taking place on 19 June 1782. The inventory valued the possessions at £130.7s.0d. (£130.35). At auction £124.18s.4d. was raised. Mr Southwood's papers indicated how the purchases were paid for. The gold coins used were guineas and half guineas – £1.1s.0d. and 10s.6d. respectively. The sum of £84.0s.3d. was settled in cash consisting of 63 guineas, 26 half guineas, £7.7s.0d. in silver and 3d. in brass. Just under £41 was not paid at the time. Obviously the auctioneer knew these purchasers.

Aerial view of Hemyock, early 1980s, setting it off well in its agricultural surroundings. This view is taken looking from the south-east with Churchills and Prowses in the foreground. Higher Mead, East Mead, Redwoods Close and Culm Meadow have yet to be built.

✌ Haymaking ✆

Left: *A full load of hay which just needs its sides raking down before being hauled to the hay rick at the farm. The photograph (c.1920) was taken in an area that is now the Eastlands Estate.*

Below: *Haymaking Scene at Mackham Farm. A field of hay is being dried and gathered with hand-held rakes. The weather was obviously 'catchy' (showery) because two pooks (heaps) can be seen in the background. This was done to protect almost dry hay from being spoilt by rain. Mackham, or Lower Mackham as it is now called, has been farmed for some years now by David and Meg Palmer.*

Right: *Haymaking scene featuring Cissie Gunn enjoying a mug of cider from the wicker-covered ferkin.*

Left: *Haymaking scene on Churchill's Farm, (where Prowses is now). The hay can be seen in rows behind the wagon. Note the wagon rope hanging down from the rear lade, this would have been used to rope the load down when it was full of hay. Ted Tartaglia on wagon, Bill Granger by the horse, Jean Clarke on right (who now lives in Canada) and unknown young lady.*

Right: *A field of wheat being harvested at Churchill's Farm, c.1923. Some of the sheaves are already stooked. Adults, left to right: Bill Granger, Bob Lowman, George Salter, James Clapp, Jack Granger; children: Jack Granger, Winnie Smith and Cissie Granger (being carried).*

Left: *Mr Bert Hill driving his rare, three-wheeled Allis-Chalmers tractor, turning a field of hay with an Acrobat haymaking machine. The tractor was in use on Churchill's Farm for many years. It has been restored, is still in Hemyock and is taken to many agricultural shows.*

Right: *A scene at Ashculm(e) Farm, 1926. The lad in front is Fred Lawrence, the men left to right are Harry Trott, Bob Tait and Percy Clist (who was killed in the war).*

Mackham Farm, early 1900s.

The same scene at Mackham, with two farmers – Gilbert Forbear in the waistcoat and a friend, late 1930s or early 1940s. Note the siting of the dung heap in front of the door to the house. After being built up for a winter, the dung was spread on the fields in the spring.

Two carthorses in the Square.
The man on the horse is riding in the normal sideways fashion as carthorses had backs
uncomfortably wide to straddle!

Five heavily pregnant Wessex Saddlebacks being driven through the Square in the 1960s. Bert Hill in
front is carrying a bucket and broom to ensure that the road is kept clean! Lloyds Bank on the left was still
in operation – before Egypt House (centre right) was demolished to provide a village car park.

Red Devon cattle in the Square. Two shops can be seen on the right, Mr Carrick's and Miss Hide's. The thatched cottages behind the Pump were burnt down. The smithy is on the left, c.1910.

Dennis Farmer with his dairy cows outside the milking parlour at milking time, c.1973.

CHAPTER SEVENTEEN

Scouts & Guides

The story of scouting in Hemyock began about 1920 when the first Hemyock Troop was formed by Mr J.B. Goddard and Mr W.J. (Bill) Griffiths. The Troop lasted for about four or five years and was then re-formed in the late 1930s by Bob Thorne of Wellington. One of the first scout camps was at Blue Anchor in Somerset in 1941. This group lasted until the early 1950s. The first Hemyock Girl Guides were formed in 1941 by Miss Thelma Lowry and the Brownies in 1943 by Miss Ida Wide and Freda Board (later Bright). The Brownie pack was officially recognised on 16 May 1945 and Barbara Hole later became the Brown Owl.

During the war years the 1st Hemyock Guides, Scouts, Brownies and Wolf Cubs did more than 'their bit' by putting on a series of 'variety entertainments' for the village. On Saturday 11 April 1942 they performed a show produced by Mr W.J. Griffiths assisted by Miss T.D. (Thelma) Lowry and Mr R.L. Thorne. A programme for this show cost the princely sum of 2d. A reminder of wartime austerity was noted on the back of the programme which read as follows:

Considerable difficulty has been experienced, owing to Wartime conditions, in obtaining the necessary costumes for the Historical Pageant. The Audience is asked, therefore, to be kind enough to overlook any mistakes in the costumes.

The audience undoubtedly made allowances and thoroughly enjoyed the show. It must have been quite an event and had, quite naturally, a patriotic theme running through it. The various acts included 'Flags of the British Isles' performed by the Guides and Scouts, 'A Sword Dance' performed by the Wolf Cub Pack, 'A Guider's Nightmare' by the Guide Company, and 'Peter-King's Scout' with M. Graves, P. Beaven, S. Graves, R. Griffiths, B. Small, A. Webber

and N. Lowman. There were a number of other acts but the highlight must have been 'England – An Historical Pageant' with an interesting cast of characters; 'Britannia' played by B. Cundict, M. Graves and Mr Stradling were 'Ancient Britons', 'Julius Caesar' was played by A. Webber, 'William the Conqueror' by N. Lowman, 'Queen Elizabeth' by B. Bird, 'Francis Drake' by P. Pike, a 'Spanish Grandee' by J. Leckie, 'Napoleon' by R. Smith, 'The Duke of Wellington' by R. Trickey, 'Adolf Hitler' by R. Griffiths, with B. Hole and P. Wide as '1st Guide' and '1st Scout'. Noticeably the foes of England were represented and a Spaniard, Napoleon and Adolf Hitler received their just desserts. Six months after the village youngsters gave their performance, the Eighth Army under Montgomery defeated the forces of Rommel at El Alamein.

On 30 April and 1 May 1943 the Company of Scouts and Guides staged 'The Masque of Empire' written by Hugh Mytton. The problem of costumes experienced in 1942 might not have been as great because in 1943 these were created by the 'Masque of Empire Society'. What a splendid show this must have been with characters bearing the names of the Patron Saints of England, Scotland, Wales and Ireland, plus various individuals cast as the Commonwealth Countries. The time setting for the play was 'The Eve of Empire Day'. Just over three months later the Allied conquest of Sicily led to the downfall of Mussolini.

The patriotic theme continued in April 1944 with the 'Gang Show'. This time much of the story line was devoted to the Armed Forces, the second act being entitled 'Till Victory'. Members of the cast depicted the 'Spirit of the Army', 'Spirit of the Royal Navy', 'Spirit of the Royal Air Force' and so on with the Merchant Navy and some of our allies, 'Spirit of the USA', Russia, China, and, importantly, 'Spirit of the Industrial Workers'. Two months after the 'Gang Show' came D-Day, and the Allied landings in Normandy.

In April 1945 the 1st Hemyock Guide and Scout Groups produced something in a lighter vein with

Camp of the 1st Hemyock Scouts at Blue Anchor, c.1941.

Guide Group in the early years of the war.
Left to right, back: Jill Leckie, Thelma Lowry, Ann Cubitt, Barbara Cundict, Sheila Graves,
Mary Graves, Juliet Summers, Barbara Hole, Mary Stradling, Mrs Almond;
middle: Freda Obermeister, ?, Sheila Lowman, Joyce Cubitt, Rose Pike;
front: Betty Dimmock, ?, ?, Daphne Lowry, Josephine Hare (?), Joan Hake.
Some of the unnamed young ladies may have been evacuees.

Left: *A gathering of Hemyock and Danish Scouts, Guides, Cub Scouts and Brownies, July 1977, pictured with their leaders outside Hemyock Parish Hall.*

Below: *Wartime Scouts and a Cub. The Cub, David Redwood, is flanked by brother Brian on the left and Ted Tartaglia on the right.*

Above: *1st Hemyock Scouts, Venture Scouts and Leaders in Denmark, July 1986. Skip Lowman is pictured in the front, and behind him are Ashley Alford, John Northam, Alan Holway, Linda Holway and Gerald Petticrew.*

Right: *A Scout meeting in the Church Rooms, 1967. Skip Lowman is flanked by Senior Scouts Brian Milton and Martin Pring.*

hopes that the war was nearing an end. 'Perhaps' was a musical revue with numbers such as 'A Nightingale sang in Berkeley Square', 'She'll be coming round the Mountain' and 'Swinging on a Star'. A month later the war in Europe had come to an end and in August, after the Allies had dropped atomic bombs on the Japanese cities of Hiroshima and Nagasaki, that nation surrendered on 2 September 1945.

It is important to put the wartime activities of the Scouts and Guides in context. The youngsters, together with their leaders and other adults from Hemyock, were all too aware of what was happening on the world stage. Members of their families or friends and other people from the village were away serving their country in different parts of the world. The importance of producing these shows indicates the spirit that existed not just in Hemyock but throughout the country.

Norman Lowman and Ray Griffiths at Blue Anchor camp, 1941.

Naturally the Scouts and Guides were continuing their normal activities and apart from producing variety shows they also did their bit for the war effort. One of the tasks undertaken by the scouts was the collection of newspaper, etc., which they normally did on a Saturday morning. This involved taking a cart around the village and outskirts filling it with paper – they even pulled the cart up Pencross and other local hills during their 'collection round'.

The shows did not cease when the war ended. In 1946, for example, the groups staged the 'War Scrapbook of John Citizen', another very imaginative production. The characters included 'Announcers', 'Shelterers' and a chorus that included rabbits, Hitler, servicemen, Home Guard and citizens from a wide range of countries. In 1949 another production entitled 'A Peacetime Parade' continued the tradition of history and wartime effort but most of all was staged as a celebration of peace.

The principal producer of these shows was the late Bill Griffiths but, as always with such ventures, there were a number of other individuals who played a key role; Marian Lowman, who acted as stage manager, and Mrs H. Cubitt, who with the Scoutmaster Bob Thorne was responsible for music, and there were many others too numerous to name.

The Scout Troop continued until the early 1950s when there was a break until the Spring of 1960 when

a supply teacher, Elizabeth Sutton, came to Hemyock. She was a trained cub scouter and decided to form a pack, ably assisted by Phyllis Salter. The Rector of Hemyock allowed the Cubs to use the Church Hall for their meetings but the initial plans were soon put in jeopardy when Miss Sutton discovered she was being posted away from Hemyock. Who could replace her? The answer came in the shape of a man whose name was to become synonymous with scouting in Hemyock for nearly 40 years, the late Ron (or Cecil) Lowman, known to all as 'Skip'. In later years he was to say that Elizabeth Sutton thought he was the ideal candidate because she often saw him wearing shorts. Whatever the reason he was persuaded to apply for a Cub Scout Leader's Warrant. Skip Lowman, a man with no previous experience of scouting, tackled his task with considerable enthusiasm and vigour. The new 1st Hemyock Troop was formed in 1960 and became extremely successful. Phyllis Salter was also involved from those early days. In 1964 a Senior Scout Patrol was formed and in 1966 two young men became the Troop's first Queen's Scouts.

By 1968 the strength of the Troop was 124 consisting of 61 Cub Scouts, 43 Scouts, 12 Venture Scouts (including 8 Queen's Scouts) and 8 Scouters and Instructors. The advances made by the 1st Hemyock Troop were quite remarkable in such a short space of time and very much due to the efforts of Skip Lowman. Some indication of the impact this gentleman made in scouting circles is shown by a statement made by a District Commissioner Colin Greensmith and quoted from the *Scouting* magazine of January 1971:

I have never known a Scouter who can get so much out of boys and young men. He inspires them to believe in themselves and their capabilities. He trusts them implicitly to carry through whatever task they undertake.

These words really do sum up Skip. Many youngsters became involved in scouting because of his infectious enthusiasm and never regretted it.

In 1972 the Hemyock Scouts and Guides, Cub Scouts and Brownies established a link with their opposite numbers in the town of Tønder in South

Jutland, Denmark. This was the beginning of a relationship that continues to this day. During some years the youngsters travel to Hemyock from Denmark and other years the groups from Hemyock travel to Denmark. The reciprocal visits have led to many friendships not only between the young folk of both communities but also many adults whether Scout and Guide leaders or the people of Hemyock and Tønder who have taken the children into their homes and hearts. It is always obvious when the Scouts and Guides from Denmark have arrived in Hemyock because the village is suddenly full of very blond youngsters exploring their surroundings and the Danish flag flies from the church tower. The friendly Vikings are back again.

Over the years many of the youngsters who began as Cubs or Brownies have progressed to become senior scouts, guides and leaders and the same will no doubt be true in the years ahead. The success of the movement is largely thanks to the enthusiasm of its leaders, not only Skip, but also many other leaders past and present, leaders such as John Northam, who took over from Skip Lowman when he retired, Frank Batten, Norman Holbrook, Ashley Alford, Barbara Hole, Margaret Wheaton, Janice Fuller (Bawler) and Pat Keith – these are only a few of the many too numerous to mention here. It goes without saying that the different Scout and Guide groups have always received considerable support from people within the village, including Polly Eden and her late husband John, also Heather Stallard and her late husband Robin, who so often opened up their homes for the youngsters, both English and Danish.

In 1986 John and Polly Eden received the Chief Scouts Commendation for Good Services as did Elizabeth Lowman and Jean Ruddy. In 1987 Skip Lowman was awarded the British Empire Medal for his services to scouting. He died in 1998. At a Service of Thanksgiving in his memory at St Mary's Church on 21 November 1998 one of the most moving, but enjoyable parts of the service was Skip's 'Elephant Dance' demonstrated by Scouts past and present.

The Scouts, Cubs, Guides and Brownies have always played an important part in village life. Apart from their own activities they involve themselves in fund-raising for a number of charities and often help with community projects. One of the most important events in the life of Hemyock is the Scouts' Annual Jumble Sale which usually raises over a £1000 and attracts people from far and wide. There is no doubt that the spirit of Scouting and Guiding is alive and well in Hemyock and hopefully will continue to be so for generations to come. It is impossible to do justice to the subject in so few words but perhaps, one day, somebody with an intimate knowledge of the movement will write a comprehensive history of Hemyock's Scouts and Guides. Now that would be a challenge!

Left: *Programme for 'The Masque of Empire', performed in 1943 by the 1st Hemyock Guides, Scouts, Brownies and Cubs.*

Right: *Programme (inside) for 'Perhaps', a musical revue performed by the 1st Hemyock Scouts and Guides in 1945.*

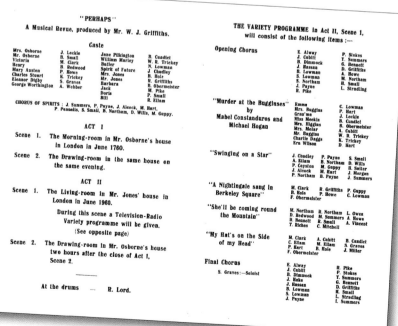

Above: *Guides and Brownies, late 1940s. Left to right, back: Mary Salter, Margaret Pring, Jane and Margaret Moore, Beryl Doble, Margaret (?) Guppy, Brenda Warren, Julie Summers, Marilyn Woodman, Margaret Dunn; 3rd row: Pam Lowman, Ruth Hold, Sally Eastick (?), Sylvia Wright, Diane Mitchell; the front two rows include: Susan Pring, Margaret Doble, ? Guppy and Anne Trenchard.*

Left: *Evelyn Doble making a presentation to Barbara Hole on the occasion of her retirement as Brown Owl, 1968. The next Brown Owl, Janice Fuller, is standing on the right.*

Right: *This was a scouting event called 'Operation Snowdrift', c.1966, and the photograph was taken at Wrangway near the Wellington Monument.*

CHAPTER EIGHTEEN

The Simcoe Connection

It is over 200 years since the name Lieutenant-General John Graves Simcoe was first linked with Hemyock. Simcoe was a hero of the American War of Independence and the first Lieutenant-Governor of Upper Canada (the present-day province of Ontario). He was undoubtedly one of the best-known historical figures to be associated with Hemyock over the centuries.

Simcoe was born at Cotterstock, Northamptonshire in the year 1752, during the reign of King George II. His father, John, was a naval captain married to a woman named Katherine (née Stamford). Young Simcoe's godfather was a naval officer friend of the family, Samuel Graves, hence John 'Graves'. Graves eventually attained the rank of Admiral and made his home at Hembury Fort House near Honiton. The house and its location were to play a significant role in John Graves' life in later years.

In 1759 his father Captain John Simcoe was in command of a ship sailing with General James Wolfe to take on the French forces, under General Montcalm, at Quebec. Unfortunately Simcoe died during the voyage and was buried at sea before the fleet reached their destination. Wolfe went on to defeat Montcalm on the Plains of Abraham, a victory that played a decisive role in the future history of Canada, a history in which John Graves Simcoe would play his own part over 30 years later.

After the Captain's death his widow moved to Exeter with her two young sons John Graves and his younger brother Percy. The move may have been prompted by the presence of Admiral Graves and his wife only a few miles from the Cathedral city. Sadly Percy Simcoe was drowned in a swimming accident in the River Exe shortly after the family moved.

John Graves attended Exeter School then went on to continue his education at Eton followed by a brief spell at Merton College, Oxford. After Oxford, he toyed with the idea of following a legal career but eventually settled for a military life. In April 1770 he became an ensign in the 35th Regiment of Foot (later the Sussex Regiment) serving with them in England, Wales and Ireland. His military career took off with the commencement of the American War of Independence or, as Simcoe and many others called it, the American Rebellion. By now a Lieutenant Simcoe had sailed with his regiment to Boston where he arrived in June 1775, the day after the Battle of Bunker Hill (in which many of his regiment, having already arrived, had taken part).

Shortly after arriving in America Simcoe became a Captain in the 40th Regiment of Foot (later the 2nd Somersets) and was in constant action. He was a man of quite innovative ideas, one being to form a negro battalion drawing on the slaves in Boston. This notion was quickly dismissed by his superiors. After the Battle of Brandywine, in which he was slightly wounded, Simcoe was given command of a provincial corps known as the Queen's Rangers. The Rangers mainly consisted of Loyalists (loyal to Britain and King George III). The corps was supplemented by British troops and consisted mainly of infantry with some cavalry. They were principally used for scouting, skirmishing and very often missions behind enemy lines, but the corps also figured in a number of major engagements. The Queen's Rangers fought in green rather than the traditional British 'Redcoats', their dress sometimes leading to them being mistaken by the Americans for their own men. Simcoe took full advantage of the error and under his inspired leadership the Rangers became a force to be reckoned with. They could almost be likened to the 'Special Forces' of today.

Simcoe had been given the local rank of Lieutenant-Colonel making quite a name for himself as a brave and effective leader. On one occasion he narrowly avoided being killed by an Indian Chief, being saved by one of his men. American Indian tribes fought on both sides in this war and were extremely effective warriors. Simcoe was wounded on at least two more occasions and once had his horse shot from beneath him and was taken prisoner by the Americans. He remained in captivity for some months before being 'exchanged' and returning to the fray. One of Simcoe's brainwaves was the idea of ordering a small force of his men to go behind the American lines and take General George Washington prisoner but the plan was never followed through by his senior officers. It is interesting to speculate how the course of the war would have been altered had Washington in fact been taken prisoner. As it was, the British forces under General Cornwallis surrendered at Yorktown in October 1781 and Simcoe set sail for England after six years of hard campaigning. He spent a short time in London before returning to Devon where he was welcomed home as a war hero. Such was his fame that he was made a Freeman of Exeter in February 1782.

The long campaign, coupled with the injuries which he had received, had taken their toll on him both mentally and physically and he was very much in need of rest and recuperation. His mother had died during the war so Simcoe went to stay with his godfather, Admiral Graves, at Hembury Fort House. Here Simcoe found himself in the company not only of the Admiral but also of the Admiral's niece, a 19-year-old heiress named Elizabeth Posthuma Gwillim – 'Posthuma' because her father died before she was born and her mother had died shortly after childbirth. John and Elizabeth fell in love and were married at Buckerell Church in December 1782.

The newlyweds purchased the Wolford Estate near Dunkeswell and it was at Wolford that they built their new home, Wolford Lodge. For the next decade Simcoe spent most of his time developing and enlarging his estate, and getting to know the people of Devon and the Blackdown Hills. He had always been interested in history, archaeology and geology, and it was at Wolford that he was now able to pursue his interest.

During this time Simcoe and his wife became familiar with Hemyock and its people. Their estate manager, John Scadding, was probably of the Scadding family who lived in Hemyock back in the 17th century. Apart from building their home and creating a large estate the Simcoes also began to raise a large family, five daughters and a son being born between 1784 and 1791.

Portrait of Colonel John Graves Simcoe by George Theodore Berthon, reproduced by kind permission of the Government of Ontario Art Collection.

Simcoe always maintained a keen interest in the welfare of the Loyalists who had fought with him in America, especially those who made their homes in Canada after the conflict. He also kept himself abreast of the political situation in North America, always fearing an American invasion of Canada. In 1790 he became Member of Parliament for St Mawes in Cornwall which gave him a doorway to more active involvement in Canadian affairs.

In 1791 an Act of Parliament was passed dividing that country into Upper Canada (the present-day province of Ontario) and Lower Canada (the present-day province of Quebec). Upper Canada had quite a small English-speaking Protestant population whereas in Lower Canada the inhabitants were mainly French-speaking Catholics.

Simcoe had, by now, acquired some extremely influential friends, both in and out of Parliament, a situation that no doubt had some bearing on him being appointed the first Lieutenant-Governor of Upper Canada in 1791. On 26 September 1791 Simcoe set sail from Weymouth for Upper Canada together with his wife and their two youngest children Sophia and Francis. They left their other children at Wolford in the care of a governess. After a rough Atlantic crossing the Simcoes wintered in Quebec before travelling on to Upper Canada the following spring. It is worth bearing in mind that much of Upper and Lower Canada was nothing more than wilderness in the 1790s, and travel was either by sledge or on foot in the winter and for the rest of the year on foot or horseback, or by canoe or bateau on the lakes. Extremes of climate added to the problems and it was tough going for much of the time. The Simcoes remained in Upper Canada until the autumn of 1796 when they returned to England. Their health had suffered a great deal during their years in Canada, with Elizabeth coming close to death on one occasion and Simcoe himself suffering badly. They also lost a daughter who was born in Upper Canada and died in infancy. Fortunately the two children they took with them survived; in fact their son Francis seemed to thrive on the new way of life and enjoyed the company of the Canadian Indians a great deal.

Whilst in Canada Lieutenant-Governor Simcoe oversaw the creation of a British-style legislature and legal system, and created English-style counties and militia. He also initiated legislation that would eventually lead to the abolition of slavery in Upper Canada and is credited with founding what is now the City of Toronto although he had given it the name of Fort York in honour of the Duke of York.

On his return to England in 1796 the Government decided to send him on another mission as Military Commander of British Forces in San Domingo (modern Haiti). San Domingo was a French Royalist colony, one of its richest in fact, built on the back of slave labour. With the onset of the French Revolution the situation had changed and there had been an uprising by the slaves under their leader Toussaint L'Oevurture aided by a number of French revolutionaries.

The British Government had agreed to help the Royalist French but things had not thus far been going well, hence the appointment of Simcoe. It is ironic that Simcoe, a man opposed to slavery, should have found himself fighting to put down a slave revolt. On his arrival in San Domingo Simcoe realised that the British involvement was a lost cause and did not hesitate to inform his superiors in England of his thoughts.

The main enemy faced by Simcoe and his men was the climate and the tropical diseases such as yellow fever and malaria; the slaves were a secondary consideration. The British losses to disease were far greater than those resulting from military action. Simcoe had arrived in San Domingo early in 1797 but he was back in England by the autumn. The British presence in the colony did not continue for very long after his return.

At home fears were mounting of the threat of invasion by Napoleon's armies in France. Experienced officers such as Simcoe, by now a Major-General, were needed to prepare England for this eventuality and he was accordingly given command in the West of England. Initially his area of command took in Devon and parts of Somerset but in 1801 he was given command of all of the western counties with the rank of Lieutenant-General. It was during this period of his career that he began to establish closer ties with Hemyock.

Simcoe's military responsibilities were many and varied. Firstly and most importantly he had to create a well-trained and effective fighting force to meet the feared invasion. This force consisted of regular Army troops, never enough as far as Simcoe was concerned, the militia and the volunteer corps. Simcoe gave instructions for hard training to attain fitness, strict discipline and the efficient use of weapons. He was very keen on the use of the bayonet and ordered special training in this particular military skill. Military exercises and reviews were organised on Woodbury Common, Curry Moor and other locations in Devon and Somerset. Hemyock had its own volunteer corps which is discussed in detail in

Chapter Twelve. Simcoe was also responsible in helping the civil authorities to prepare the civilian population for evacuation in the eventuality of the French landing on native soil.

An additional responsibility for Simcoe was aiding the civil authorities in dealing with the food riots of 1801, which caused considerable problems throughout the West of England and beyond. Even members of the volunteer forces were rioting. The population of Hemyock were, however, keeping their heads down. The Revd John Land of Hemyock wrote to Simcoe stating that although the people of the village were suffering because of the high food prices they did not take part in 'the tumultuous and disgraceful proceedings' that were proceeding apace in nearby Wellington and elsewhere. There was in fact considerable sympathy for the poorer people, high food prices had lead to riots in the first place and efforts were made to deal with the problem with a minimum of force. Simcoe even made a handsome donation to help the poor of Honiton.

Shortly after taking command in the South West the General purchased Hemyock Castle and the farm, also acquiring the lordship of the manor in the process. He also bought up other properties in the village and parish. The Land Tax Returns for 1802, for example, show that apart from Hemyock Castle he was the owner of Serles Close and Moores (the 'occupier' or tenant being John Manley), and also Gorwell (a farm on the edge of the parish which was occupied by William Holway). Hemyock Castle was very much in a state of disrepair when Simcoe purchased it and he was determined to restore it to something of its former glory. He apparently considered it possible that the fortification was Roman in origin and in March 1802 wrote to a John Voss of Culmstock (presumable a local antiquary) setting out some of his ideas and seeking that gentleman's opinion. Simcoe had sent Voss a drawing of an old Roman castrum near Cairo which he felt supported his viewpoint. On 27 March Voss penned the letter to Simcoe which is shown overleaf.

Was Voss trying to be diplomatic by going along with the idea of Roman origins advanced by the General? Certainly Voss's original opinion of the castle dating from the 11th or 12th century was probably nearer the mark.

Another site in the parish of Hemyock that interested Simcoe was the mound at Simonsburrow, reputed to be the burial place of an Anglo-Saxon warrior Sigemund interred there in the 7th or 8th century. In 1806 Simcoe was visited at Wolford Lodge by a distinguished Swiss geologist Jean Andre de Luc. This gentleman wanted to visit friends in Somerset and intended to travel via Simonsburrow. Simcoe generously provided him not only with a horse for his journey but the services of the Simcoe family footman cum coachman John Bailey. Later in life Bailey wrote the 'Memoirs' of his life with the

FROM JOHN VOSS TO GENERAL SIMCOE
27 MARCH 1802

Sir,

I beg leave to thank you for the Drawing you were so good as to send me of the old Roman Castrum near Cairo, and should have returned it to you, but Mr Scadding informed me that he understood I was to keep it – The plan is so similar, in most of the material Points to that of Hemyock Castle, that altho' I had always considered the Castle at Hemyock as the work of the 11th or 12th Centuries, yet as Pococke, whose authority as our Antiquary, is unquestionable, refers the Castle at Cairo to the Roman Pera, I've no Reason why the Castle at Hemyock may not be the work of the Romans, while they were in Possession of this Island.

I apprehend it is supposed that Seaton was a frequent Place of Landing by the Romans, and Hemyock is nearly the Centre between Seaton and the Bristol Channel at Minehead, and a Chain of strong positions between these Two Places would keep the whole Province which was called Britannia prima in subjection. The extremities of the Black Down Hills, Hembury Fort and Castle St. Neroche are nearly in these lines, and particularly before the time of artillery, would, I should suppose, have been considered as Dominating Points; and might also, have been used as Castra Astiva and the Castle at Hemyock might have been used for the purpose of a Castrum Hybernum for the troops to retire to in the Winter. There is a Road which is now called the Post Road, and which is still to be traced in different Points between the South Coast, and the Bristol Channel & which I understood was generally supposed to have been a Roman Road.

I beg to excuse my troubling you with these observations and which your better Judgement may probably discover to be perfectly unfounded – I am Sir, your most obe'dt

Humble Servant, John Voss.

Simcoe family over many years. The original of his work is in the possession of a Simcoe descendant, Mrs Margaret Partridge. Bailey was semi-literate and his narrative is a little difficult to follow. Extracts quoted in this book are, therefore, paraphrased to make them a little more understandable. Bailey described the Simonsburrow aspect of the journey as follows:

So we started off together by Wolford, through Dunkeswell and Hemyock, in the Culme Valley, four miles from Dunkeswell and went as far as Wellington in Somersetshire the first day. This journey took us a long time as M. de Luc wished to see a little of the country, and there is one place in particular where he was engaged for a considerable time. It was Simonsborough; it lies between Hemyock and Wellington, and at this place there was a large heap of stones, supposed to be many thousand waggon loads, and it appeared they had been there many hundred years, for no one could give any account how they came there. M. de Luc was very much interested in viewing these stones, for it was wonderful how it could be placed to such a great height, and where they could have all been brought from.

Indeed, many people have been fascinated by the long-lost historical site over the years.

In his book *Tales of the Blackdown Borderland* published in 1923 F.W. Mathews discusses the 'great cairn of stones' at Simonsburrow (or Simonsborough). He writes of local legends which told of the cairn being protected by the 'evil one'. Many had tried to penetrate the barrow over the years because legend had it that there was a crock of gold buried there. Sadly it will never be known who or what was buried there because in 1870 a local road contractor, James Bale, cleared the whole site and utilised the stones for his own commercial purposes. The name Simonsborough has varied considerably over the centuries. The earliest written record was c.1190 when it was known as 'Simundesbergha' (Sigemund's hill).

When the threat of a French invasion faded Simcoe sought an active overseas command without success. In 1806 he was offered the position of Commander in Chief in India, a position he accepted with some reluctance. Before leaving for India he was given a special mission in Portugal. Unfortunately the ship he sailed in had been recently painted and the paint fumes brought on a severe asthma attack which forced him home from Portugal without delay. He landed at Topsham and was conveyed to the home of his friend Archdeacon Moore in Cathedral Close, Exeter, where he died before he could be re-united with his wife and family. On 4 November 1806 General Simcoe was buried with full military honours at Wolford Chapel. The funeral procession travelled from Exeter, along what is now the A30, through Fenny Bridges and Honiton to Wolford. The route was lined with soldiers and salutes were fired at various stages of the journey as a mark of respect. In Exeter Cathedral there is a monument to General Simcoe by the famous sculptor John Flaxman, a monument which also records the death of Simcoe's eldest son, Francis Gwillim Simcoe, who died at the Siege of Badajoz. In Cathedral Close there is a plaque marking the site of the house where General Simcoe died.

Following his death in 1806 the Simcoe family connection with Hemyock continued for many years. Mrs Simcoe acquired further properties in the village including Millhayes. Apparently fuller's earth was discovered on one of her properties although it is not known which one. There is no evidence to suggest that Mrs Simcoe made any commercial use of this discovery. Before her husband's death the Simcoe family had been increased by the birth of another son, Henry Addington Simcoe (named after the General's close political friend and ally Henry Addington, later Viscount Sidmouth), and also two daughters Katherine and Anne. Another boy had died in 1799 at the age of nine months.

Interestingly none of the Simcoe daughters married until after the death of their mother in 1850. Then, in 1851, the youngest daughter Anne married a gentleman by the name of John Alford. The marriage took place in Paddington, which was then a village in Middlesex on the outskirts of London.

Elizabeth Posthuma had enjoyed travelling very much, visiting many parts of England and Wales usually accompanied by one or more of her daughters and often by the faithful family retainer John Bailey. Like many travellers passing through Hemyock she encountered one of the familiar local problems, flooding at Millhayes. In his memoirs Bailey recalls one such incident in the following terms:

I went with Mrs Simcoe and Miss Caroline to attend a missionary meeting in Wellington but on our way home it came on to rain very much so that there was a deep flood when we came to Millhayes, the waters were very deep. Mr. Manley said it was not safe to go through as the main stream ran close to the road and if I should chance to drive one foot off the way we would be right in the main stream which was more than ten feet deep. Mrs Simcoe asked what should be done. I told her we could first see the deepness of the water so Mr. Manley sent one of his horses through. The water was up to the horse's side so I told Mrs Simcoe we could quite trust our horses. I thought 'Venture makes the merchant'. Old William Selway was with us so we jumped on the dickey and started off but just as we got about half way through poor old Selway was quite frightened; he said the wheels were quite under the water, he could not see them. I told him not to say anything and not to be frightened so I gave the horses a flick with the whip. They gave a plunge or two in the water and we were soon out of danger and got safe to land and arrived home without any hurt.

It appears that Mr Manley was the farmer at Millhayes. The modern traveller, in his or her horse-less carriage, trying to drive through floods that still occur at Millhayes now and then will fully sympathise with those travellers of 150 years ago.

Mrs Simcoe was very much a philanthropist and contributed generously to the rebuilding of the church at Dunkeswell and she also financed the building of a new church at Dunkeswell Abbey. It is believed that she also gave money too towards the rebuilding of St Mary's Church in the 1840s. Her correspondence shows that in 1822 she discussed with a friend the subject of giving financial aid to a Mrs Collins of Hemyock to assist with the education of Hemyock children.

Above right: *Artist's impression of Mrs Simcoe based on an early portrait.*

Main: *Hemyock Castle, 2001.*

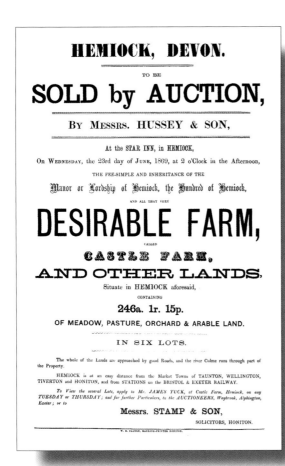

Whether this aid was forthcoming is not known, but judging by Mrs Simcoe's reputation for charity, it seems likely.

The Simcoes' eldest son, Francis Gwillim Simcoe, followed in his father's footsteps and joined the Army. Unlike his father, however, he actually fought against the forces of Napoleon in the Peninsula War. He met his death in the breach at the Siege of Badajoz on 6 April 1812, aged 21. He had never married. The General's second son, Henry Addington, chose a career in the Church and became the parish priest at Egloskerry in Cornwall. It was he who preached the first sermon when Hemyock Church was re-opened on Wednesday 28 July 1847. Henry died in 1868, the father of five sons, none of whom produced a male heir subsequently. The male line of the Simcoe family died out at the end of the 19th century, but there are a number of descendants on the female side of the family surviving at the beginning of the 21st century.

The last firm Simcoe link with Hemyock ended with the sale, by Simcoe's grandson Captain John Kennaway Simcoe, of their Hemyock properties in 1869. The auction took place at the 'Star Inn, Hemiock' (as it was then spelt) on Wednesday, 23 June, 1869, at 2 o'clock in the afternoon. The auctioneer's sales catalogue described the estate as:

The fee-simple and inheritance of the Manor or Lordship of Hemiock, the Hundred of Hemiock and all that very Desirable Farm, called Hemiock Farm, and other lands situate in Hemiock aforesaid...

In all there were six lots which are of considerable local interest. Lot 1 consisted of Castle Farm, orchards, closes and some cottages with gardens. The principal tenant was a James Tuck (a yearly tenant from Lady Day) and three cottage tenants, the Revd F.J. Kitson, William Coles and William Govier. A Robert Hembrow was a leaseholder of part of Lot 1. Lot 1 was sold subject to the annual payment of £1 at Christmas to the poor of the parish of Hemyock. Lot 2 was 'all those Cottages and Gardens called Passby' with adjoining orchards and closes of land. All of these were in the tenancy of James Tuck. Lot 3 was 'All those valuable Closes of Land called The Crownhills and Pudding Meads situate near the village of Hemiock' where James Tuck was the tenant. Lot 4 was 'all those desirable Closes of Land situate in Hemiock aforesaid and at or near Shuttleton.' Here also James Tuck was the tenant. Lot 5 was 'All that tenement called Holcombe Wood with the Closes of Land called Fourways.' Holcombe Wood was in the occupation of Mrs Mary Blackmore and James Tuck again had the tenancy of Fourways. The final lot, No. 6, consisted of a 'Cottage and Garden Closes of Land and a Plantation situated at Coniger; a Cottage and Garden plus Closes of land at Newcot and Four Closes of Land called Newlands, situated at or near Coniger.' The cottages and gardens, etc. at Coniger were leased to a John Hitchcock and James Tuck was tenant of a number of the closes. The Newcot properties had been granted on a 99-year lease (from 1833) to John Stoneman, but, 'now, determinable on the death of Francis Manley Stoneman aged 46 years.' Two closes of land included in this Lot were occupied by John Hembrow as tenant.

So, with this auction, ended the principal links between the Simcoe family and Hemyock although some people from the village worked for the Simcoes their descendants and heirs at Wolford Lodge for many years afterwards. The Simcoes are remembered by the name 'Simcoe Place' on the recently built housing development Culm Meadow in Hemyock.

CHAPTER NINETEEN

Echoes From 1900

The Tiverton East Ruridecanal Magazine *for the year 1900 contains fascinating items of news from parishes in the area then covered by the Rural Deanery of Tiverton. One such parish was Hemyock. Obviously much of the content related to church news within each parish but so often the local happenings were strongly influenced by world events such as the Boer War. The magazine also serialised, in a dozen parts, a story by H. Rider Haggard, 'Doctor Therne'. The following are some extracts from the monthly news items about Hemyock – some amusing, some sad – which give a good idea of activities within the community 100 years ago.*

In January 1900, the Rector of Hemyock, John de Burgh Forbes wrote the following:

Since the dark days of the Crimean War, no year has opened so sorrowfully as the present one. High and low alike are mourning the loss of loved ones fallen on the field of battle. Widows and orphans, the maimed and invalided, are appealing for the sympathy, the prayers, the generous help of their brethren in the great Family of Christ. Let us take great care that our ears are opened to these sad sounds, and that, to the very utmost of our power, we assist in the great work of administering to their needs. Already, by means of the Red Cross working party, a considerable amount of material has been made up into such articles as are much needed by the sufferers in the various hospitals, and we propose that this good work shall be continued into the spring.

On Wednesday, 3rd January, a concert on behalf of the 'Soldiers and Sailors' Widows and Orphans Fund' will take place in the Board School, at 7p.m. The programme promises to be an exceptionally attractive one, and during the course of the evening, an opportunity, which we are sure none will fail to avail themselves of, will be given of subscribing to the Funds of the Society.

He was, of course, referring to the Boer War which had broken out in October 1899. When the item appeared in the magazine a British force and many civilians had been under siege at Ladysmith, which was finally relieved in February 1900. One of the British regiments fighting in South Africa was the Devonshires. The Boer War theme continued in February:

In accordance with the terms of the 'Royal Letter' and the wish of the Bishop of Exeter, at all services on Sunday, Jan. 7th, an opportunity was given of contributing to the Transvaal War Fund, and the result, amounting to £4.2s. has been sent to the Mansion House (London). During the continuance of the war, a short service of Intercession immediately succeeds the ordinary Evening Service in the Parish Church, on the first Sunday in each month.

At such Intercession all those who are natives of Hemyock, or known to be connected with any of the parishioners are remembered by name.

A most successful Concert, on behalf of the Devon Branch of the Soldiers, Sailors' Wives and Families Association, took place in the Board School on Wednesday Jan. 3rd. In spite of bad weather there was a large and most appreciative audience. The first and third parts of the programme included Glees by the Choir, songs by Miss Riding, Miss Macrone and Mr. Chester Master, and solos on the violin by Miss E. Furze, who most kindly took the place of Mrs Terry (a victim to influenza) at very short notice. It is needless to add that 'encores' were very frequent. In the second part, after a most admirable rendering of 'The Handy Man' by Miss New, and the singing of the inevitable 'Absent-minded Beggar', by the Rector (in the most regrettable absence of Mr. E. Crease through a domestic bereavement), a tambourine collection on behalf of the Fund realised the substantial sum of £5.7s.6d.

The article went on to record the fact that so far the parish had raised over £20 for this cause.

In March the magazine made reference to a Church Sunday School prize-giving and treat in December where, amongst other activities, the rector exhibited a series of lantern slides illustrating the stories of *Robinson Crusoe, Cinderella* and *The Tale of a Tub*.

The following items also appeared:

On the first Sunday in the New Year the Culm Davey Sunday School commenced work under the able superintendence of Miss Lutley, of Chapel Farm. This together with Mr and Mrs Gill's most successful school at the Symonsborough Mission Room, makes a third centre of Church work among Christ's little ones of the Parish.

And continuing the war theme:

It will interest our readers to know that the Weekly Working Party has been very busy indeed. Up to the present time the following articles have been despatched to those who have the care of the sick and wounded in South Africa; 24 shirts, 26 pairs of socks, one pair of stockings, six warm waistcoats, ten sleeping helmets, and 3 'tam o'shanter' caps.

The April issue reported the ill health of the rector who, on medical advice, had gone to Italy for about two months. The Revd W. Pullen had undertaken to be responsible for the Parish Church and Culm Davey Chapel services during his absence. Miss Forbes remained at the Rectory and, it was noted, was to be at once 'informed of any cases of illness'.

In May an epidemic of pneumonia brought sad times to the people of Hemyock:

The last few weeks have brought deep sorrow into many of our Hemyock homes. The prevailing epidemic of pneumonia, consequent upon influenza, has proved fatal in many cases. Among those who have passed away while still in the prime of life is Mr Gill of Symonsborough. Though only residing in the parish a comparatively short time, he had won the esteem and affections of all, and his loss will be deeply deplored throughout the whole parish.

The June 1900 edition of the magazine was taken up with a letter to the parishioners from the Revd Forbes describing his sojourn in Italy. The July issue reported that he had presided at the Annual Church Parade and Dinner of the Rational Sick and Burial Association on Whit Monday. The war effort was continuing:

On Tuesday June 12th the Rector and Miss Forbes entertained all those who had been assisting at the weekly 'Red Cross Working Party' to tea at the Rectory.
The following is a complete list of articles made at these gatherings, and which have been sent off for the use of the troops at the front; 28 shirts, 16 warm waistcoats, 27 pair knitted socks, 1 pair knitted stockings, 12 knitted helmets, 3 knitted 'tam o'shanter' caps.

The people of Hemyock also managed to raise five guineas for the 'Indian Famine Fund'.

In August 1900 there was much to report. The first item noted that the hay harvest had kept all busy during the past month and 'generally speaking' the crop was a very good one. The choirs of the Parish Church and Culm Davey Chapel had been well represented at the Choral Festival in Exeter Cathedral on the 26 June, although:

...much to the regret of the Rector, some were unable to accept his invitation to be present at the practices and take part in the services.

A little rap on the knuckles for some individuals here one suspects.

Events from overseas once again figured in the news:

Many of our readers will be glad to hear that the Rector has quite recently received a very cheery and interesting letter from their old friend Sergt. Mark Matthews of the Imperial Yeomanry. It seems that his Battalion has been engaged in all the more recent operations of Lord Robert's force and, though under fire at Thaba'nchu, Springfontein, Bloemfontein and Pretoria, he has been so fortunate as to escape without a wound.

So it would appear that at least one Hemyock man was in action in the conflict.

Other problems in far-off places were the subject of some concern to the people of Hemyock as the magazine indicated:

The state of affairs in the Far East is now also a cause of great anxiety in many English homes, and all those who have relatives or friends in China claim our warmest sympathy.

The writer was referring to the Boxer Rebellion. The 'Boxers' were fanatical Chinese nationalists, who in 1900 attacked the various foreign legations in Peking murdering European missionaries and thousands of Chinese who had converted to Christianity. The attacks had been instigated by the Empress Dowager. Peking was captured by an international punitive force on 14 August 1900, probably at about the same time as the parishioners of

Hemyock were reading their *Ruridecanal Magazine*.

Purely domestic matters also had to be considered:

The order for the closing of the Churchyard has been extended for another six months to the 1st February 1901. By that date it is to be hoped that the much talked of Cemetery will be an accomplished fact.

and:

It is to be feared that the disturbance of the village street caused by the laying of the new sewer must have caused a good deal of inconvenience. However, when the work is completed Hemyock will be the proud possessor of a more complete system of drainage than any of her neighbours.

The magazine served well as a notice board for locals:

It would be well to remind both parents and children that, during the holidays, the weekly contributions to the Boot Club must be brought to the Sunday School, at 10.30 each Monday morning.

For more information on the Boot Club readers are referred to Chapter Ten.

In September the magazine concentrated on more mundane matters such as the Annual Meeting of the Sunday School Teachers and an outing to Teignmouth of the same with the eldest Sunday scholars.

The October issue described an old custom in danger of being forgotten:

Among the many old customs, now rapidly disappearing, is that of observing 'Revel Sunday'. The origin of this custom seems lost in obscurity, but from time immemorial it seems to have been kept up with more or less in spirit in every parish in this part of England.

It is interesting to learn that in former days different Churches, even though situate in the same parish, 'revelled' (if this be the right expression) at different times. For instance, at our Parish Church, 'Revel Sunday' is always the first Sunday after September 14th, Holy Cross Day, whereas our little sister at Culm Davey was wont to keep hers in the spring. In support of this statement we quote an ancient rhyme kindly contributed by one who often heard it in his youth:-

'God bless ye! God save ye!
Sunday after St. George's Day
[April 23rd]
Is revel up to Culm Davey!'

It is by no means improbable that theses quaint lines point us to the original dedication of the little Church on the hill, and that its full style and title ought to be, not Culm Davey Chapel, but 'St. George's Culm Davey'.

However, as it has borne the former name for certainly 300 years, it is scarcely likely that any would now like to see it altered.

There is reference in October's magazine to the 'Clothing and Coal Club' and again to the 'Boot Club'. Apparently the total contributions in one year had exceeded £100 which included a 'bonus' contribution, this being an incentive to thrift. The contributions had been expended on clothing, fuel or shoe leather. The writer in the magazine commented:

While the venture was merely an experiment, the bonus came from a private source, but as it was now plain that these clubs supply a real need, and are extensively patronised by those for whose benefit they were intended, it is proposed to open a regular 'bonus fund', and give all employers of labour in the parish an opportunity of entering into the good work which is being done.

An interesting item appeared in November relating to Church repairs:

Except the restoration of the Chancel, which was carried out by the late Rector soon after his induction to the living, but very little has been done either to the exterior or interior of the Parish Church since 1847. It is therefore but natural that a good deal in the way of repairs is necessary, and we heartily congratulate the Churchwardens in having taken the matter in hand. The work which they recently caused to be done outside will keep the sacred edifice weather-tight during the winter months, while the handsome new matting imparts warmth and comfort to the interior.

We should dearly like to devise some means by which the many draughts, which at the present moment are so fertile a source of colds, might be excluded. This, however, is impossible until such a sum of money is forthcoming as will suffice to reglaze the windows, the leading in several of them being quite worn out.

The year 1900 closed with routine Church business together with information such as the fact that the 'Lantern Lecture' 'Wanderings in Paris' had been well attended in November and that the December talk was to be on the subject of Palestine.

Little could the Hemyock folk of 1900 or their descendants have realised that the years ahead were to bring two World Wars and numerous other conflicts around the world against which the Boer War and Boxer Rebellion would pale into insignificance.

CHAPTER TWENTY

'Perlycombe'

We can imagine many readers of our Hemyock book saying 'Where or what is Perlycombe?' The answer is quite simple: Perlycombe is the pseudonym given to Hemyock by one of the great Victorian novelists R.D. Blackmore in his book *Perlycross*. To a certain extent Blackmore did for Devon and parts of Somerset what Thomas Hardy did for his native county Dorset.

Blackmore is known internationally for his novel *Lorna Doone*. Much filmed and televised, this tale of romance, adventure and passion was mainly set on Exmoor, the title probably being one of the best known in English Literature. Across the world thousands have heard of the scene when Lorna is about to marry her true love John Ridd in Oare Church and is then shot by the evil Carver Doone.

Like Thomas Hardy, Blackmore sets his stories in real villages or towns but gives them fictitious names. In Perlycross (Culmstock) Blackmore places his villages on the River Perle (the Culm), Uffculme becomes Perliton and Hemyock Perlycombe – and the local town of Wellington in Somerset becomes 'Pumpington'. Many look on *Perlycross* as Blackmore's best work after *Lorna Doone*.

Blackmore was born in Berkshire in 1825 where his father John Blackmore was the curate-in-charge of Longworth Parish. The family were of Devon stock descending from a John Blackmore of Parracombe who died in 1689. Three months after his birth Richard's mother died. In 1831 his father remarried and became the curate at Culmstock. Richard was initially educated at home and then spent some time at a preparatory school in Bruton, Somerset, before attending Blundells School in Tiverton and then Oxford. Much of his early life was, therefore, spent in the rural heart of Devon that was later to feature in *Perlycross*. After Oxford, Blackmore was called to the Bar and spent a number of years practising as a conveyancer.

He married in 1853 but for health reasons gave up legal work and turned to teaching. He then decided for a complete career change, purchased some land in Teddington, Middlesex, and became a gardener and horticulturist. He had started writing in the 1850s and his first work was published in 1854. For the rest of his life he devoted himself to his market garden and writing. *Lorna Doone* was not published until 1869 and *Perlycross* late in his career, in 1894.

Blackmore became friendly with a family by the name of Coward in Teddington and was godfather to the family's first son Russel. Unfortunately this boy died in 1897 aged seven. When the Cowards had a second son, Nöel, in 1899, Blackmore was asked to be his godfather. He declined because several of his many godchildren, including Russel Coward, had died in their infancy and Blackmore felt that he might have had a negative influence over their lives. Nöel Coward of course went on to become far more famous than the man who had declined to be his godfather!

The story of *Perlycross* deals with events in the village of Culmstock and surrounding villages and countryside. The theme of the plot hinges on the disappearance of the body of Sir Thomas Waldron from a vault beneath the Parish Church and an accusation of body-snatching against the local doctor, an unfounded accusation as it proves. Unlike *Lorna Doone* there is little love interest in the tale but Blackmore's descriptions of people, the rural way of life and the countryside is him at his best.

As always in these rural communities there was considerable rivalry between neighbouring villages and in one chapter Blackmore describes how things became pretty difficult between the parishioners of Perlycross and Perlycombe (Hemyock) over the matter of the parish boundaries. The practice of 'beating' or 'perambulation' of the bounds is still carried out in some places as a custom but until well into the second half of the 19th century the bounds were perambulated or beaten as a matter of course in all parishes. Officers of the Vestry, the parish incumbent, village notables, local schoolchildren and many others checked the parish boundary stones and other markers to ensure that none had been moved and that all was in order. Importantly, the walk also served to ensure that the younger members of the community were aware of exactly where the boundary was and that the local knowledge would thus be passed on down through the generations.

For the parishioners of Perlycross all was not well on one of these regular beatings. It was discovered that the people of Perlycombe had made some changes and 'stolen' some Perlycross territory. This was almost tantamount to a declaration of war. In one chapter of his book Blackmore describes the events of a certain St Clement's Day when one of the principal characters, Dr Jemmy Fox, is out walking with his sister Christie. On hearing a great din they discover that it is the population of Perlycross out bound beating, and as the doctor explains to his sister the problem between the neighbouring parishes has often led to fighting – 'they beat their bounds, and often break each others heads upon Saint Clement's Day'. The doctor elaborates:

The business has always been triennial. But the fighting grew more and more serious, till the stock of sticking plaster could not stand it. Then a man of peaceful genius suggested that each parish should keep its own St Clement's day, at intervals of three years as before; but in succession, instead of all three at once; so that no two could meet on the frontier in force. A sad falling off in the spirit of the thing, and threatening to be better for the lawyers, than for us. Perlycombe had their time last year; and now Perlycross has to redress it. Our eastern boundary is down in that hollow; and Perlycombe stole forty feet from us last year. We are naturally making a little stir about it.

Jemmy Fox goes on to explain how the beaters would start in two companies from Perle-Weir, one lot to the north and one to the south, both continuing around the boundary until meeting each other somewhere at the back of Beaconhill. All told this entailed a distance of some 30 miles.

The doctor and his sister arrive on the scene of the disturbance with all of the beaters in indignant uproar and the village parson crying out 'Thou shall not move they neighbour's land-mark'. The narrator continues:

Some fifty yards before them was a sparkling little water-course, elbowing its way in hurried zig-zag down the steep; but where it landed in the fern-bed with a toss of tresses some ungodly power of men had heaved across its silver foot a hugeous boulder of the hill, rugged, bulky, beetle-browed – the 'shameless stone' of Homer. And with such effect, that the rushing water, like a scared horse, leaped aside, and swerving far at the wrongful impulse, cut a felonious cantel out of the sacred parish of Perlycross! Even this was not enough. To add insult to injury, some heartless wag had chiselled, on the lichened slab of boulder, a human profile in broad grin, out of whose wicked mouth came a scroll, inscribed in deep letters- 'P.combe Parish'.

Clearly somebody in Perlycombe had a pretty good sense of humour even if it was not appreciated by the inhabitants of Perlycross.

As Blackmore goes on to explain, the 'Perlycrucians' managed to move the offending boulder back into Perlycombe territory. It would be an interesting exercise to try and identify the exact location of this particular incident. It does seem likely that Blackmore based this account on fact, at least to some extent. If that were the case then some of those Perlycombe folk must have descendants living in Hemyock today.

There is a little postscript to the Blackmore story which is perhaps best described as typical of the 'it's a small-world syndrome'. A friend of one of the authors of *The Book of Hemyock* lived in Teddington some years ago. Her home backed on to 'Blackmore's Grove' and was built on the site of the novelist's old orchard. In later years this lady was researching her family tree and discovered that she herself had roots in Hemyock, Culmstock and Clayhidon back in the early 1800s. Her ancestors included Wrights, Frys and others. This would have been at the time when Blackmore lived at Culmstock and was spending some of his boyhood years exploring the Culm Valley.

Unlike Blackmore we have used the real names of places and people in our volume and it is hoped that no readers will detect any traces of fiction. We also trust that it has proved to be an informative and enjoyable read that will perhaps whet the appetite of those eager to investigate the history of our parish – there is still much to be discovered!

R.D. Blackmore

In October 1996 we made our first exploratory visit to St Herblon. Mavis Clist is 3rd from the left and Brian Clist is 3rd from the right. The link is obviously well forged.

Departure from Annetz, April 2000, after a very successful exchange.
The photograph shows some of the English party with their French hosts.

The official signing of the charter between our communities whilst the French were visiting us in Hemyock in June 2009. The charter was signed by the four French Mayors, and the Chairmen of our two Parish Councils. The charters are displayed in Hemyock Parish Hall. The previous year identical charters were signed in France whilst we were visiting.

Twinning

In May 1996 a party of five French people came to visit us in Hemyock to find out if Hemyock and St Herblon would like to twin with each other. In October 1996 Brian and Mavis Clist went to visit the French. Subsequently the French and the English decided to twin with each other, and the resulting twinning became very successful. On the English side we became the Upper Culm Twinning Association, most of our members come from Hemyock and Clayhidon. St Herblon is the largest of four communes adjacent to the river Loire. On alternate years either the French or the English visit each other over a long weekend. We stay with each other during the visit.

Twinning is successfully established on both sides of the Channel, firm and lasting friendships continue.

The St Ivel Hall

The last few years Brian Clist's chairmanship of Hemyock Parish Council saw the culmination of two huge projects that greatly improved the future of our village.

Both were achieved at very low expenditure, in fact for just £1 each! One was the acquisition of about 12 acres for much needed playing fields, the other was the purchase of the St. Ivel Hall. On page 71 of this book we saw that the old factory site had been purchased by Bloor Homes and was to be used for the construction of houses. Unusually from the outset the Parish Council was involved in the planning process, and at an early meeting in Tiverton Bloor Homes discussed the details of their plans, in addition to housing we were told that the Factory Hall could be used for light industry. At this stage Brian Clist mentioned that it could also be used as an additional village hall, there was no response, but when the plans were submitted it was written that the St. Ivel Hall would be donated to Hemyock Parish Council! What a tremendous asset for the village this would become.

It took several years for the plans to materialise, in the interim it was said that the site was polluted. After prolonged negotiations the site was declared free of contamination and some 50 houses were built at Millhayes. The Factory Hall remained empty for several years, some vandalism took place, eventually following an idea from Dr Meads the hall was converted into "The Blackdown Healthy Living Centre" and is a great benefit to the village. Internally a number of rooms have been built leading to two larger rooms, together with a kitchen at the end. The Centre houses an old persons organisation called the Cameo Club that covers the whole Blackdown Hills and meets twice a week. A number of medical conditions are addressed by means of classes that are well attended.

A range of buildings opposite the Centre, that were the garages for the milk collection lorries, is currently being converted for the benefit of our young people.

The latest estate to be built in Hemyock was at Churchills Farm, just 100 yards from the centre of the village, where some 30 houses were constructed. An archaeological survey was carried out before the new estate was built and remains of a large medieval pottery discovered, thousands of pieces of pottery were found, and also the site of a medieval iron smelting area appeared.

The Twenty-first Century

New apartments built on the site of the old tennis courts.

There have been a number of changes in the village during the past ten year including a number of new homes located at Millhayes, Longmead, Churchills and elsewhere. The most recent development has been a small block of apartments on what were the old tennis courts located behind Hemyock Parish Hall. Obviously these new developments have increased the population of the village. In the Census of 2001 the population was given as 1821. A survey carried out by the Hemyock Parish Council regarding housing needs in the parish in March 2011 estimated a rise in the population to 2211 in 2010. It can be anticipated the population has probably increased since 2010. The growth of the population has led to more cars and other vehicles in the village, much in line with a similar increase across the country.

One of the principal developments within the parish has been at Longmead, with new housing and new sport and recreation facilities, created by the Hemyock Parish Council, opened in 2007. There are now two football pitches, 3 tennis courts two of them

floodlit, a multi games area with a superb adventure playground for children. In addition there is an excellent modern pavilion. These facilities would be the envy of many other communities.

Apart from the new sporting and leisure benefits Hemyock has retained its recreation field adjoining the parish hall and of course, Hemyock's first rate bowling green. The recreation field is a delightful large, well cared for, open space in a central location. It is ideal for walking, sitting and enjoying the views, with another play area with swings etc. for younger children. The 'Rec' has the benefit of a well managed cricket field where the Hemyock cricketers are able to display their talents, and hopefully will do so for many years to come, so upholding a wonderful English tradition.

At 12.30pm on Saturday 2 June 2012 a group of local ladies, colourfully attired for the occasion, paraded through the village on their horses by way of an 'opener' to the Diamond Jubilee celebrations. Fortunately the weather was kind for this particular event. On the Saturday evening there was a 1950s style music and dance extravaganza in the parish hall with music from that era provided by Jason Baxter and 'friends'.

Longmead Field proved to be the ideal location for many of Hemyock's Diamond Jubilee Celebrations. On Sunday 3 June 2012 at 11am there was an open air service of Thanksgiving for the Diamond Jubilee of Her Majesty the Queen. The service was led by the Reverend David Burton, Priest in Charge, of St. Mary's Hemyock and the Preacher was Steve Williams, Pastor of Hemyock Baptist Church. During the service the singing was led by the Hemyock Church Choir conducted by Ron White, the accompanist was Nigel Atkinson. There were other contributions to the service from members of St Mary's Church and Hemyock Baptist Church. Fortunately a covered stage had been erected for the occasion, keep-

Three new tennis courts at Longmead.

Jubilee horse parade

Open air service of Thanksgiving.

Members of Hemyock Junior School Choir.

ing the participants dry. The congregation was also sheltered under a semi-circle of gazebos.

After the service there was more singing, first by five very young children from the Hemyock Junior School Choir who, given their age, performed extremely well. They were followed by the Hemyock Singers, as good as ever, who roused their enthusiastic audience with stirring and patriotic music. The audience were only too happy to join in with many old favourites such as 'Land of Hope and Glory'. This session of music was perfect for the occasion and afterwards everybody enjoyed a picnic. It is as well the gathering had some sort of protection because the weather turned rather wet but it could not dampen people's spirits. Despite the inclement

Above: The congregation take cover at the open air service
Left: A participant of the 'decorated toddler pram push'.
Bottom left: Classic cars on show.
Bottom right: The Bottle Top Boogie Band provided entertainment.

weather there was more music played by Gordon's Algiers Strutters Jazz Band during the afternoon, enough to warm anybody's heart.

There was an improvement in the weather for the Jubilee celebrations that continued on Monday 4 June with a Spring Bank Holiday 'Fun Day' at Longmead Field. The fun started with a 'decorated toddler pram push' followed by a Children's Fancy Dress Competition. These events were followed by something for the adults with foot tapping music from the 'Bottle Top Boogie Band'. Other activities included 'Hemyock's Got Talent' hosted by the Valley Arts. A number of classic cars were on show during the day, all very well cared for by their proud owners. There were also burgers and hotdogs available from Kittow Meats and the local touring fish and chip van.

The Hemyock Singers, one of the ongoing traditions, have entertained the village for many years, performing choral works and traditional shows ranging from Gilbert and Sullivan to popular musicals such as *My Fair Lady* and *Scrooge* and *The Wizard of Oz* and much more. All ages were encouraged to be involved and youngsters who joined when teenagers, or younger, stayed with the group well into adulthood. In more recent times the Hemyock Singers have concentrated on choral works and a new group, 'Valley Arts' was formed by a number of the original Hemyock Singers, and they have been joined by other local people over the years. Valley Arts have performed a number of popular pantomime style shows and this year their production will be *Ali Baba and the Forty Thieves* to be presented at the parish hall in October.

One of the great improvements in the village was the recent construction of an extremely sturdy raised walkway along the road between the southern edge of the village and the Millhayes area. This walkway came into use in 2010. For many years prior to its construction pedestrians had to brave walking on this busy road, a road that has become even busier in recent times. Many of the vehicles using the road are commercial and include large lorries from other parts of the country and overseas. The road is often used as a route through to the industrial estate at Dunkeswell to the south of Hemyock.

The other difficulty there had been for pedestrians, including parents with prams and pushchairs etc. taking their children to school, in fact any users whether on foot or in a vehicle has, over the years, been the flooding from the River Culm by the bridge. Fortunately, following remedial work on the north side of the bridge this risk has been greatly reduced but every now and then when there is continual heavy rain, nature has the final laugh such as with the torrential downpours in April 2012 that caused flooding all over the country. Even the new walkway was nearly submerged as will be seen in the photograph. Where Hemyock Railway station once stood on the north side of the bridge there is now the BMX

New walkway at Millhayes during the floods of April 2012

track used by young village enthusiasts.

A popular addition in the last few years is the Hemyock History and Archiving Association. The history group meets once a month and nearly always has a guest speaker. The subjects are very wide ranging, from local history to family history and personal memories. For example a most interesting meeting was held on 14 June 2012 when Ted Frost described his role as a bomber pilot in the Second World War. These meetings, held in the Church Rooms, have proved extremely popular. Visits have also been organised by the history group to the Tiverton Museum, the Weather Centre in Exeter and other interesting venues. The archiving aspect of the group has included gathering photographs, articles, documents etc., in fact anything of historical interest relating not only to Hemyock but the Blackdowns Hills in general. Much of this data has been preserved on a computer database for the benefit of future generations. A very valuable project.

Sadly a number of the people who provided information and photographs for the first edition of this book are no longer with us. One of these individuals was Doctor John Griffin who died on 19 April 2012. A family doctor for many years in Hemyock, he is greatly missed. Dr Griffin, known locally and affectionately as 'Doctor John' retired from the practice in 1992. He was summed up by a local as 'Quite a character'! His father and grandfather had also been doctors before him. Dr Griffin was extremely interested in local history and regularly attended meetings of the Hemyock History Group.

Brian Clist's family have been farming in Hemyock for over three hundred years. They would be astonished to see how Hemyock has developed over that period, especially during the last thirty years, the time Chris Dracott and his wife have lived in Hemyock. One can only speculate as to what changes will take place in the village in the next decade. Readers of this book who have the benefit of a computer and wish to learn and see more about Hemyock can go to the following websites:

hemyock.org, and blackdown archives.org.uk